W9-ATM-016

GREAT DECISIONS 2009

FPA gratefully acknowledges the generosity of ENI for underwriting the World Map.

• ------------------------------------

Preparation of this year's book was underwritten by a generous
grant from the Freeman Foundation.

Next Fall - Mexico
Active Minds - Lecture w/ Q&A

THE AUTHORS ARE RESPONSIBLE FOR FACTUAL ACCURACY
AND FOR THE VIEWS EXPRESSED.
FPA ITSELF TAKES NO POSITION ON ISSUES OF U.S. FOREIGN POLICY.

GREAT DECISIONS IS A TRADEMARK OF THE
FOREIGN POLICY ASSOCIATION

©COPYRIGHT 2009 BY FOREIGN POLICY
ASSOCIATION, INC., 470 PARK AVENUE SOUTH,
NEW YORK, NEW YORK 10016.
ALL RIGHTS RESERVED.
RESEARCHED AS OF DECEMBER 5, 2008.

PRINTED IN THE UNITED STATES OF AMERICA.
LIBRARY OF CONGRESS CARD NUMBER: 58-59828.

ISBN: 978-0-87124-226-6

PRINTED BY DARTMOUTH PRINTING COMPANY
HANOVER, NEW HAMPSHIRE

DESIGN: AGNIESHKA BURKE

GREAT DECISIONS

Animating our 90-year history at the Foreign Policy Association is a keen awareness of the importance of an education in democracy. To paraphrase Alexis de Toqueville, democracy is not inherited but taught and learned anew by every generation. As yet another change of leadership in Washington takes our country in new directions, what better time to reflect upon democratic renewal?

Accepting the call to engaged citizenship is critical to a robust democracy. As President Dwight Eisenhower observed in his first inaugural address, every citizen "plays an indispensable role....No person, no home, no community can be beyond the reach of this call..., [for] whatever America hopes to bring to pass in the world must first come to pass in the heart of America."

Indeed, any lasting success in foreign policy depends upon reaching a broad audience—an informed citizenry willing to support informed leaders. A vigorous democracy is sustained by the ability of the public to have access to information that can be utilized to broaden individual and collective choices. And it is not knowledge per se, but sharing knowledge that unleashes power. This is a compelling rationale for the democratic form of government; great decisions in the public sphere benefit from the deliberations of informed communities.

From its inception, the American contribution to self-government has rested on the premise that an informed citizenry is vital to a participatory democracy. For James Madison, the "diffusion of knowledge is the only guardian of true liberty." And Thomas Jefferson admonished, "If a nation expects to be ignorant and free, in a state of civilization, it expects what never was and never will be."

In the era of globalization, knowledge of the world is increasingly imperative. Among major liberal democracies, no country has been more forthcoming in embracing the global economy than the United States. This places the American polity at risk for an increasingly divisive income-distribution challenge, which in turn places increasing importance on our educational system. The growth of international trade and the movement of 2 million people daily across national borders have far-reaching implications. For one thing, to compete successfully in this environment requires a renewed commitment to excellence: excellence in our educational system, excellence in government, and excellence in citizenship.

Such an agenda will be illusory if we are insular. What is troubling about our online networking culture is how, at this late date, so many people are wired and yet disconnected from the greater world—the world beyond America's shores. This is a world we have engaged in militarily in recent years in such far-flung places as Kosovo, Somalia, Afghanistan and Iraq. Global markets now account for a larger percentage of revenues for many American companies than domestic markets. So-called "intermestic" issues that straddle domestic and international life like global warming, pandemics and terrorism are not going away anytime soon. A capacity to see the world whole, and to appreciate the values and aspirations of all its inhabitants, is no longer a luxury but an urgent necessity.

I am struck by the extraordinary breadth of this issue of **Great Decisions**. A contribution to sustain this vital program can be made at **www.fpa.org**. Thank you more than ever for your continued participation.

Noel V. Lateef
President and CEO
Foreign Policy Association

The U.S. and rising powers
by Michael Schiffer

In the 21st century, there is more and more global competition for power and resources. What role will the U.S. play? What kind of relationship will the U.S. have with the rest of the world?

A destroyer of the South China Sea Fleet of the Chinese Navy fires a missile in the South China Sea on Nov. 17, 2007. Dozens of warships were deployed in a competitive training exercise to improve combat capability of the fleet. AP PHOTO/XINHUA, ZHA CHUNMING

The likely emergence of China and India as new major global players—similar to the rise of Germany in the 19th century and the U.S. in the early 20th century—will transform the geopolitical landscape, with impacts potentially as dramatic as those of the previous two centuries. In the same way that commentators refer to the 1900s as the 'American Century,' the early 21st century may be seen as the time when some in the developing world, led by China and India, come into their own.

National Intelligence Council
Mapping the Global Future (2007)

In 1999, in the wake of the Asian financial crisis, the meltdown of the Long-Term Capital Management hedge fund spooking the markets and economic crises in Russia and Brazil, the cover of *Time* magazine featured "The Committee to Save the World": the chairman of the U.S. Federal Reserve and the secretary and deputy secretary of the U.S. Treasury. With the cold war over and with what U.S. Secretary of State Madeleine Albright (1997–2001) termed the "indispensable nation" enjoying a unipolar moment of primacy on the world stage, the conceit of the magazine cover—that the U.S. was the world's sole great power—did not seem much of a stretch.

Now, just a decade later, that conceit seems the relic of a bygone era. While there is no ques-

tion that the U.S. remains the world's most powerful actor, with unparalleled military, economic, diplomatic and cultural strength, other major powers—China, India, the European Union (EU), Japan and a resurgent Russia—have appeared on the horizon along with a host of others, like Brazil and South Africa, as increasingly important players. America's unipolar moment, it seems, was brief, and the world now appears to be moving rapidly toward multipolarity or what one analyst has termed the "post-American" era.

In part, this is a function of U.S. policy miscues during America's era of supposed ascendancy, but it is more fundamentally related to deep structural changes in the distribution and diffusion of power around the globe that have been years, if not decades, in the making. It is

MICHAEL SCHIFFER *is program officer in Policy Analysis and Dialogue at the Stanley Foundation, where he is responsible for programs on Asia and a range of other U.S. national and global security issues.*

not necessarily that the U.S. is losing power in an absolute sense, but rather that the rapid rise of "the rest" across so many dimensions is creating new *relative* differentials, with the U.S. comparatively less powerful now than it was even just a few years ago. Moreover, changing technology is creating—and redistributing—new forms of power around the globe.

Lessons from history

Classic international relations theory holds that during periods of "power transition," when shifting power relations between nations create new patterns of power distribution, there are dangers that a misalignment of communications, expectations, perceptions and legitimacy among major powers can lead to breakdowns and the potential for conflict throughout the international order.

Indeed, a common source of instability is the result of friction between rising powers, which may believe they have been deprived of a "seat at the table," and dominant powers unwilling to relinquish their positions, regardless of new realities.

From the decline of Spanish hegemony ushering in the Thirty Years War (1618–48) through the first and second world wars and the end of the British Empire, periods of power transition seem more often than not to be characterized by upheaval and violence be-

fore a new global equilibrium settles in.

The system can also come under stress, perhaps paradoxically, if rising powers fail to be responsible stakeholders in the global order and play the critical role of major powers in providing public goods and maintaining system stability. When dominant powers in decline find themselves unable to underwrite a well-functioning system, rising powers are called on to mind the gap. For example, following World War I, the U.S. retreated into isolationism and walked away from incipient international organizations and norms, failing in many significant ways to live up to its obligations as a rising power to uphold the global order. Although the causes of World War II were many, complex and varied, the vacuum created by the failure of the U.S. to engage and play a constructive role—providing the clout that the declining powers of Europe, drained by the Great War, no longer could—was surely among them.

Although some analysts contend that a clash between rising and dominant powers is inevitable, there is nothing automatic or mechanistic in this process. Policy choices and decisions—great and small—matter.

What makes a major power?

Defining which states constitute the major powers of any era is never an

easy task and can be quite subjective. Broadly speaking, however, major-power status can be considered to be a function of the combined capabilities of force, wealth and ideational influence that a state can bring to bear upon the actions of others. Although major-power status is often seen as a function of superior military might, at least in general discussions, military power is just one dimension of the question.

For example, political scientist Kenneth Waltz has suggested a set of five different measures to assess a state's power: its population and its territorial extent; its natural resources; its economy and economic capacity; the stability and facility of its political system; and its military strength. British historian Paul Kennedy likewise identified population size, urbanization rates, level of industrialization, energy consumption and industrial output as key measures of power in the 20th century, and as the basis of a nation's military power. Other analysts offer similar sets of criteria by which to measure and track state power.

At the broadest level, much of the current public interest in the question of rising powers has been sparked by the remarkable economic growth of China and India. The scope and implications of the recent emergence of these two new players on the global scene can be clearly seen through an economic prism.

Traditional power

For over a decade, China's economy has grown annually at a 10% clip. By 2050, China's economy will have grown 50-fold and will have overtaken the U.S. as the world's largest economy (although the U.S. will still be richer because of its per capita gross domestic product, or GDP). India's economy grew at close to 8% a year during the last decade, and if present trends continue, it will be one of the top three economies of the world by mid-century.

Spurred by the explosive growth in China and India, the world has been witnessing a transition from a global economy dominated by Europe and the U.S. to one dominated by the Asia-

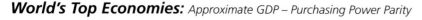

World's Top Economies: Approximate GDP – Purchasing Power Parity

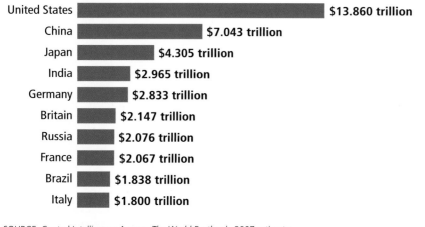

United States	$13.860 trillion
China	$7.043 trillion
Japan	$4.305 trillion
India	$2.965 trillion
Germany	$2.833 trillion
Britain	$2.147 trillion
Russia	$2.076 trillion
France	$2.067 trillion
Brazil	$1.838 trillion
Italy	$1.800 trillion

SOURCE: Central Intelligence Agency-*The World Factbook,* 2007 estimate

LUCIDITY INFORMATION DESIGN

People hold placards and burn firecrackers to celebrate the India-U.S. nuclear deal, in Ahmadabad, India, Sept. 6, 2008. Nations that supply nuclear material and technology overcame fierce obstacles and approved a landmark U.S. plan to engage in atomic trade with India, a deal that reverses more than three decades of American policy. AP PHOTO/ AJIT SOLANKI

emphasize the ability to operate in the South and East China seas and, indeed, even beyond.

China's military growth in the past few decades has been tremendous and spurred serious concerns in some areas regarding the country's intentions. Indeed, looking at China solely though the prism of certain military modernization statistics, Beijing appears to be rising, and rising fast, soon to have, as a recent Pentagon report put it, "the greatest potential to compete militarily with the U.S." on a global scale.

Going nuclear

Another measure of military power in the new global era relates to the development and possession of nuclear weapons—and being treated as a legitimate "nuclear weapons" state, which the 1970 Treaty on the Non-Proliferation of Nuclear Weapons (NPT) limits to the U.S., Russia, China, France and Britain. India has chaffed at this distinction for many years, and for many, the U.S.-India nuclear deal was as significant for its tacit acknowledgement

Pacific. The U.S. may still be China's single-largest trading partner, but if the 27 states of the EU are considered as a whole, trade between the EU and China now eclipses that between the U.S. and China. With these changing trade patterns come significant changes in the flow of information, ideas, politics and diplomacy. These changes are leading, in some quarters, to a sense of "Asian triumphalism," as Singaporean diplomat and scholar Kishore Mahbubani phrases it. According to Mahbubani, Asians who for centuries have been bystanders in world history are now ready to become codrivers and join the West in shaping global economic institutions, from the International Monetary Fund (IMF) to the World Bank.

Although economic growth has recently received considerable attention, for many, military power remains the gold standard for status as a major power. Perhaps no state serves as the poster child for burgeoning military muscle as much as China whose military has made a quantum leap in recent years, following in the wake of its dynamic economic expansion, marked by more than a decade of double-digit growth in its military budget due to a significant increase in efforts to enhance military capability.

One sign of China's growing mili-

tary power can be seen in efforts by the Chinese Navy to extend its offshore capabilities and increase its strategic maritime depth, building a fleet with modern submarines and new destroyers while revising its naval doctrine to

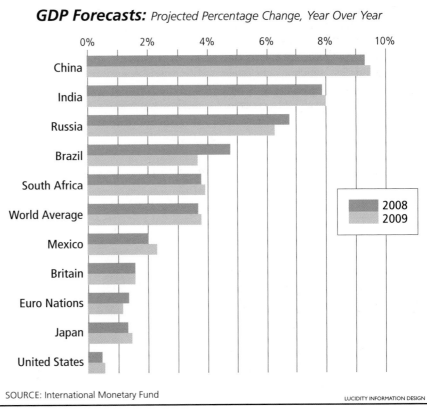

GDP Forecasts: *Projected Percentage Change, Year Over Year*

China
India
Russia
Brazil
South Africa
World Average
Mexico
Britain
Euro Nations
Japan
United States

2008
2009

SOURCE: International Monetary Fund

LUCIDITY INFORMATION DESIGN

NOTE: *Chart does not take into account global economic crisis of fall 2008.*

of India as a nuclear weapons state—as too important to be outside the club, if not quite in and of it—as anything else, but with this acknowledgement coming at considerable potential cost to the future health and endurance of the nonproliferation regime itself.

Other major-power aspirants, such as Brazil or South Africa, have had nuclear programs in the past, but opted not to develop nuclear weapons, pursuing major-power status via other avenues. Japan, of course, has disavowed both nuclear weapons and offensive military power under its Peace Constitution, but in recent years has not been shy about its status as a "virtual" nuclear power, able to "go nuclear," at least technically, on short notice. So long as nuclear weapons are seen as having currency as an indicator of major-power status (it is possible to have nuclear weapons and not be a major power, but is it possible to be a major power without nuclear weapons?), there is likely to be some tension between responsible nonproliferation norms and major powers' orientation toward their own potential nuclear aspirations.

Petro-power

Another significant dimension of power, as in eras past, are energy and natural resources, which appear likely to remain prominent features of new power modalities in the 21st century. In the context of the cross pressures of climate change and the need for emerg-

Brazil's President Luiz Inácio Lula da Silva holds up samples of biodiesel during his visit to Petrobras oil company in Rio de Janeiro, Oct. 26, 2007. AP PHOTO/RICARDO MORAES

ing economies to maintain high levels of growth, energy-related questions— and the limiting factor that a lack of access may create—are critical, cutting several different ways for states that are aspiring to major-power status.

There can be little question, for example, that Russia's reemergence on the world scene following its precipitous decline in the post-cold-war decade has been fueled almost exclusively by the riches accumulated from growing global demand for, and rising prices of oil and natural gas. (Senator Richard Lugar (R-IN) has described a new era of "petro-superpowers," whose strength and influence is in direct proportion to their hold on oil and gas supplies.) Others, such as Brazil, likewise appear ready to leverage their access and expertise with new and alternate energy such as biodiesel, or, like Japan, to assert a position of world leadership through the development of new technologies for energy efficiency or alternate and renewable fuels.

Beyond the economic and military dimensions of power there is a range of other factors, such as demographics, that are also part of the traditional calculus of major-power status. Demographics are again a factor in the perceived rise of China and India, the two most populous states on the planet with seemingly endless supplies of labor, providing both with considerable influence on the global stage. Conversely, on the other side of the linkage is Russia. In recent years, the Russian people have faced several very serious health issues including high rates of HIV/AIDS and alcoholism, resulting in a declining life expectancy rate, now estimated at 65 years overall; 59 years

World leaders at the G-8 summit, July 9, 2008, in Toyako, Japan. From left to right: IEA Executive Director Nobuo Tanaka, IMF Managing Director Dominique Strauss-Kahn, UN Secretary General Ban Ki-moon, Italian Prime Minister Silvio Berlusconi, British Prime Minister Gordon Brown, German Chancellor Angela Merkel, Russian President Dmitry Medvedev, French President Nicolas Sarkozy, Indonesian President Susilo Bambang Yudhoyono, Brazil's President Luiz Inácio Lula da Silva, South African President Thabo Mbeki, Japanese Prime

for men. With a fertility rate of only 1.4, well below the normal replacement rate, Russian demographic trends are on the decline, which poses an interesting question about whether it is possible to be a major power and, at the same time, endure a demographic crash.

Legitimacy of 'power'

A final factor to consider in major-power status lies in the simple acknowledgement of that status by the other players in the international system. One way to measure the emergence of Brazil as a global player can be found in the increasing frequency with which Brazil, previously excluded from the council of the powerful, is recognized as a member of the club. Since 2003, Brazil has had observer status at G-8 (Group of Eight leading industrialized nations) meetings and U.S. policymakers in recent years have taken pains to refer to Brazil as a global partner and key regional power in Latin America. This sort of "recognition" is not just empty rhetoric, but has important practical and concrete applications. First, recognition and a drawing in of rising powers by the established order is a critical element in assuring that eras of power transition are smooth and peaceful. Second, given that the outcome of great historical events has often been determined when the dominant powers meet to discuss them, such as the Congress of Vienna (Nov. 1814–June 1815) following the Napoleonic wars, or the

Paris Peace Conference in 1919, who is invited into the room— and given a seat at the table—is of more than a passing interest to those invested in the outcome.

In today's global system, the United Nations Security Council is the authorized and legitimized space for such a concert of powers and permanent membership on the council—currently reserved for China, France, Russia, Britain and the U.S.—confers status as a global stakeholder. This is precisely the problem for aspirants like India, Japan, Germany, Brazil and others who see permanent council membership as a club that no longer reflects the true distribution of global power.

This "acknowledgement" of great-power status feeds directly into two additional features of major-power status that are critical to both the exercise of a state's power and to the proper functioning of the international community: legitimacy and the provision of public goods.

Indeed, as one analyst has noted, "A nation's material power can be measured in fairly simple terms. On the one hand, military and economic strength may be arduous to acquire, but relatively easy to gauge. Moral authority, on the other hand, is more subjective and has no indices equivalent to GDP

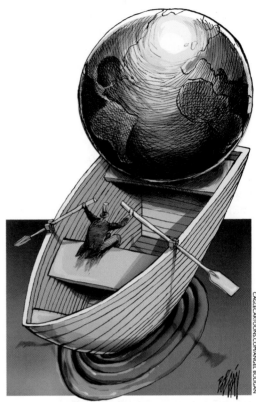

or naval fleet tonnage. Yet the moral high ground is politically a very powerful place, and it cannot be unilaterally claimed or declared. In other words, legitimacy is in the collective eyes of the beholders." For a major power, legitimacy, though harder to measure than these other metrics of power, can prove to be just as useful in the pursuit of interests. If power has to do with the ability to influence the actions of oth-

Minister Yasuo Fukuda, U.S. President George W. Bush, Chinese President Hu Jintao, Mexican President Felipe Calderón, South Korean President Lee Myung-bak, Indian Prime Minister Manmohan Singh, Canadian Prime Minister Stephen Harper, Australian Prime Minister Kevin Rudd, EU President José Manuel Barroso, World Bank President Robert Zoellick and OECD Secretary-General José Ángel Gurría Treviño. AP PHOTO/PABLO MARTINEZ MONSIVAIS

ers, being seen as legitimate in one's actions and goals can play a critical role in shaping the reaction of others to one's policies, gaining support and shaping outcomes.

Power in a new era

Beyond these base features—wealth, military power, demographics and the like—the elements of major-power status must also be relevant to the realities of the new era and its defining features. Traditional concepts, like the geopolitical importance of spatial and geographic location that were stressed by analysts in the 19th and early 20th centuries, for example, became less relevant in an age of ballistic missile technology that rendered traditional force-space ratios irrelevant. Although many traditional elements of power remain crucial, the realities of a globalized, digitalized world of the 21st century have introduced new power dimensions that have allowed some unlikely countries to contend for major-power

status. While not a comprehensive enumeration, some of these new elements of power are the nature of soft power, globalization and innovation.

In an era of instantaneous global communications, soft power can be seen as playing an increasingly important role in a major power's portfolio. The concept of soft power was developed by Joseph S. Nye, Jr., dean of Harvard's Kennedy School of Government, who summarized it as "… the ability to shape the preferences of others…. [It is] leading by example and attracting others to do what you want." This persuasive attractiveness plays out through popular culture, public diplomacy and the power of national ideas and ideals. American soft power helped further U.S. goals in the cold war. Today, many analysts point to China's marketing of its soft-power assets—be it as an exciting place to do business, an interesting culture or an alternative political model with notions of nonintervention and state

sovereignty—as essential to its rise.

But other rising powers also benefit from the increasing importance of soft power in shaping today's world. Indeed, in some ways it is the increasing importance of soft power that has allowed them to aspire to major-power status. Brazil has emerged on the world scene not only due to its vibrant economy, but also its vivacious culture, with the image of Brazil—its music and its beaches—helping to create an effective "brand" that leverages its economic potential in trade and its diplomatic profile in regional and global affairs.

The interconnectedness of the global economy and trade has likewise changed the complexion of traditional measures of economic power and the accumulation of national wealth. The level of worldwide trade, measured as a ratio of exports to GDP, is twice as high today as it was a century ago. Foreign direct investment and cross-ownership—of real estate, corporate assets, stocks and bonds—between the

Who are the rising powers?

SINCE THE POPULARIZATION of the concept of great powers in the 19th century, academics have tended to apply the term to European powers, with the U.S. and Japan as exceptions. Thus the 1884 Congress of Berlin divided up Africa among the European colonial powers; the Paris Peace Conference in 1919 saw Europe—along with the U.S. and Japan—redraw the map of much of the world in the wake of World War I; and Tehran (1943) and Yalta (1945) saw the Allied powers remake the world again following World War II.

As the world enters the 21st century, the global landscape is shifting. Few would argue with the idea that the U.S., EU and Japan remain among the ranks of today's major powers. Likewise, few would contest the idea that China and India have emerged and have converted their rising influence to major-power status. Russia, as always, remains "a riddle wrapped in a mystery inside an enigma," possessing some elements of major-power status—its vast energy resources, its nuclear arsenal—while other features, such as its demographic decline, argue for a less certain status.

Beyond these six, debate remains over how to measure the relative power and influence of rising powers like Brazil or South Korea, which clearly possess some elements of power but perhaps not enough—or not enough yet—to be included in the ranks of the globally influential.

Another is Turkey. Its claim to major-power status rests in part on its strategic location between Europe, Asia and the Middle East. Like real estate prices, power can, at least along one dimension, also be derived from "location, location, location." Turkey's geography provides it strategic influence on critical issues like energy. It also has conceptual influence, offering a model for secular Islamic development and politics. Turkey's continued political evolution will be a key marker for navigating between Europe and the Islamic world. Turkey will clearly exert considerable and perhaps decisive influence on some of the key issues facing the international community in the decades ahead. Turkey appears to have a claim on rising-power status in some respects, yet at the same time, its economy and military, while regionally influential and significant, seem to fall short as measures that provide the basis for global major-power status.

Regardless of how one may choose to answer the question of who is in, who is out and why, it seems reasonable nonetheless to conclude, as Secretary of State Condoleezza Rice (2005–2009) acknowledged in a speech in 2006, that "in the 21st century, emerging nations like India and China and Brazil and Egypt and Indonesia and South Africa are increasingly shaping the course of history." Indeed, with China and India seemingly on their way to great-power status, the political consolidation of Europe and the rise of "middle powers" such as Brazil and South Africa, the world is arguably witnessing a shift in power dynamics that has been unparalleled in 200 years.

major powers is unprecedented, creating truly global flows of capital, people and goods. When the New York Stock Exchange catches a cold, London, Tokyo and Shanghai all sneeze—and vice versa.

The creation of new financial structures and instruments has also changed the potential utility of national wealth accumulation (for example, through trade surpluses) as a tool of state power. Projecting power is no longer simply about being able to translate wealth into military force. China holds approximately $600 billion in U.S. treasuries and China's total foreign currency reserves of some $1.9 trillion, as of October 2008, seem to give it potential economic clout, even if analysts remain divided on exactly how China might operationalize this potential leverage in useful ways.

Human capacity

A third feature of the new global order is an emphasis on innovation and the ability of a nation to compete in producing the scientific and technological breakthroughs that lead to economic (and other) power that will shape and influence the way people live. This is demonstrated by a debate often popularized through misleading statistics about how many engineers China or India is producing versus a decline in engineers produced in the U.S. When seen through the prism of inter-

Panasonic's new eco-house system is seen on display in Tokyo, Japan, Feb. 13, 2008. The superclean technology creates energy from the chemical reaction of hydrogen combining with oxygen in the air to form water. Developers say fuel cells for homes reduce emission of global-warming gases by a third, compared to conventional electricity, due to their energy efficiency AP PHOTO/JUNJI KUROKAWA

national patent applications, the U.S. still stands head and shoulders above the rest, with some 53,000 patent applications in 2007, compared to 28,000 for Japan and just 5,000 for China.

An emphasis on innovation also opens the door for new players on the world scene, who may lack some of the traditional prerogatives of major powers, to seek influence and leverage. South Korea, for example, is a global leader in new and emerging technologies like cloning, robotics and biotechnology, fields that seem destined to have as much influence in shaping the decades ahead as the automobile

sector did in shaping the last century. South Korea is now on track to become the world's ninth-largest economy, and with some 90% of its homes wired for high-speed internet, to cement its place as a hub in the networked world of the 21st century.

These elements may not be definitive for determining major-power status in the years and decades ahead, but measuring the ability of states to pursue their interests and shape events through these new and alternative dimensions of power will be a critical factor in discerning the character of the world to come.

New global challenges

This era of rising powers and shifting global-power dynamics is defined not just by new elements of power status, but also by a host of new and shared global challenges. The ability of current and emerging powers to navigate these challenges—together or alone—will help define the 21st century.

First, there is the challenge of energy and natural resources. As rising powers place increasing demands on the world's resources and commodities—think energy and food, but also

water and a fragile ecosystem—will the 21st century see a return of geopolitical competition and mercantilist economics?

Looking at the "new international energy order," defense analyst Michael Klare argues that America's sole superpower status is falling to the increasing influence of "petro-superpowers" like Russia and "Chindia," and he warns of the danger of a new cold-war environment driven by energy competition. To head off potentially disastrous competition, Klare urges a

U.S. diplomatic initiative to build collaboration with China (rapidly moving to second place in carbon emissions) to develop alternative energy resources, such as biodiesel fuels; ultralight, ultraefficient vehicles; and an innovative plan to use new coal plants (currently in development) to strip carbon waste that can then be buried.

Indeed, the International Energy Agency's 2007 World Energy Outlook report concluded that growing demand from India and China is transforming the global energy system. Without cooperative and collaborative mechanisms in place, major powers now compete around the globe to lock in long-term secure energy supplies.

The international energy market has also long depended on the notion that the U.S., in its role as global police officer and provider of public goods, would be willing to use force, if needed, to manage its operation. As energy security analysts Daniel Moran and James A. Russell have noted in their examination of the militarization of energy supplies, "international markets have always been sustained indirectly by the armed forces of major participants, above all by the great maritime powers (first Britain, now the U.S.), whose interest in the expansion of global commerce was and is backed by armed forces that secure an essential piece of the system: free transit of goods across the high seas."

Thus, as a recent Stanley Foundation analysis brief concludes, the energy market has never been immune to political and strategic influence. Oil has been used as a weapon by oil-producing states in the past, and its price (along with that of natural gas) is reflective of a range of political pressures to which a perfectly efficient, private, agnostic market would be indifferent.

Closely related to energy security is climate change. Global emissions of "greenhouse gases" (gases that trap heat in the atmosphere) nearly doubled over the last 30 years, driven in large part by the economic growth of China, India and other rising powers (and by the failure of major powers to curb their behavior). With the threat of climate change mounting — warming temperatures, an increase in severe and unpredictable weather events, in some places, drought and the spread of tropical diseases — the global community will have to cut greenhouse-gas emissions dramatically in the coming decades simply to mitigate the worst effects of climate change.

However, for many rising powers a mandate to cut emissions is tantamount to putting the brakes on economic growth — a trade-off that may have unacceptable political consequences if mounting unemployment leads to social unrest. From the perspective of rising powers, any climate-change regime that does not demand severe concessions from already established powers — countries that have already had the opportunity to reap the benefits of industrialization — would be viewed as unfair and illegitimate.

In an era of concentrated power,

solutions to a challenge like climate change can be imposed on others. Yet in an era of diffused power, with different perspectives and interests, the questions remain as to who determines what a just and fair climate-change regime is and how it is enforced.

A third key global challenge lies in nuclear nonproliferation. Under the NPT, states without nuclear weapons pledged not to acquire them, while the five nuclear weapons states agreed to take actions to reduce their arsenals with the aim of eventually giving them up. The NPT and the core understanding animating it held for close to 30 years, deterring new states from acquiring nuclear weapons. However, in the two decades that have followed the cold war, stresses have increasingly threatened the "grand bargain" that buttressed the NPT regime for most of the second half of the 20th century. Those stresses include proliferation activities by a number of NPT signatories like North Korea and Iran that allow them to develop nuclear-weapons capability while remaining in compliance with the NPT; the international community's treatment of nonsignatories like Israel, India and Pakistan; and the shortcomings of nuclear-weapon states like the U.S. and Russia to reduce their stockpiles.

A common characteristic of the strains facing the nonproliferation regime is their connection to the changing global order. If it were ever the case, it is certainly true today that the U.S. can no longer dictate the rules of the nuclear game. Russia is resurgent and unwilling to blithely accede to U.S. wishes. Regional power dynamics and security competition drive nuclear ambitions. Furthermore, the status associated with the possession of nuclear weapons makes it valuable for states seeking a seat at the global head table. The widespread reconsideration of nuclear energy in the context of climate change further complicates nonproliferation efforts.

A fourth challenge shaping the new era is the rise of terrorism and nonstate actors. In many respects the rise of terrorists with global reach can

The United Nations Security Council discusses the situation in the Middle East, Sept. 26, 2008, at UN headquarters in New York City. Saudi Arabia, the Arab League and the Palestinian president urged the Security Council to save the faltering Middle East peace process by demanding an end to Israeli settlements in Palestinian territory. AP Photo/David Karp

be seen as the dark underbelly of globalization. Terror networks that may have their origin in a very specific political grievance are now able to operate worldwide through new information technologies, buoyed by global black markets of weapons and drugs which provide resources and material that "super-empower" what might otherwise have been troubling, but localized, manifestations of extreme and violent ideologies.

According to a recent Stanley Foundation paper, Joseph McMillan, a former Department of Defense official, has described such nonstate groups as "armed bands" that benefit from the globalization of information: "The information revolution is a major facilitator of almost anything a terrorist group would want to do, from collecting intelligence to propagating its ideological message to recruiting, indoctrinating and training new personnel.... Thorough indoctrination in what soldiers would call 'the commander's intent,' coupled with the most sporadic of communications, could yield an unprecedented degree of fluidity and unpredictability in terrorist operations."

A fifth challenge lies in the question of whether, as in eras past, internal domestic or cultural factors in major powers may be leading to a world in which there are multiple competing ideological frameworks, each with its own set of rules, interpretation and enforcement mechanisms. Political scientist Samuel P. Huntington famously put forward his "clash of civilizations" theory in 1993. More recently, Robert Kagan, neocon political commentator, has proposed that a division exists in the world between Western democracies and an "axis of authoritarianism" centered in China and Russia. Kagan suggests that a new, long struggle between ideologically opposed major powers is on the horizon. Bulgarian political scientist Ivan Krastev, in the *American Interest,* offers his concept of a clash of civilizations between postmodern states and premodern illiberal ones, pointing to a Europe that is seeking to move be-

A worker uses a blowtorch on a construction site in Beijing, China, Jan. 24, 2008. For over a decade, China's economy has grown annually at a 10% clip. By 2050, China's economy could overtake the U.S. as the world's largest economy. AP Photo/Greg Baker

yond the use of force as a mechanism to arbitrate disputes and a Russia still reliant on flexing military muscle.

Krastev's suggested ideological clash was read by many as the subtext of Russia's actions against Georgia in the summer of 2008, which were seen as a return to a 19th-century "sphere of influence" approach. Russia's military actions were in essence an announcement that it was not to be challenged in setting and enforcing the rules in what it terms its "near abroad," and an exclamation point on an announcement that Russia was resurgent as a major power. Following the dissolution of the Soviet Union in 1991 and a decade in which Russia's economy was in shambles and its military second-class, it had seemed that Russia was destined to be a second-tier power. Yet there can be little doubt now that Russia was flexing its military muscle as a reminder that it must still be counted in the top tier.

There is an undeniable danger in major-power rivalry that breaks down along these sorts of ideological lines. Different and competing approaches to questions of sovereignty, legitimacy, intervention, the use of force and other normative practices, and the resultant implications for the shape of global order, is a formula that, lack-

ing the existence of broadly accepted ameliorative mechanisms seems destined to create friction, rivalry and perhaps even worse consequences.

A new global order?

Thus, a final challenge for the new era of multiple rising and major powers lies in reinvigorating—or recreating—the structures of global governance that reflect power alignments in the international system at a given historical moment. As power relations evolve, global governance structures must either prove themselves sufficiently plastic to cope with new realities or risk rupture, to be replaced by new institutions and norms reflecting new realities.

Are there areas of convergence and/or divergence in the ways that major and rising powers view the current international civil order and its shared rules? Can effective multilateral approaches be developed for global governance in an era of multiple and rising powers?

In the aftermath of World War II, the U.S. helped establish a system of global institutions, norms and other mechanisms that were both capable and adequate to address the challenges of global-problem solving and adjudication, and also reflected

CAGLECARTOONS.COM/FREDERICK DELIGNE

the alignment of interests and powers in the world as it then stood. The five permanent members of the Security Council were the victorious powers of the war (with the exception of China), but they are no longer, some 60 years later, the five strongest or most important global players.

Reshaping institutions

Since the norms of the international order are ultimately enforced by the major powers in a period of transition, the rules of the road can become ambiguous and it can be difficult to determine who plays the role of enforcer if different powers have different views. Thus the risk of conflict becomes higher. In many important respects the current gridlock in international institutions such as the UN and World Trade Organization (WTO) can be seen as a reflection of changes in power dynamics and the diffusion of power.

More recently, the global financial crisis in the fall of 2008 has thrown this question of the adequacy of international institutions to capably meet the challenges of the new global order into sharp relief.

British Prime Minister Gordon Brown summed up the conventional wisdom about the shortcomings of the post–World War II system of financial institutions—known as the Bretton

Woods system—when he said in October 2008, "The old postwar international financial institutions are out-of-date.... We need cross-border supervision of financial institutions; shared global standards for accounting and regulation; a more responsible approach to executive remuneration that rewards hard work, effort and enterprise but not irresponsible risk taking; and the renewal of our international institutions to make them effective early-warning systems for the world economy."

In the wake of the financial crisis, numerous commentators concluded that the G-8 should exercise a coordinating and aligning role in the international community. But as the functional challenges of the crisis made clear, the G-8 as presently constituted does not have the right set of players gathered around the table. Many have ideas for how to determine the right set of players. Robert Zoellick, president of the World Bank, has proposed the creation of a G-14, drawing in additional stakeholders who would put their national interests at risk in addition to bringing their economic and financial power to bear. Others have suggested different configurations and geometry. Underlying all the proposals is a sense that no matter what set of players, the *right* set of players reflecting new power equities and realities needs to be woven into the institutional

architecture in order for it to prove adequate to the challenges of the new era.

The end of unipolarity?

The financial crisis also appears to have highlighted another significant feature of the new era. After more than a half century in which the U.S. set the standards for the shape and functioning of international institutions, other powers are now asserting their prerogatives. The U.S., with its power in relative decline, has been compelled to accept that others are now setting the rules of the game. A newsmagazine cover story on "the committee to save the world" in the fall of 2008 would likely have featured European political leaders and central bankers playing the key roles in shaping the policy response, leaving the U.S. to accommodate, and in the unfamiliar position of following, not leading.

An additional consideration is how to restructure multilateral organizations to reflect the reality of new- and emerging-power dynamics. Though these institutions often serve as shock absorbers, smoothing relations among contending powers, there is also some danger that during periods of power transition, regional and global institutions may themselves become mechanisms for furthering competition among powers. Something of that dynamic was visible when Japanese and Chinese competition and rivalry played out in the run-up to the launch of the East Asia Summit in 2005. Japanese and Chinese interest in the institution waxed and waned in perfect proportion to one another, each clearly measuring the potential of the institution in zero-sum terms rather than as a way to ameliorate and smooth over competition.

In the end, global and regional systems are the mechanisms that allow nations to participate in multilateral, cooperative action. Managing today's transnational threats and challenges requires a cross-regional, principled and multilateral "coalition for global governance" that incorporates as many of today's middle and rising powers as possible.

One of the salient features of the challenges of the new era—be it nonproliferation, terrorism, energy or architecture—is that the very essence of the problem presented to the international community is shared and common.

The U.S. role in a multipolar era?

As this new world has started to come into focus, increasing amounts of ink are being spilled in response to the question of the strategic options available to U.S. policymakers.

Broadly speaking, several schools of thought have arisen about how the U.S. should react and deal with the changed and changing global circumstances. One school, citing the dangerous and turbulent nature of the world, stresses "primacy," advocating that the U.S. maintain unrivaled military power to protect its interests and that it allow, in the words of the 2002 National Security Strategy of the U.S., "no peer competitors." A second school, though it does not emphasize primacy, underscores the inevitability of a clash among the major powers, driven either by "realism" or cultural and civilizational issues. A final school acknowledges the reality of what has been termed the "post-American era," but is divided over the best response, with some advocating the embrace of a multipolar world and a networked future, while others promote a retreat to isolationism, with good fences making for good neighbors.

As Mona Sutphen and Nina Hachi-

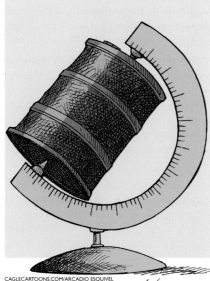

CAGLECARTOONS.COM/ARCADIO ESQUIVEL

gian, coauthors of *The Next American Century,* have argued, the best bet for the U.S. may be to take advantage of the new global reality and view other major powers—both established and emerging—not as competitors but as potential collaborators in dealing with global challenges. In a world of multiple major powers, a focus on strategic collaboration, while hedging in case things go sour, is likely to prove beneficial over the long haul, especially given the number of serious transnational issues that confront the world today. What might such an approach look like?

Collaboration and recognition

First, the U.S. needs to appreciate the multidimensionality of the rise of other major powers. The real challenge of a China or an India is not so much in the military sphere, but rather along other dimensions of power—economic, cultural, diplomatic—where they will be "peer competitors" of the U.S. in the international community.

Second, the U.S. needs to appreciate the reality that power is relative and that the changing balance of power in today's world is due at least as much to the erosion of American power—such as the decline in U.S. soft power in the context of Iraq—as because of the rise of other major powers.

Third, as other major powers seek to integrate and embed themselves in international institutions and seek positive relations not just with the U.S. but with each other, it will be difficult, if not impossible, for the U.S. to construct alignments that might hold down any one, let alone all, of the other major powers.

Fourth, so long as there is uncertainty about the strategy and objectives of any of the rising powers, the U.S. will be neither friend nor foe of that power. There can and should be cooperation on issues where there is a mutuality of interests. Confrontation can be avoided, but strategic transparency will be needed if the U.S is to pursue positive relations.

Fifth, the goal of U.S. policy is not to try to prevent others from rising, but

rather to strengthen the mechanisms that will cushion the impacts of these changes in power distribution around the world. The U.S. should engage other major powers in enforcing international norms and standards—to be "responsible stakeholders" in the international community. The U.S. can build or expand areas of cooperation, such as climate change or the prevention of pandemics, where there are obvious shared interests. Additionally, the U.S. can strengthen its own ability to compete by getting its own house in order, addressing fiscal imbalances and pressing domestic issues that undermine core strengths (such as an educated and skilled workforce) and the U.S. position in the world.

Lastly, the U.S. needs to recognize that its own worldview will be critical to defining this new era, even as American power appears to be in relative decline. Whether the U.S. approaches these issues as zero or non-zero sum will shape and influence the views of other major powers, and over time, the world and the views of other major powers will tend to reflect the U.S. approach, for better or for worse.

Why should the U.S. seek such a collaborative and cooperative approach? The basic reason, according to Sutphen and Hachigian, is simple: given the realities of the challenges the U.S. faces in the 21st century, there is nothing that it can do on the global stage that could not likely be done better with the cooperation of others.

The U.S. cannot determine the future or the choices of other major powers. That task ultimately belongs to them. But by working with other major powers to tackle shared global challenges, the U.S. has a once-in-a-generation opportunity to shape the environment in which these powers make their choices while peacefully integrating these states into a rules-based international order—and, in the process, embedding them into the web of norms and responsibilities that come with being active players on the world stage. ●

OPINION BALLOTS AFTER PAGE 64

QUESTIONS

1. If the 21st century brings increased competition for resources, what does this mean for the U.S.?

2. Do you believe that the U.S. can influence how countries like China, India and others wield their power? If so, how?

3. Are there any areas of power where the U.S. should maintain its dominance? If yes, which ones?

4. Can the power structures of existing organizations like the United Nations be adapted to accommodate rising nations? If not, are there other venues to accommodate them?

5. What role should the U.S. have in dealing with the global challenges of energy security, climate change, nuclear proliferation and terrorism?

6. Do you think a clash between the U.S. and other rising or dominant powers can be avoided? If yes, how? If not, why?

7. Does the changing global order demand more collaboration and cooperation from the U.S.? If not, what relationship should the U.S. seek with the rest of the world?

8. Should the U.S. seek a collaborative and cooperative approach to global challenges? What are the advantages and disadvantages of doing this?

9. How should the U.S. react to changing global circumstances? Should the U.S. view the emergence of powers like China and India as a threat or as an opportunity? Explain your answer.

NOTES: ....
....
....
....
....
....
....
....
....
....
....

READINGS

Diamond, Jared, **Collapse: How Societies Choose to Fail or Succeed.** New York, Penguin Books, 2005. 592 pp. $18.00 (paper). An innovative study of ecological factors that can lead to and create societal crisis and collapse.

Emmott, Bill, **Rivals: How the Power Struggle Between China, India and Japan Will Shape Our Next Decade.** San Diego, CA, Harcourt, 2008. 352 pp. $26.00 (hardcover). The book explores the opportunities and challenges for the U.S., China, India and Japan, including patterns of political culture as well as economic, military and political power, with possible policy options and outcomes, to create a stable, prosperous and secure Asia, and globe, in the decades to come.

Hachigian, Nina, and Sutphen, Mona, **The Next American Century: How the U.S. Can Thrive as Other Powers Rise.** New York, Simon & Schuster, 2008. 368 pp. $16.00 (paper). The authors argue that while the U.S. may have some conflicts with "pivotal powers"—China, Europe, India, Japan and Russia—by and large, they want what the U.S. wants: a stable world and better lives for their citizens.

Kennedy, Paul, **The Rise and Fall of the Great Powers.** New York, Knopf, 1989. 704 pp. $18.00 (paper). A groundbreaking study tracking the rise and fall of great powers and empires through history, drawing insights about the necessary elements of state power, and how great powers, through imperial overstretch, for example, can seal their fate.

Klare, Michael T., **Rising Powers, Shrinking Planet: The New Geopolitics of Energy.** New York, Metropolitan Books, 2008. 352 pp. $26.00 (hardcover). Klare explores the contours of energy competition in the 21st century, identifying and analyzing the major players as well as the new playing field, the danger of armed conflict and environmental disaster and warning of the danger of a new cold-war environment if the major powers are unable to develop cooperative structures and alternative energy resources.

Mahbubani, Kishore, **The New Asian Hemisphere: The Irresistible Shift of Global Power to the East.** New York, PublicAffairs, 2008. 336 pp. $26.00 (hardcover). The author proposes a new Asian century in which Asians move from being bystanders to drivers of world history and argues that Asia wants to replicate, not dominate, the West. Accordingly, tensions can be avoided if the world accepts key principles for a new global partnership.

Soderberg, Nancy, and Katulis, Brian, **The Prosperity Agenda: What the World Wants from America—and What We Need in Return.** Hoboken, NJ, Wiley, 2008. 272 pp. $27.95 (hardcover). The authors argue that a new, integrated U.S. national security strategy with emphasis on improving the lives of people around the world will prove effective in helping defeat terrorism, increasing America's leverage against its enemies, weakening dictatorships and, most importantly, saving the lives of millions.

Zakaria, Fareed, **The Post-American World.** New York, Norton, 2008. 288 pp. $25.95 (hardcover). Zakaria argues that while it is true that America is losing the ability to dictate to a new world that is rising, it has not lost the ability to lead. The danger, as Zakaria sees it, is that just as the world is opening up, America is closing down.

TO LEARN MORE ABOUT THIS TOPIC AND TO ACCESS WEB LINKS TO RESOURCES GO TO www.greatdecisions.org/topic1

Afghanistan and Pakistan

by Barnett R. Rubin

With a new President in the White House, the U.S. military focus is likely to shift to Afghanistan and Pakistan. Are there realistic goals for U.S. involvement in this complex area?

Newly elected president of Afghanistan, Hamid Karzai, gives a speech during a session of the Loya Jirga (grand council) in Kabul, Afghanistan, June 14, 2002. Karzai was elected Afghan head of state by a landslide at the Loya Jirga assembly after setting out his vision to rebuild the war-shattered nation. AP PHOTO/BEHROUZ MEHRI/POOL

In 2009 Afghanistan will both face a new U.S. Administration and hold its own presidential and provincial elections. President Barack Obama's Administration will have little time to work with the United Nations and the Afghan government to stabilize or reverse a fast-deteriorating situation. Presidential elections are scheduled to be held in late 2009 in Afghanistan, but with both security and government control in decline, the government and international community might be unable to carry out a credible electoral process in much of the southern part of the country. This could threaten the foundation and legitimacy of the post-Taliban regime. In Pakistan, a newly elected civilian government faces an uphill battle to establish, let alone consolidate, its power, and the Pakistani Taliban continues to provide al-Qaeda with a secure base, creating an additional area of concern.

The recent upsurge in violence is only the latest chapter in Afghanistan's 30-year war, which started as a cold-war ideological battle, morphed into a regionally fueled clash of ethnic factionalism and then became the center of the broader conflict between the international establishment and a transnational Islamist insurgency. Afghanistan has been a flashpoint—shattered by the successive collapses of the British and Russia-Soviet empires, the disappearance of cold-war regulatory mechanisms and the growth of a globalized, nonterritorial terrorist network.

The problem originated with Afghanistan's position as a buffer state within the sphere of influence of British India. As the British Empire moved northwest from the Indian subcontinent toward Central Asia, it first tried to conquer Afghanistan and then, after two Afghan-Anglo wars, settled for making it a buffer against the Russian empire to the north. The Afghan state was formed not to provide security and gover-

BARNETT R. RUBIN *is the Director of Studies and Senior Fellow at the Center on International Cooperation, New York University. He is also chair and founder of the Conflict Prevention and Peace Forum of the Social Science Research Council. He served as adviser to the UN Special Representative of the Secretary-General during the UN Talks on Afghanistan that produced the Bonn agreement in November-December 2001 and has advised the UN on the monitoring of assistance and the drafting of the Constitution of the Islamic Republic of Afghanistan, the Afghanistan Compact, Afghanistan's Millennium Development Goals, and the Afghanistan National Development Strategy.*

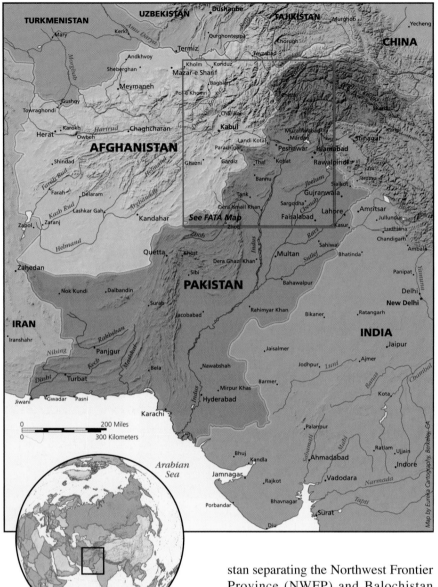

nance to its people but to enable a foreign-subsidized elite to control the territory as a first line of defense against foreign empires and neighboring states. Hence the paradox of modern Afghanistan: a country that needs to decentralize governance to provide services to its scattered and ethnically fragmented population has one of the world's most centralized governments.

The British established a three-tiered border settlement. The first frontier was the line separating the areas of India under direct British administration from areas under Pashtun tribal control—today the line within Paki-stan separating the Northwest Frontier Province (NWFP) and Balochistan from the Federally Administered Tribal Agencies/Areas (FATA). The second frontier was the Durand Line, separating the tribal territories from the area under the administration of the Emir of Afghanistan—now the line that Pakistan and the rest of the international community consider to be the international border. The areas under the control of the Afghan state were stabilized through British aid.

In the 20th century, however, the weakening and dissolution of these empires eroded this security arrangement. The Third Anglo-Afghan War, in 1919, concluded with the recognition of Afghanistan's full sovereignty. The independence and partition of India in 1947 changed the strategic stakes in the region once again. Afghanistan claimed that Pakistan was a new state, not a successor to British India, thereby concluding that all treaties, including those regarding the frontier, had lapsed. It did not recognize the Durand Line as an international border and called for the self-determination of the tribal territories as Pashtunistan. At the same time, Islamabad was aligning itself with the U.S. in order to balance India—which led Afghanistan, in turn, to rely on aid from Moscow to train and supply its army.

Afghanistan's ruling dynasty collapsed in 1973, when the king was overthrown by his cousin, Daud, who was in turn overthrown and killed by Communist military officers in an April 1978 coup. When the Soviet Union intervened militarily in December 1979, the fight expanded into the major military confrontation of the cold-war endgame. The U.S., Pakistan, Saudi Arabia and others spent billions of dollars supporting the Afghan mujahidin (guerrilla fighters) and their Arab auxiliaries, creating a regional and global infrastructure for jihad (or holy war).

After 1991, as the U.S.S.R. dissolved and the U.S. disengaged, regional powers fueled a conflict among ethnically organized militias. Drug trafficking boomed on the ruins of the economy, while Arab and other non-Afghan Islamist radicals strengthened their bases and networks. Pakistan supported the rise to power of the Islamic fundamentalist Taliban, while the resistance, organized in a "Northern Alliance" of feuding former mujahidin and Soviet-supported militias mainly from non-Pashtun ethnic groups, held some pockets bordering on Central Asia.

The U.S. government was utterly unprepared to respond to the attacks of Sept 11, 2001. Immediately following 9/11, a panicked Bush Administration developed a response focused on counterterrorism. The Administration prioritized destroying al-Qaeda's bases in Afghanistan and assuring that it would not find sanctuary in another state. The military strategy consisted of providing money and arms to, and coordinating air support with, Afghan ground commanders. The U.S.-led operation began with bombing on Oct. 7, 2001.

Several weeks after 9/11, the State Department proposed that the U.S. ask the UN to take charge of sponsoring a political transition and a reconstruction program despite Administration hostility to "nation building." U.S. President George W. Bush (2001–2009) accepted such a framework because the U.S. was initially to be involved only in supporting the UN effort.

The UN-sponsored Bonn Agreement named an interim authority for six months and provided a framework to restore political legitimacy to the Afghan state by gradually making the government more representative. It also contained declaratory goals for restoring and increasing the effectiveness of the Afghan state. The new government was inaugurated on Dec. 22, 2001. The remaining leadership of the Taliban and al-Qaeda fled to Pakistan or remained in remote areas of Afghanistan.

The interim authority chosen at Bonn had a six-month term. Its primary task, besides reestablishing basic administration, was to convene an Emergency Loya Jirga (ELJ) to choose the "transitional" administration that would succeed the "interim" one. (Loya Jirga, a Pashto phrase meaning grand council, is a centuries-old Afghan institution.) As the ELJ would be the first nationally representative body to be convened in Afghanistan in decades, the hope was that it would choose a far more representative government than the interim administration appointed at Bonn. However, the main commanders and mujahidin leaders, in attendance though not as elected delegates, dominated the proceedings.

The continued power of these leaders resulted from the U.S. counterterrorism policy. The Taliban were not an international terrorist organization but an Afghan movement that had gained control of most of the country; yet they did not participate in the Bonn Conference, since the conference occurred as they were being forcibly removed from power. Neither, in succeeding months, were there any efforts to incorporate them into the peace process.

Under the Bonn Agreement, the transitional authority appointed a commission to draft a new constitution, to be submitted to a Constitutional Loya Jirga (CLJ) within 18 months of the ELJ. The CLJ met from Dec.14, 2003, to Jan. 4, 2004, and adopted a presidential system with a bicameral legislature and a powerful (if unreformed) judiciary. It reaffirmed Afghanistan's historical centralized administrative structure, while for the first time recognizing its ethnic plurality.

Within six months of the CLJ, the government was to hold free and fair elections to choose a "fully representative government." Both practical and political imperatives led to holding the presidential elections separately from the legislative elections. Hamid Karzai was elected president of Afghanistan for a term of five years in October 2004 and was inaugurated two months later. The National Assembly and provincial assemblies were elected in September 2005. The National Assembly convened in December 2005, marking the end of the Bonn process.

The international military presence changed during that period. The U.S., which did not want a "peacekeeping" force in the same space as its "war fighters," had opposed the expansion of the International Security Assistance Force (ISAF), a UN-mandated force established in accord with the Bonn Agreement, until the summer of 2003. Provincial Reconstruction Teams (PRTs) were devised as a partial solution to the challenge of security in the provinces. PRTs—initially all coalition-led—consisted of deployments of several dozen troops with a few embedded aid officials, whom the military protection would enable to start reconstruction, thus building public support and improving security.

The North Atlantic Treaty Organization (NATO) took over command of ISAF on Aug. 11, 2003. Over the next two years, NATO-led ISAF expanded by establishing more PRTs

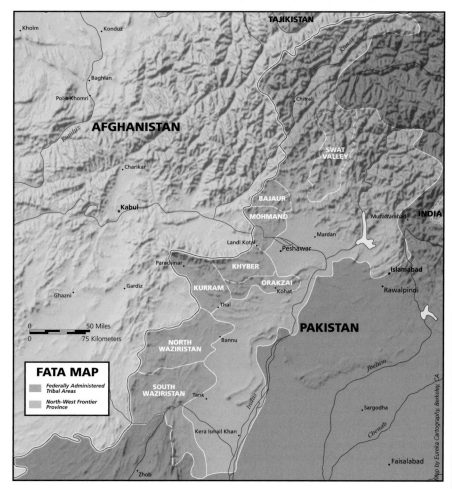

Glossary of terms

AFGHANISTAN COMPACT: The outcome of the London Conference on Afghanistan in 2006. It was the result of consultations by the government of Afghanistan with the United Nations and the international community and established the framework for international cooperation with Afghanistan for the following five years.

ANA: The Afghan National Army is a service branch of the military of Afghanistan currently being trained by the coalition forces. The ANA is being equipped with modern weapons and provided with newly built state-of-the-art housing facilities. As of May 2008, the Afghan National Army comprises at least 76,000 active troops.

ANSF: Afghanistan National Security Forces, comprises ANA, Afghan National Police, National Directorate of Security (NDS) and other forces.

BONN AGREEMENT, BONN PROCESS: Under the "Bonn Agreement," an Afghan Interim Authority was formed and took office in Kabul, Afghanistan, on Dec. 22, 2001, with Hamid Karzai as chairman. The Interim Authority held power until an emergency Loya Jirga (grand council) in mid-June 2002 that decided on the structure of a Transitional Authority. The Transitional Authority, headed by President Karzai, renamed the government the Transitional Islamic State of Afghanistan (TISA). One of TISA's primary achievements was the drafting of a constitution that was ratified by a Constitutional Loya Jirga on Jan. 4, 2004.

DURAND LINE: Named after Sir Mortimer Durand, the foreign secretary of the British Indian government, it is the term for the 2,640 kilometer (1,610 mile) border between Afghanistan and Pakistan. After reaching a virtual stalemate in two wars against the Afghans, the British forced Emir Abdur Rahman Khan of Afghanistan on Nov. 12, 1893, to come to an agreement under duress to demarcate the border between Afghanistan and what was then British India (now North-West Frontier Province (NWFP), Federally Administered Tribal Areas (FATA) and Balochistan provinces of Pakistan).

FATA: The Federally Administered Tribal Areas or Agencies (FATA) in Pakistan are areas outside the four provinces bordering Afghanistan, comprising a region of some 27,220 km² (10,507 sq mi). The Tribal Areas comprise seven agencies, namely Khyber, Kurram, Bajaur, Mohmand, Orakzai, north and south areas of Waziristan and six FRs (Frontier Regions) namely FR Peshawar, FR Kohat, FR Tank, FR Banuu, FR Lakki and FR Dera Ismail Khan. The constitution of Pakistan provides for a form of indirect rule in FATA, in which tribes represented by elders are collectively responsible for security under the control of political agents appointed by the governor of NWFP.

NORTHERN ALLIANCE: "NA" is a name used for the UF (the United Front), which was formed by an alliance of groups supported by Russia and Iran that opposed the Taliban and had recognized the ISA. In 2001 the UF succeeded in occupying those areas of northern and western Afghanistan, as well as the capital, Kabul, from which the Taliban and al-Qaeda had been dislodged mainly by the U.S. air war.

NWFP: The North-West Frontier Province (NWFP) is the smallest of the four main provinces of Pakistan. The NWFP is a Pashtun-majority province.

PASHTUNISTAN: The idea of an independent country constituting the Pashtun -dominated areas of Pakistan and Afghanistan. Pashtun nationalists believe this historic homeland was divided in 1893 by the Durand Line, a border between British India and Afghanistan.

PASHTUNS: An Eastern Iranian ethno-linguistic group with populations primarily in eastern and southern Afghanistan and in the North-West Frontier Province, Federally Administered Tribal Areas and Balochistan provinces of western Pakistan. The Pashtuns are typically characterized by their usage of the Pashto language and practice of Pashtunwali, which is a traditional code of conduct and honor.

PRT: A Provincial Reconstruction Team is a unit introduced by the U.S. government, consisting of military officers, diplomats and reconstruction-subject-matter experts, working to support reconstruction efforts in unstable states. PRTs were first established in Afghanistan in late 2001 and as of 2008 operate there as well as in Iraq. While the concepts are similar, PRTs in Afghanistan and Iraq have separate compositions and missions. Their common purpose, however, is to empower local governments to govern their constituents more effectively.

TTP: Pakistan's Taliban movement, known as Tehrik-e-Taliban Pakistan, is an umbrella group for regionally based militant organizations along the northwest border with Afghanistan.

---

throughout the country in four stages. Most troop contributors, except for Canada, Britain, the Netherlands, Denmark and Poland, imposed limitations on their troops that prevented them from engaging in combat or being deployed where there was such a risk.

To establish new Afghan security forces, the U.S. convened meetings in 2002 of the G-8 (leading industrialized nations) in January (Tokyo) and April (Geneva). The U.S. limited its involvement to building a new Afghan National Army (ANA). Different aspects of security-sector reform (SSR) were assigned to other G-8 members;

Germany for police; Japan for demobilization, disarmament, and reintegration (DDR) of militia forces; Britain for counternarcotics; and Italy for justice. There was no mechanism to coordinate among different areas of SSR or to assure that each sector received adequate resources. The result was a relatively successful ANA. The other security sectors lagged badly behind. When the U.S. finally realized that it could not succeed in Afghanistan with a solely counterterrorism approach (around 2005), it gradually moved into all the other areas.

Drug trafficking flourished amid insecurity and corruption. In 2002, Afghanistan produced 3,400 metric tons of raw opium; by 2007–2008, this amount had jumped to an estimated 8,200 tons. British-led support for counternarcotics became increasingly dominated after 2005 by the U.S., which sought (misguidedly) to emphasize eradication in order to deny Taliban funding. The Japanese-funded DDR program demobilized the regional warlord-based military forces (the Afghan Military or Militia Force, AMF) that had originally been incorporated into the ministry of defense, but it made little progress in dismantling the vast network of armed patronage networks that formed the real infrastructure of politics and power in Afghanistan. The justice system, if anything, actually deteriorated, as the influx of drug money and money from contracting for foreign organizations increased corruption beyond levels Afghanistan had previously witnessed. Attempts to reform and strengthen the civil service also made little progress, despite some successful national programs.

Economic reconstruction and development also lagged. Consistent with its "no nation-building" policy, the Bush Administration did not allocate any new money to Afghanistan reconstruction the first year (FY2002), limiting its contributions to humanitarian assistance already allocated. The reconstruction effort proceeded through a series of conferences: donors pledged $4.5 billion in Tokyo (2002), $8 billion in Berlin (2004), $10.5 billion in London (2006) and $21 billion in Paris (2008), though there is considerable overlap in these figures. Through 2004, however, annual aid to Afghanistan amounted to only about $50 per capita, less than any other postconflict reconstruction or nation-building effort since World War II. Primary education and health made

Afghan policemen keep watch behind a pile of burning narcotics in Kabul, June 25, 2008. AHMAD MASOOD/REUTERS /LANDOV

significant progress. By 2008 half of Afghan school-age children were enrolled, 35% of whom were girls; the ministry of public health had developed a basic package of services and infant mortality had declined by 22%. Some 85% of the population was said to live within a day's journey of a health clinic offering basic services. The government reversed the Taliban's strictures on women, who returned to their jobs and played important public roles.

Some major infrastructure projects were completed, notably the rehabilitation of the ring road, the country's major highway. Telecommunications was another success story. Starting in 2001 with almost no functioning telephones, Afghanistan had four mobile telecommunications providers and 5.4 million users by 2008. Open media also sprang up in an unprecedented way. The official estimates of gross domestic product showed robust growth, but the benefits appeared to accrue disproportionately to a small group of people who became far richer than any group in previous Afghan history. In Kabul and other urban areas, increased wages were offset by climbing prices of housing and other necessities, while the insurgency-affected areas received little if any benefits.

The Afghanistan Compact, adopted at an international conference in London in January 2006, was intended to compensate for some of the shortcomings of the Bonn Agreement by declaring international commitment to a comprehensive state building and development program for Afghanistan. It did not, however, address the political conflicts at the core of the crisis either within Afghanistan or between Afghanistan and its neighbors.

The insurgency escalated steadily in both quantity and quality. Through the summer of 2006 the number of security incidents nearly tripled over the previous year. The Taliban launched a major offensive in Kandahar province. Though finally turned back by ISAF at the cost of high casualties, the offensive showed a new level not only of military operations but of political sophistication, seeking to undermine already soft support for deployment among troop-contributing countries. The number of attacks continued to rise in 2007 and 2008. By July 2008, it was estimated that the government controlled 62 of 365 districts in Afghanistan, the Taliban more than 50, with the rest either contested or supplying no information.

The region and its neighbors

One condition for the stabilization of Afghanistan has been the formation of an Afghan state that enjoys sufficient resources and legitimacy to control and develop its territory, while developing a geopolitical identity that does not threaten its neighbors—especially Pakistan, whose deep interpenetration of Afghan society and politics enables it to play the role of spoiler whenever it chooses. Such a project would require political reform and economic development in FATA.

The Bush Administration's reliance on the Northern Alliance to overthrow the Taliban put in power those whom Pakistan most mistrusted. Afghanistan's geopolitical situation has pushed it back toward closer relations with India, with whom Washington has also become closer. The current conflict has thus recreated the situation in which Pakistan uses Pashtun Islamist armed groups based in FATA and Balochistan to exert pressure on Afghanistan and Kabul's patron, which is now the U.S. The stakes for Pakistan itself, however, have become higher, as the leadership of al-Qaeda has also found refuge in FATA, and Pakistani militant groups have coalesced into a Pakistan Taliban Movement (TTP, in its Pakistani acronym).

Pakistan's military has treated the various wars in and around Afghanistan as a function of its national security and institutional interests: balancing India, a country over eight times its size in population and economic resources, and whose elites, in Pakistani perceptions, do not fully accept the legitimacy of the existence of Pakistan; neutralizing the nationalism of cross-border peoples (Pashtun and Baloch), which it suspects India of supporting in order to break up Pakistan, as in the Indo-Pakistan War of 1971–72; and strengthening its domestic Islamist allies to wage asymmetrical warfare on Afghanistan and India. Pakistan has charged the

Pakistani Taliban with serious terrorist acts, including the assassination of Benazir Bhutto, the former prime minister who was in the midst of campaigning for the office once again, on Dec. 27, 2007.

Pakistan's goal in Afghanistan has been to bring the country under its influence or hegemony by supporting Pashtun Islamists against nationalists to preclude any Indian influence there. Pakistan would then benefit from "strategic depth" and a secure border. Some in Pakistan have also dreamed of uniting the two countries under Islamabad's suzerainty, and eventually joining with Central Asia.

On Sept. 19, 2001, then President Pervez Musharraf announced to the Pakistani public his decision to support the U.S. military intervention in Afghanistan and end *overt* support to the Taliban. He justified the about-face by saying it was necessary to save Pakistan, as otherwise the U.S. would ally with India. Supporting the U.S. effort also gave Pakistan a voice in deciding the postwar settlement, in which Pakistan hoped the Taliban would play a role.

Under U.S. pressure, Pakistan for the first time since independence sent the army into FATA to search for al-Qaeda, leading to several clashes with local militants who had given refuge to the fugitives. Pakistan's willingness to arrest Arab leaders of al-Qaeda, however, disguised its continued toleration of the Taliban. The Taliban leadership was kept secure, but largely inactive, in Pakistan. Reacting to what in retrospect appears as a minor increase in Taliban activity in the summer of 2004, President Bush confronted Musharraf during the UN General Assembly meeting in New York in September 2004 and demanded that he rein in the Taliban to assure that the Afghan presidential election could take place securely, which Bush saw as a necessary

precondition for his own reelection.

In 2005, Pakistan and Afghanistan's other neighbors saw the deterioration of Iraq and the decision to turn military command over to NATO in Afghanistan as signs that the U.S. might soon disengage from Afghanistan. The signing of a Declaration of Strategic Partnership by Presidents Bush and Karzai in May 2005 indicated that if the U.S. did not disengage, it would treat Afghanistan as a base for power projection into the region. The U.S. also initialed a deal with India on nuclear cooperation, which was approved by the U.S. Congress on Oct. 1, 2008. This agreement was taken as a sign by Pakistan that the U.S. was aligning itself with India, precisely the outcome it had hoped to prevent by joining with the U.S. against the Taliban.

The escalation of cross-border activity by the Taliban led President Karzai to issue several statements that the real "war on terror" was not in Afghanistan but in the places outside of Afghanistan where the terrorists were trained and armed, by which he meant Pakistan. The Bush Administration, however, focused its attention on Iraq and the al-Qaeda leadership, largely ignoring the resurgence of the Afghan Taliban and the development of the Pakistani Taliban.

By 2006, however, the U.S. had concluded that, at best, Pakistan had decided not to disrupt the Taliban's command and control in Quetta, the capital of the Pakistani province of Balochistan, and FATA. Under increased pressure, President Musharraf claimed that his government would negotiate with tribal elders in FATA to assure that they controlled Taliban activity, but he did nothing about the Taliban leadership in Balochistan while the agreements in FATA led to an increase in attacks across the border in Afghanistan.

Western, Afghan and Indian officials had differed for several years over the extent to which Pakistan's aid to the Taliban is ordered or tolerated by the highest levels of the military, but in July 2008, after the suicide bombing of the Indian Embassy in Kabul, the U.S. government leaked to the press that the Central Intelligence Agency (CIA) had intercepted communications showing Pakistan's Inter-Services Intelligence Directorate (ISI) sponsorship of the attack.

The regional implications of Afghanistan, however, go beyond Pakistan. India's activities in Afghanistan are very supportive of the Afghan government, which it sees as a strategic ally against Pakistan. Indian paramilitary construction companies are engaged in building strategic roads near the Pakistan border. Some of these roads will link Afghanistan to the Persian Gulf through Iran, thus greatly reducing landlocked Afghanistan's dependence on Pakistan for transit to the sea. Pakistan also claims that India is using its consulates in Afghanistan to support Baloch nationalist insurgents and even some "Taliban" activity.

In 2001 the Bush Administration had cooperated with Iran to overthrow the Taliban both diplomatically and on the ground, but it rejected initiatives from Iran to intensify the cooperation and broaden it to other areas. Instead, the Administration placed Iran on the "axis of evil" list, along with Iraq and North Korea. Iran continues to play a supportive role in Afghanistan through its aid program, which has provided over $600 million since 2001, as well as extensive trade. As it has come to see the U.S. presence as more threatening, however, its behavior has changed. After the signing of the Declaration of Strategic Partnership in 2005, Iran asked Afghanistan to sign a similar declaration, promising its territory would not be used against Iran. The U.S. prevented Afghanistan from moving forward with these negotiations.

In the context of the international effort to curb Iran's nuclear ambitions, Washington has repeatedly stated that "all options are on the table" including the military option, which Tehran interprets to mean forcible regime change, as the U.S. carried out in two of Iran's neighbors. Consequently, the current hard-line regime places a higher priority on preventing the U.S. from succeeding in order to forestall any forcible "regime change" in Tehran. It has apparently given symbolic quantities of weapons to anti-NATO insurgents in western Afghanistan and has signaled its intention to respond massively in Iraq, Afghanistan and Lebanon, as well as the Persian Gulf, to any attack on Iran.

Russia, China and the Central Asian states remain ambivalent. All support the fight against al-Qaeda and the Taliban and think that the U.S. is acting in their interest in fighting them. They nonetheless oppose the consolidation of a U.S. or NATO presence on the Asian landmass—including bases in Kyrgyzstan and Uzbekistan. The heads of state of the Shanghai Cooperation Organization (SCO—Russia, China and the Central Asian states except Turkmenistan) responded to the strategic partnership by asking the U.S. to set a timetable for dismantling its bases in Central Asia. China, however, is poised to extend its search for raw materials and energy to Afghanistan. It has agreed to invest $3.5 billion in developing a copper mine in Logar, south of Kabul, an area now strongly contested by the Taliban, and is likely to spend several billion dollars more on the infrastructure needed to operate the mine and other facilities. ●

The actors in the war on terror

The Bush Administration has conflated al-Qaeda, terrorism and regional actors under the rubric of the war on terror, crafting a policy that drives these actors together rather than dividing them. Instead of identifying all Islamist groups that use violence with "terror/al-Qaeda," Washington must seek to distinguish local and regional actors with potentially negotiable political goals (Taliban and other insurgents) from al-Qaeda.

Al-Qaeda is the only Islamic militant organization whose modus operandi is to launch large-scale terrorist attacks on the territory of the U.S. and its allies. Al-Qaeda depends for its operation on a safe haven, now located in the FATA region of Pakistan, on the Afghan border. From here it has exploited the contested and loosely governed status of the Afghanistan-Pakistan frontier to reconstitute its leadership infrastructure and support insurgencies in both countries.

Pakistani Taliban

The al-Qaeda safe haven in Pakistan is protected by Pakistani Pashtun tribal militant groups, most of whom have joined the TTP umbrella organization. The Pakistan Taliban is a threat because it is hosting al-Qaeda and may also threaten the integrity of the state and military of nuclear-armed Pakistan. Both the U.S. and Pakistan governments claim that TTP is responsible for the assassination of Benazir Bhutto, among other terrorist acts. TTP collaborates with al-Qaeda; Afghan Taliban; predominantly non-Pashtun (mostly Punjabi) militant groups originally trained and equipped by the ISI to fight in Kashmir; Uzbek and Chechen militants who have fled to the area; and armed groups mostly concerned with profit from criminal activity. TTP has built a support base using extensive funds from various sources including al-Qaeda, Persian Gulf donors, drugs and other trafficking; intimidation (killing tribal elders), and supplying public services, especially justice, as there are no other courts in FATA.

TTP claims that it wants only a free hand for jihad in Afghanistan and responds violently in Pakistan only when the Pakistan Army turns against it at the behest of the U.S. TTP and its affiliates have become de facto authorities in the tribal agencies and have infiltrated and threatened much of the NWFP, including the city of Peshawar. Their allies have also staged shows of force in Islamabad and carried out terrorism throughout Pakistan. Nonetheless, Pakistan retains a core of state organization, including its powerful army.

Afghan Taliban

Afghanistan has no such core. One of the poorest countries in the world (on a par with the poorest in Africa, poorer than Haiti), it also has one of the weakest governments. Afghanistan has been stable historically only when it had a legitimate government subsidized by great powers and not contested by neighbors.

The Afghan Taliban is an international security threat only insofar as it may provide a safe haven for al-Qaeda, which has never been one of its strategic goals. It recruits support in Afghanistan based on government corruption and predation, civilian casualties caused by coalition/NATO operations (especially air power), resentment of the expulsion of Pashtuns from North Afghanistan, intimidation, supplying of justice, consistent and reliable organization and ability to pay some fighters. A significant minority of Afghans (up to 25%) consider it a religious obligation to fight against foreign troops in Afghanistan.

Mullah Muhammad Umar, the leader (amir) of the Taliban, is most likely in or near Quetta. He leads the Quetta Shura (council), which directs operations in southern Afghanistan and loosely oversees the rest of the movement. A second center of Afghan Taliban leadership (formally subordinate to Mullah Umar), based in North Waziristan Agency, is the network commanded by Jalaluddin Haqqani, a

former anti-Soviet commander much favored in the 1980s by the CIA, and his son, Sirajuddin. The Haqqanis collaborate more closely with al-Qaeda and TTP than does the Quetta Shura and are responsible for military activity in eastern Afghanistan and the boldest attacks inside Kabul. Another center of Afghan insurgency is Gulbuddin Hikmatyar's Hizb-i Islami (Islamic party—the mujahidin group that got the most CIA funding in the 1980s), based in northwest Pakistan and northeast Afghanistan. While Hikmatyar plays a relatively small role in the armed insurgency, his former party members have a strong presence in the Afghan government, parliament, professions and universities, and their allegiance in case of crisis is unclear.

All of these Afghan groups were closely supported and monitored by the ISI and had bases and logistical structures in Pakistan for many years. U.S. intelligence finds evidence that the connection continues, while Afghan and Indian intelligence charge that the ISI directly organizes the most spectacular attacks, using these groups, as well as TTP, as implementation partners.

Pakistan's goals

Pakistan has been dominated by its military, as a result of which its civilian political institutions are weak and fragile. This in turn provides a rationale for the military to preserve control of national security policy, whether or not a civilian government has been elected, as it considers politicians incompetent and corrupt. The Pakistan military's national security doctrine revolves around the Indian threat. Pakistan needs military supplies from the U.S. to maintain a balance or a level of deterrence with India; therefore it enlisted in the cold war and the war on terror, always with the fundamental goal of countering India. The Pakistan military holds as part of its doctrine that the U.S. is an "unreliable ally" that uses Pakistan when it needs to but has a fundamental inclination toward India, based on India's strategic importance and antipathy to Islam.

In addition to the Indian threat, Pakistan's military policy toward Afghanistan derives from the British doctrine that Afghanistan is within the security perimeter of the subcontinent. Pakistan also perceives a threat from Afghanistan, as Kabul has never explicitly accepted the border between the two countries or renounced its claim to the tribal areas. Many Pakistanis suspect that India, Afghanistan and the U.S. plan to dismember Pakistan (with Afghanistan and India each absorbing a portion) as India did in 1972. Hence Pakistan's strategic goal in Afghanistan is to eliminate both Indian influence and Pashtun ethnic nationalism, while maintaining the dependence of the U.S. on Pakistan for security cooperation.

Pakistan's strategy for opposing Pashtun nationalism is to support pan-Islamic groups based among Pashtuns in FATA and Balochistan, including the Taliban, through whom Pakistan projects asymmetric power into both Afghanistan and Kashmir. The military has simultaneously supported largely Punjabi Islamist groups to fight in Kashmir, and the two fronts and groups of militants are increasingly linked. The military believes that its nuclear deterrent has created a defensive shield against conventional Indian retaliation for such actions. Although the TTP presents a potential threat to Pakistan, it can also be useful to the Pakistan military in pressuring or destabilizing the civilian government.

Since the 1980s, Islamabad has sought U.S. support to incorporate Afghanistan into its sphere of influence. After the U.S. "abandoned" Pakistan in 1990, the Pakistan military supported the Taliban to ensure that its neighbor had a friendly government. This was not the original goal of the Taliban, but as their dependence on Pakistan grew, their goals changed.

As concern over al-Qaeda's base in Afghanistan grew after the 1998 bombings of U.S. embassies in Kenya and Tanzania, the Pakistan military argued with the U.S. that it should engage with and recognize the Taliban in order to gain its cooperation against al-Qaeda. It failed to deliver al-Qaeda to the U.S. before 9/11, but blames the U.S. for failing to engage the Taliban. The military then allied with the U.S., once again hoping to make the U.S. its security partner in Afghanistan. Pakistan's military argued that it could help install a "moderate" Taliban government, but the Pakistan military failed to deliver such a government or al-Qaeda; instead some of the senior military leadership secretly encouraged the Taliban to resist, leading to a series of high-level dismissals.

In the view of Pakistan's military, the U.S. has done a poor job of stabilizing Afghanistan, has done nothing to meet Pakistan's security needs there, is once again using Pakistan for its own strategic purposes and will abandon Pakistan for India as soon as feasible; all this despite Pakistan's loss of hundreds of troops fighting al-Qaeda (not the Taliban) in the tribal areas and delivering many high-value al-Qaeda targets to the U.S. Hence the Pakistan military regards its nuclear deterrent as more essential than ever, especially as the U.S. has recognized India as a legitimate nuclear power, whereas Pakistan still suffers stigmatization because of its record of proliferation. The military continues to argue that only it can deliver al-Qaeda to the U.S., but that it will be able to do so only when the U.S. engages the Taliban and includes them in the government of Afghanistan, in particular, handing the Taliban hegemony over the area neighboring Pakistan (and presumably closing the Indian consulates there). Support for the Afghan Taliban's military and terrorist efforts provides bargaining leverage.

The U.S., NATO and UN are poorly structured to meet this integrated transnational threat. Initially, the role of the UN Assistance Mission in Afghanistan was to oversee and monitor implementation of the Bonn process, in addition to facilitating the delivery of humanitarian assistance and providing good offices. After negotiating the Afghanistan Compact in 2006, its mandate shifted to improving coherent delivery of support by interna-

NEW AXIS OF EVIL

BIN LADEN'S CHAUFFEUR..   BIN LADEN'S MAID..   BIN LADEN'S INTERIOR DESIGNER..

U.S.

CAGLECARTOONS.COM/TAB

Caglecartoons.com
tabtoons@telus.net

tional actors to the government and monitoring progress toward fulfilling the compact's benchmarks.

NATO assumed command of ISAF on Aug. 11, 2003. By mid-2008, NATO had deployed over 52,000 troops across the country. The U.S. maintains some 36,000 troops split between NATO's Eastern Command (19,000), in addition to training forces for the ANA and special forces pursuing terrorist targets (17,000). National caveats imposed by most NATO troop contributors remain a contentious issue, preventing their contingents from engaging in combat or being deployed to the south or east where there was such a risk. In 2008, Canada, which has operational responsibility for Kandahar, threatened to withdraw its troops if additional forces are not deployed.

The command and control arrangements in Afghanistan are not unified, and there is little civilian capacity within the U.S. government to deliver major programs as part of a coordinated strat-

egy. Counterinsurgency is supposed to be 20% military and 80% civilian, but the actual allocation of resources is reversed. Further complicating matters is a complex and poorly coordinated international effort (U.S., UN, NATO, EU, various donor and troop-contributing countries) that can at times be unwieldy and contradictory, despite the formal coordination mechanisms.

Although militants including al-Qaeda are using Pakistan as a strategic headquarters, there was no multilateral framework to manage relations with Islamabad until the formation of the Friends of Pakistan group at the UN during the visit of President Asif Ali Zardari to the 2008 General Assembly meeting. The U.S. has mainly used aid to the military and occasional pressure to seek cooperation in counterterrorism efforts in the border region. There is also no U.S. or multilateral framework to address Afghanistan-Pakistan relations (except for a nonfunctional commission for tactical military cooperation) or any of the re-

An Afghan election official registers Afghan men for their voter identity card at the voter registration office in Parwan province, north of Kabul, Afghanistan, Oct. 6, 2008. Afghanistan has begun registering voters for 2009 presidential polls, an election likely to be the most dangerous and challenging since the Taliban were ousted from power in 2001. AP Photo/Rafiq Maqbool

gional fallout of this situation on Iran, India, Central Asia, Russia, China or the Persian Gulf.

The Afghan institutions established through the Bonn process have now lost much of their legitimacy as a result of failure to deliver security or justice. The new Administration will walk right into the middle of the legitimacy crisis, as the Afghan constitution requires presidential elections in 2009. (Other elections are also required, but they are not as crucial for legitimacy.) Karzai remains the front-runner, though a consensus of Afghan and international opinion has concluded that he has serious shortcomings as a leader. Furthermore, under current conditions, it is probably impossible to hold a contested election whose results would be accepted as legitimate. Security conditions are likely to reduce participation in the predominantly Pashtun south and east while there is little faith in the integrity of the process.

Policy considerations

The core challenges in the region that create the conditions for an al-Qaeda safe haven are first, the lack of legitimacy and capacity of the Afghan state; second, the Pakistan military's perception of the post-9/11 political arrangement there as a security threat; and, third, the political conflict between the two states over the status and management of the border region. The international community has many goals in Afghanistan, but it is time to make these goals commensurate with its resources by reducing the former and increasing the latter. Following are the basic lines of policy to be considered for a more secure and self-sufficient Afghan state that will not become a haven for international terrorism.

To strengthen the government's legitimacy, a vigorous effort is necessary to integrate the insurgency into the current political framework. Two of the biggest obstacles to such a political settlement have been the lack of clarity as to whether the U.S. plans a long-term or permanent occupation of Afghanistan and the Bush Administration's frequent conflation of the Taliban/insurgents with al-Qaeda, stating that all who "harbored" global terrorists (even unknowingly) will be treated in the same way as the terrorists themselves. As a result of the latter policy

and related detention practices, the Afghan government has been unable to guarantee the security of several senior Taliban leaders who have sought to lay down their arms. To remove the first obstacle, the U.S. should clarify that international combat forces will remain only to secure the area from the global terrorist threat (though stabilization forces may remain at the Afghans' request). To remove the second, the U.S. and its allies should state clearly that it views Taliban or other insurgents with a purely Afghan agenda as "Afghans who have not yet joined the peace process" rather than as "those who harbored terrorists and will share their fate." The U.S. must set up transparent and speedy mechanisms to review detentions to assure trust in this declaration.

Legitimacy will also require a thorough cleansing of the Afghan administrative apparatus of criminal elements, which will have to be a main priority for the next Afghan president. As many of those who will have to be dismissed lead or can raise armed groups, the president will require strong backing of the international community for these reform measures.

Immediate improvements in security are also required. Some experts estimate that up to an additional 30,000 troops may be necessary. They must be deployed to cooperate with Afghan National Security Forces (ANSF), which includes the ANA, Afghan National Police (ANP), National Directorate of Security and other forces to provide security to the population. However, as the U.S. and NATO members deploy troops, their rules of engagement should be changed to reduce, if not eliminate, the threat of civilian casualties.

There appears to be a consensus in favor of accelerating training and expanding the size of the Afghan National Army and Afghan National Police. The ANA functions relatively well, though without the backbone of U.S. Embedded Training Teams (ETTs) and a payroll funded by U.S. supplemental appropriations, it would not work. Creating an effective police force must be a top priority, as this is the face of the Afghan government's authority and its ability to prove it can provide law and order on a daily basis. For the police to provide security to the population, rather than just act as a paramilitary force, the judiciary, including both the courts and the attorney general's office, will have to also be a top priority.

Counternarcotics and economic development have to be considered together, as narcotics production is the largest industry in the country. The drug industry provides all the public goods needed for production and marketing of a cash crop (extension services, finance, guaranteed purchase and marketing) and is a major source of employment. Afghanistan has become a monetized economy and farmers will not return to subsistence agriculture. The economic alternative to the drug industry is not another "crop," but the capacity to finance and market other commercial crops, agro-based industries and above all, jobs. Interdiction and law enforcement should be aimed at the upper end of the value chain and coordinated with the reform of the administration, in addition to counterinsurgency. In the limited areas of Afghanistan where alternatives are in place, there is no need for crop eradication, as people do not grow poppy. Where such alternatives are not in place, crop eradication leads to support for the insurgency rather than a shift in economic activities (which is not yet possible). Therefore the role of crop eradication should be greatly reduced and targeted closely where alternatives exist, as provided for in the Afghan National Drug Control Strategy.

The Afghanistan National Development Strategy provides a framework for the investment needed to improve governance and raise standards of living. While the international community should increase the level of assistance, the most important issue is its effectiveness. A far greater share of assistance should be provided through the Afghan government budget, combined with oversight mechanisms against corruption and targeted capacity building of the Afghan administration.

Afghanistan, the transnational insurgency and al-Qaeda's presence in FATA are intrinsically related to the deterioration of security and governance throughout Pakistan, the strategic posture of Pakistan's security establishment (including its nuclear deterrent) and the weakness of civilian forces in Pakistan. They cannot be addressed without a comprehensive strategy for Pakistan and its region, including Afghanistan.

Asserting the authority of the Pakistani state in FATA, NWFP and Balochistan will require military action, but such action, as in Afghanistan, requires complementary civilian efforts (governance and development) to have sustainable results. Pakistanis must see such action as serving their own interest; U.S. aid to the military for counterterrorist action (though there is little evidence it was so used) strengthened the dictatorship.

Framework for Pakistan

Pakistan presents a greater threat of both global terrorism and nuclear proliferation than does Iran, and policy toward Pakistan must enjoy a comparable level of attention. Pakistan policy requires high-level multilateral engagement by all states affected by the situation, which includes the members of NATO, Russia and China. The international community should engage in multilateral consultations in the appropriate forums to forge consensus. These forums should include the UN Security Council and the North Atlantic Council of NATO. The cooperation of SCO should also be sought.

This consensus should be less confrontational than the framework on Iran: it should highlight the international importance of stabilizing Pakistan under democratic governance and present itself as a forum for assisting the government with its self-proclaimed objectives. While Pakistan has refused an international troop presence, President Zardari initiated and co-chaired the Friends of Pakistan group at the UN. The group initially focused on providing economic and se-

curity assistance to the country. Within this framework, the international community could work with Pakistan to integrate FATA and improve governance and security in all provinces.

This denser comprehensive engagement with Pakistan should also serve as a forum for frank discussion of Pakistan's concerns and activities in Afghanistan. The international community should explore what it could do to assure Pakistan that it wants a stronger and more stable Pakistan, not a weaker, fragmented or defanged Pakistan. At some point, the issue of parity on nuclear issues with India may be raised, though this would require addressing concerns about Pakistan's past proliferation activities.

To the extent that Pakistan moves toward integrating FATA and reducing Taliban and al-Qaeda activities there, the international community could also work with Afghanistan to resolve other outstanding issues, including the Durand Line. Pakistan will not respect a border Afghanistan does not recognize, but Afghanistan cannot recognize a border for which Pakistan does not take responsibility. As Pakistan increases border security, Afghanistan should be encouraged to recognize the Durand Line, perhaps through the Afghanistan-Pakistan Jirga process.

As part of the defrosting of U.S.-Iran relations, a dialogue on cooperation in Afghanistan is likely to be attractive to Iranian officials and NATO. It will also place the Pakistan military on alert that it cannot count on a permanent monopoly on controlling Western access to Afghanistan.

The strategic goal of a regional policy is to generate and sustain a full regional consensus on the nonthreatening nature of the political and security dispensation in Afghanistan. All neighboring countries need not support the government, but they should not support armed contenders for power that undermine the government. This in turn will lower the threat level and the expense required for ANSF. ●

**OPINION BALLOTS
AFTER PAGE 64**

QUESTIONS

1. Why does Pakistan perceive the security arrangements in Afghanistan post-9/11 as a threat?

2. The U.S. has given billions of dollars in military aid to Pakistan since the beginning of the "war on terror." Can this aid be more effectively disbursed? Should the U.S. attach conditions or benchmarks to these funds? If so, to what goals—and how would this progress (or lack thereof) be measured?

3. Some officials have argued that implementing more development and aid projects within Afghanistan would help consolidate military gains. President-elect Obama has promised similar efforts. How can one ensure against corruption and misuse?

4. The author writes that for an effective strategic regional policy, "all neighboring countries need not support the government, but they should not support armed contenders for power that undermine the government." How can this be achieved? What can the U.S. offer to get these other players on board?

5. The author highlights some of the key areas for reform in Afghanistan, including the economic and judicial sectors. What should be the priority for the U.S.—security and the training of the police or a greater focus on nation building? Does the U.S. have sufficient resources to tackle both? Should NATO or the UN play a larger role?

6. What are the prospects for a U.S.-Iran dialogue over cooperation on Afghanistan? What are the potential benefits and costs? What would a framework of such an agreement look like? Does it appear likely?

7. Can India play a constructive role in conditions in Afghanistan and relations between Pakistan and Afghanistan?

Would this be akin to throwing fuel on the fire, or is this regional engagement necessary?

NOTES: ....
....
....
....
....
....
....
....
....
....
....
....

READINGS

Abou Zahab, Mariam, and Roy, Olivier, **Islamist Networks: The Afghan-Pakistan Connection.** New York, Columbia University Press, 2006. 92 pp. $19.00 (paper). An informative account of the cultural and religious motivations of jihadist movements and their relationship to the West and secular powers.

Bhatia, Michael, **Afghanistan, Arms and Conflict: Armed Groups, Disarmament and Security in a Post-War Society.** London, Routledge, 2008. 324 pp. $39.95 (paper). A comprehensive overview of security issues in post-9/11 Afghanistan, exploring the many facets of violence and recommendations for overcoming it.

Coll, Steven, **Ghost Wars: The Secret History of the CIA, Afghanistan and Bin Laden, from the Soviet Invasion to September 10, 2001.** New York, Penguin, 2004. 738 pp. $18.00 (paper). A revealing look at the CIA's involvement in the evolution of the Taliban and al-Qaeda in the years before 9/11.

Rashid, Ahmed, **Descent into Chaos: The United States and the Failure of Nation Building in Pakistan, Afghanistan, and Central Asia.** New York, Viking, 2008. 544 pp. $27.95 (hardcover). A condemning portrait of U.S. policymakers' unwillingness to commit the forces and money needed for nation building after routing the Taliban from power in Afghanistan.

_____ ,**Taliban: Militant Islam, Oil, and Fundamentalism in Central Asia.** New Haven, CT, Yale University Press, 2001. 294 pp. $14.95 (paper). Released prior to the 9/11 attacks, Rashid's book is considered a 'must-read' for those seeking to understand the origin and rise of the Taliban, its concepts of Islam and rule of law.

Roy, Olivier, **Islam and Resistance in Afghanistan,** 2nd ed. New York, Cambridge University Press, 1990. 284 pp. $43.00 (paper). Based on the author's visits to Afghanistan during the 1980s, the book offers an instructive reading of the Afghan response to Marxist doctrine and Soviet intervention.

Rubin, Barnett R., **The Fragmentation of Afghanistan: State Formation and Collapse in the International System**, 2nd ed. New Haven, CT, Yale University Press, 2002. 420 pp. $19.00 (paper). Drawing on two decades of research, the book examines Afghan society from the 1978 Communist coup to the fall of Najibullah, the last Soviet-installed president in 1992, and provides insights on the Taliban and Osama bin Laden.

TO LEARN MORE ABOUT THIS TOPIC AND TO ACCESS WEB LINKS TO RESOURCES GO TO www.greatdecisions.org/topic2

Energy and the global economy

by Ronald J. Bee

Then presidential candidate Barack Obama holds a news conference at a gas station in Indianapolis, Ind., April 25, 2008, about energy independence. Obama has outlined a broad energy plan, which includes a windfall-profits tax on oil companies. AP Photo/Jae C. Hong

With oil prices spiking to $147 a barrel on July 11, 2008, the U.S. mortgage and stock market meltdown and a frightening global credit lockdown, energy and the world economy have once again grabbed the headlines. October and November 2008 saw the stock market sink, taking American 401(k) pension plans with it, losing trillions in value. On Oct. 14, 2008, the Chicago Council on Global Affairs released survey results revealing that "60% of Americans believe that the next generation will be economically worse off than today's working adults" and "80% of Americans think that securing adequate supplies of energy is a very important goal for U.S. foreign policy, more than 10 points higher than the goal of combating international terrorism."

These percentages surely reflect the natural unease Americans feel in the wake of an economic downturn. Even when the economy starts to improve, energy issues will remain high on the U.S. agenda. Relying on foreign oil puts the U.S. economy at risk, raising costs in all kinds of ways when the price of oil goes up. Citizens expect the next Administration to review and reform U.S. energy policy as part of its global economic strategy. Cries for energy independence and a dizzying variety of approaches for achieving it add to the complexity. What are the choices and how will they affect American economic well-being? How do the global economy and its energy markets affect the U.S.?

Government's role?

Positions on energy and international trade usually reflect beliefs on how markets should operate and the role that government should or should not play in regulating domestic and international economics, as well as the priorities and implications attached to employing current versus alternative sources of energy. Because energy policy affects everyone's bottom line—from households to businesses to the national and international level, understanding different economic strategies to providing and trading public goods is useful. Two predominant approaches have emerged.

Free-market capitalism versus government

After reaching record highs, the price of oil is now in free fall, and the economy is in a deepening recession. How big a role should the U.S. government play in trying to stabilize the situation?

RONALD J. BEE, *the Director of the Charles Hostler Institute on World Affairs at San Diego State University, is a frequent contributor to* Great Decisions.

regulation and intervention represent the two key contrasting views of economic development. These views apply to domestic economic policy as well as to international trade. They are not mutually exclusive and their paths have crossed many times—especially when the economy worsens. Private firms and multinational corporations (MNCs) tend to prefer less government interference in their business as such rules, regulations and particularly taxes tend to reduce corporate profits.

Adam Smith, the 18th-century Scottish economist who wrote *The Wealth of Nations* at the dawn of the British Industrial Revolution in 1776, formulated three key tenets of free-market economics: division of labor, the pursuit of self-interest and freedom of trade. The 19th-century British economist David Ricardo's theory of comparative advantage posits that countries should specialize in producing what they do best and most efficiently, and trade those goods for the goods they do not. He believed, and free marketers continue to believe, that free trade and laissez-faire attitudes toward foreign competition prove a win-win for those importing goods as well as for those exporting them.

On the other side of the equation, John Maynard Keynes, a British economist from the 20th century, believed in the necessity of government intervention to provide a social safety net during bad economic times. He argued for alleviating high unemployment by government stimulus of the economy, such as spending on public-works projects. He advocated intervention by using fiscal and monetary measures to lessen the effects of economic recessions and depressions. (A recession normally means when real gross domestic product (GDP) declines for two consecutive quarters.) A sustained recession may become a depression, a rare and extreme period characterized by abnormal increases in unemployment, restrictions on credit, shrinking output and investment, numerous bankruptcies, reduced trade and commerce, and currency devaluations. The most widely known depression—the Great Depression—began with the crash of the Wall Street stock market in 1929, and lasted for most of the 1930s.

A little history

By 1927, 18 million Model T Fords had rolled off the mass production lines. A year later, the 1928 presidential election saw free-market-oriented Herbert Hoover (1929–33) promise "a chicken in every pot and a car in every garage." After the stock market crash of Oct. 24, 1929, however, that promise fell along with any remaining chicken into depression-era soup-kitchen pots as unemployment rates reached 25%. Cars became all-too-expensive luxuries that largely sat—for those who could still afford them—in their garages.

The ensuing Great Depression led to four terms of President Franklin D. Roosevelt (1933–45) and the New Deal, a sequence of programs from 1933 to 1938 that provided federal government intervention to resolve an unprecedented economic crisis and prevent similar occurrences in the future. Specifically, the government sponsored relief for the unemployed and reform of business and financial practices, which, along with the onset of World War II, ultimately led to the recovery of the overall economy.

Several institutions and programs created by the New Deal remain today: the Social Security system, which remains the primary social insurance program in the U.S.; the Security and Exchange Commission (SEC), which regulates and enforces laws relating to stock exchanges, options and securities; the Federal Insurance Deposit Corporation (FDIC), which insures checking and savings accounts up to $250,000 ($100,000 before the 2008 government bailout); the Federal Housing Administration (FHA), which provides insurance for home mortgages and seeks to stabilize the mortgage market; and the Federal National Mortgage Association (FNMA), commonly known as Fannie Mae, a stockholder-owned corporation that buys and secures mortgages to ensure that enough money remains available to institutions that lend money to home buyers. (On Sept. 7, 2008, the

ARTIZANS.COM/MIKE BALDWIN

"Tonight, an in-depth look at what each of us can do to help conserve electricity."

U.S. government announced it would take over Fannie Mae and another organization created in 1970 called the Federal Home Loan Mortgage Corporation [FHLMC], commonly known as Freddie Mac, which together owned or guaranteed about half of the American $12 trillion mortgage market.)

A global economy

American government intervention during the Great Depression, following the Keynesian strategy, played a role in restoring domestic confidence by creating jobs and financial stability. After World War II, the U.S. government, through targeted acts of altruism and self-interest, helped to restore international confidence by providing aid to Europe and Japan that allowed them to rebuild their economies within liberal democratic guidelines.

The containment of Soviet communism found its early economic application through key international U.S. government assistance programs like the 1947 Marshall Plan (also known as the European Recovery Program), the Truman Doctrine and the General Agreement on Tariffs and Trade (GATT,

1947). The Marshall Plan provided $13 billion in economic assistance "against hunger, poverty, desperation, and chaos," and became seen as one of the early jump-starts for European integration by erasing tariff and trade barriers while creating institutions that coordinated Europe as an entire region. The Truman Doctrine provided $400 million in economic aid to Greece and Turkey "essential to economic stability and orderly political processes," which also helped prevent them from falling under Soviet control. The GATT, the precursor organization to the World Trade Organization (WTO), provided an important conduit for American industry—one of the strongest and the few left undamaged by World War II— to trade American products with countries desperately in need of rebuilding their societies. Their economies also needed cheap, plentiful and reliable energy sources to fuel their renovated homes, new cars and domestic industrial growth.

By design and development, this post–World War II economic system helped secure a strong European economy that led to the creation of the

European Union (EU), the resurgence of Asian trade-driven economies that formed the Asia-Pacific Economic Co-operation (APEC), as well as a robust exchange of goods between the U.S and both regions. The EU represents 27 countries, almost 500 million citizens and 30% of the world's GDP. APEC, an economic forum for 21 Pacific Rim countries, including the U.S., represents 41% of the world's population, 56% of world GDP and 49% of world trade. In 1948, U.S. Secretary of State George C. Marshall presided over the establishment of the Organization of American States (OAS), which at that time, representing 21 countries, first set out to thwart communism in the hemisphere.

Free trade

Globalization of the world economy blossomed in the 1990s. Ricardo's comparative advantage theory became practice in China and India, as they began trading everything from shoes to software engineers with the West. The U.S., for its part, began to turn increasing focus on developing free-trade agreements (FTAs). The North America Free Trade Agreement (NAFTA), between the U.S., Canada and Mexico, came into being in January 1994. The U.S. imports most of its foreign oil from Canada, followed by Saudi Arabia and Mexico. Thus, two of the top three oil exporters to the U.S. belong to NAFTA. The OAS also hosted the first meeting of the Summit of the Americas in 1994 in Miami, Florida, a forum that has since focused on establishing a free-trade area for Latin America. When President George W. Bush took office in 2001, the U.S. had FTAs with three countries; currently that number stands at 14 (with 5 more pending congressional approval). Although those countries represent only 7.3% of the world's GDP, exports to these countries represent 42.5% of U.S. exports.

Paul Blustein, at the Brookings Institution, believes that such FTAs have run amok and do not really promote trade liberalization, but serve more as political instruments, television opportunities and veiled protectionism.

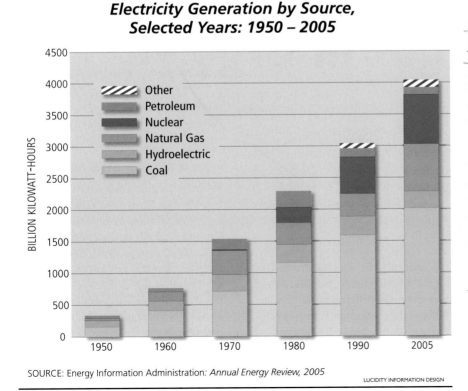

Electricity Generation by Source, Selected Years: 1950 – 2005

Other
Petroleum
Nuclear
Natural Gas
Hydroelectric
Coal

BILLION KILOWATT-HOURS

SOURCE: Energy Information Administration: *Annual Energy Review, 2005*

LUCIDITY INFORMATION DESIGN

He prefers to call them "preferential trade agreements" (PTAs) among two or more countries. "PTAs simply muck up the trading system with complexity," Blustein argues, "rather than having a big impact on trade flows. That's because they are laden with 'rules of origin' designed to make sure that products receiving duty-free treatment aren't actually made in some other country that isn't party to the pact." He would prefer trade issues be handled by the WTO, the successor to GATT, the multilateral institution established after World War II to prevent the reversion to the 1930s, when protectionism only deepened the Great Depression.

Era of interdependence

Smith and Ricardo remain alive and well today in China, which, with its median manufacturing wage in 2007 of about 53 cents per hour compared to about $15 an hour for U.S. workers, produces about 85% of the shoes Americans wear. Americans buy high quality shoes more cheaply from China than if they made them in the U.S. while China receives the business that allows it to grows its economy.

By 2000, as a sign of increasing integration, the top 500 MNCs accounted for 70% of the world's trade. MNC affiliates—both physically and "virtually" on the internet—locate overseas to take advantage of cheaper labor costs, less government oversight, less taxes, and opportunities in developing markets. "Off-shoring" or "out-sourcing" jobs overseas for everything from payroll to customer service has blossomed since the 1990s. Due to improved and cheaper global telecommunications, today a call to a computer "help desk" will more than likely mean interacting with a polite Indian or Filipino for help with software problems. Off-shored and out-sourced foreign employees are paid less by U.S. standards, which helps the corporate bottom line, and those foreign employees are usually very happy to have the work, which helps their family's bottom line.

This form of interdependence has generated more than mutual economic benefit; it ties the countries together in ways that tend to moderate behavior toward one another regardless of significant political differences. Moreover, many Americans and Chinese now own stakes in each other's companies, creating yet more global economic glue.

Financial instruments are another aspect of rapid globalization. China and Chinese companies owned over $200 billion in banks caught up in the 2008 U.S. mortgage meltdown. It also holds about $1.9 trillion dollars in foreign reserves, including almost $600 billion in U.S. treasury bonds that help finance the U.S. national debt. China has also played a key role in hosting the multilateral "six-party talks" with North Korea on ending their nuclear weapons activities. Despite differences over Chinese human rights violations in Tibet, drilling for oil in Sudan or U.S. weapons sales to Taiwan, President Bush did attend the Beijing Olympics in 2008 out of national self-interest just as much as to promote the Olympic spirit.

Globalization of the world economy still has its fare share of protectionist critics. When national economies go badly, so too does domestic support for international trade and improving the condition of those overseas. The Oct. 14, 2008, survey by the Chicago Council on Global Affairs emphasized that "a large majority of Americans (80%) view protecting the jobs of American workers as a very important foreign policy goal." Protectionism and political cries in support of it grow almost proportional to bad economic times. ●

Evolution of energy

The history of how humans have developed and used their energy resources spans the ages. The initial energy sources took a very long time to evolve, starting with human labor and use of draft animals to windmills and watermills to whale blubber being made into lamp oil. From colonial times to about 1885, wood fuel represented a significant part of the U.S. energy mix, until replaced by coal. In 1890, hydroelectric power largely generated at dams was the first "renewable" energy supplying the electrical grid. Niagara Falls, the Jensen Dam, the Tennessee Valley Authority Project, the Grand Coulee Dam and Hoover Dam still produce some of the lowest priced (under $1 per kilowatt hour) clean electricity in America.

After World War II, oil-heating boilers took over for coal-burning plants on the East Coast, oil-fired electricity plants were built, diesel trains displaced coal-fired steam engines, buses replaced streetcars and Americans all bought cars to drive on the new interstate highway system. Oil discoveries in California, Texas, Oklahoma, Canada and Mexico made gasoline plentiful and cheap. Petroleum replaced coal in 1951 as the predominant source of U.S. energy, supplanted by natural gas a few years later. Nuclear power came on line in 1957. Solar photovoltaic, advanced solar thermal, geothermal, advanced wind and biomass technologies represent further recent developments in energy sources.

Oil, gas and coal

When economies industrialized, countries became very dependent on the use of fossil fuels to run internal combustion engines and to heat and cool buildings. In addition, World War I introduced machines into warfare that ran on oil and gas. By World War II, the Axis powers of Nazi Germany, Italy and Japan shared a major strategic problem in that none had major oil reserves to run a war increasingly fought with combustion-engine machines like tanks, airplanes and submarines. Thus access to an energy supply became a national security issue.

Fossil fuels derive from the fossilized remains of dead plants and animals formed by exposure to heat and pressure in the earth's crust over hundreds of millions of years. Such fuels, hydrocarbons within the top layer of the earth's crust, range from volatile materials like methane, liquid petroleum and natural gas to nonvolatile materials such as anthracite coal. Fossil fuels have become the source of fantastic economic growth and wealth as well as the center of ongoing controversy over whether their continued burning will overheat and threaten the planet. Concerns over access to oil and gas supplies have caused regional and global conflicts abroad while domestic appeals for energy self-sufficiency have driven politics at home.

Fossil fuels represent nonrenewable sources of energy because their reserves deplete much more quickly than the millions of years it takes to form them. In 2005, The Energy Information Administration (EIA) estimated that 86% of the primary energy production in the world came from

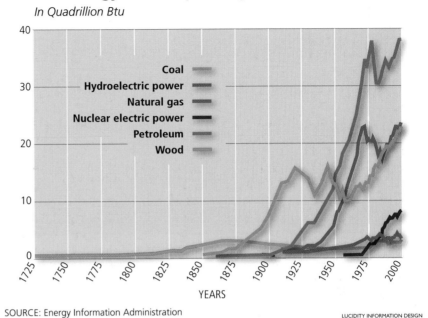

U.S. Energy Consumption by Source: 1725 – 2000
In Quadrillion Btu

SOURCE: Energy Information Administration

LUCIDITY INFORMATION DESIGN

burning fossil fuels, with 6.3% coming from hydroelectric power, 6.0% coming from nuclear power plants, and geothermal, solar, wind, wood and biomass all combined equaling 1.5%. The U.S., with about 5% of the world's population, consumes about 26% of annual global energy production.

The world's population now equals 6.7 billion people, set to increase to about 9 billion by 2050. That means the world will have the equivalent of two more Chinas to feed, clothe and provide energy for to run their homes, transportation and businesses. Energy will need to become more efficient—in exploration, development and delivery—and come at a reasonable cost, if global demographic trends continue to rise as anticipated. Otherwise, expectations of the good life will outrun resources. Sustainable development remains an important objective, and finding cost-effective energy supplies remains a key element in achieving that goal.

Foreign oil

Once, a few oil companies dominated global oil markets—that is no longer the case. Exxon Mobil, the world's largest private oil company, produced 2.6 million barrels of oil per day (mb/d) in 2007, equaling about 3.1% of the world total (85 mb/d). The combined market share of the five biggest private oil companies equals less than 12% of global production. Sovereign countries now control the vast majority of the world's oil supplies. While other sectors of the world economy are

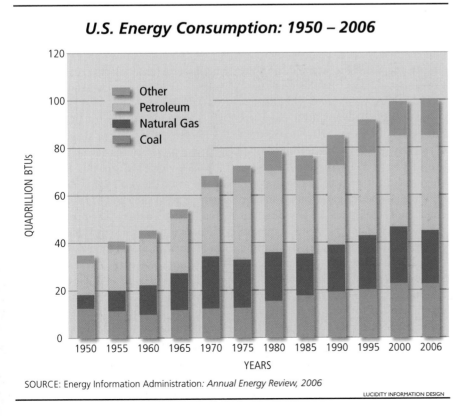

U.S. Energy Consumption: 1950 – 2006

SOURCE: Energy Information Administration: *Annual Energy Review, 2006*

LUCIDITY INFORMATION DESIGN

A worker stands in a photovoltaic solar power plant, which is under construction in Buchloe, southern Germany, June 18, 2008. Solar photovoltaic, advanced solar thermal, geothermal, advanced wind and biomass technologies represent further recent developments in energy sources. AP PHOTO/CHRISTOF STACHE

becoming increasingly globalized, in some ways, international oil markets may be taking a step in the other direction. With the rise of state-owned oil companies controlling over 75% of the world's oil reserves, national governments, especially those of oil-exporting nations, have direct control over energy supplies and how policy is formulated and wielded. At times, this may mean commercial interests will take a back seat to national or foreign policy goals, which may not create the ideal conditions for a stable energy market. Conversely, there is a noticeable lack of international cooperative mechanisms to address energy issues, even in the case of energy security or climate change, which are inherently transnational issues.

The Organization of the Petroleum Exporting Countries (OPEC), founded in 1960 in Baghdad, Iraq, grew to include 12 of the most important oil producers by 1973—Algeria, Ecuador, Indonesia, Iran, Iraq, Kuwait, Libya, Nigeria, Qatar, Saudi Arabia, United Arab Emirates and Venezuela. Angola joined in 2007. One, Indonesia, has become a net importer of oil. In 2007, OPEC produced nearly 40% of the world's oil supplies, with Saudi Arabia accounting for almost 30% of OPEC total output. OPEC aims to coordinate and unify petroleum policies among member states, including setting production levels and

prices. Two members, Angola and Iraq, do not currently participate in OPEC's production agreements.

OPEC rose to world prominence in the 1970s when, in 1973 and 1979, two oil-pricing crises took place, underscoring the importance that energy plays in driving growing economies and foreign policy.

Historical price shocks

Oct. 16, 1973, marked the day when Arab members of OPEC plus Egypt and Syria announced an oil embargo "in response to the U.S. decision to resupply the Israeli military during the [Yom Kippur] war." By this time, most industrialized economies relied heavily on OPEC oil. Arab OPEC members raised oil prices by 17%—to $3.65 a barrel. By 1974, the price almost quadrupled to $12. By raising oil prices and linking it to political behavior, OPEC changed the game on oil and the conduct of foreign policy. Double-digit inflation and a 1973–74 stock market crash served to underscore the turning point. In reaction to the oil embargo, President Richard M. Nixon (1969–74) announced "Project Independence," which aspired to achieve energy self-sufficiency in the U.S. by 1980. In a theme that echoes today's claims, Nixon believed American science, technology and industry could free us from dependence on foreign oil. Three

notable initiatives included lowering the speed limit to 55 mph, converting oil power plants to coal and completing the Trans-Alaska Pipeline.

After the 1973 oil shocks, the U.S. and other industrialized countries started building strategic petroleum reserves (SPRs) to reduce the impact of future oil shocks. The U.S. now has some 700 million barrels in its SPR, and others have cumulative SPRs of another 700 million barrels. In 2006, global oil consumption averaged 85 mb/d. This means that such SPRs could cover all demand for 16–17 days, or at a slower release into the market of 2.5 mb/d, would cover demand for about 560 days.

A second oil crisis occurred in 1979. In 1978, strikes at nationalized Iranian oil refineries cut oil production by 75%, which effectively fell to zero soon after Iranian Islamic revolutionaries ousted the shah of Iran, Mohammad Reza Pahlavi. Oil prices rose to $39.50 a barrel. Long lines appeared at American gas stations, as they had six years earlier. In July 1979, President Jimmy Carter (1977–81) outlined plans in a fireside speech to the nation to reduce oil imports and improve energy efficiency. He asked citizens to do what they could to reduce their energy use, installed solar panels on the roof of the White House (removed under the Reagan Administration) and a wood-burning stove in the living quarters. His speech called the energy crisis "the moral equivalent of war" and led directly to the Carter Doctrine in 1980 to protect the oil shipping lanes in the Persian Gulf.

Oil and foreign policy

In fact, since 1945, U.S. foreign policy has sought to protect oil supplies emanating from the Middle East. In that year, President Roosevelt promised Saudi Arabian King Ibn Saud that the U.S. would protect the kingdom in return for special access to Saudi oil. The Saudi king wanted a counterbalance to British influence in the region. He felt an affinity for Roosevelt because the American President needed to use a wheelchair and the king walked with difficulty, unable to walk up stairs because of war wounds. (Roosevelt gave Ibn Saud one of his spare wheelchairs as a token of friendship.) The protection Roosevelt promised Saudi Arabia in 1945 remains part and parcel of American foreign policy to this day.

In 1980, President Carter enshrined protection of the Persian Gulf under the Carter Doctrine by declaring that the U.S. would use "any means necessary, including military force" to protect the secure flow of oil through the Straits of

An abstract blurred view of the umbrellas of a massive number of commuters leaving the Beijing railway station during a torrential downpour. With over 1.3 billion people China's demand for oil is rising and it might match U.S. oil-consumption by the year 2010. © GIDEON MENDEL/CORBIS

Hormuz to the Western world. Carter argued this commitment was in "the vital interests of the USA."

By the time of the 1991 Persian Gulf war, President George H.W. Bush (1989–93) saw the Iraqi invasion of Kuwait as a threat to Western oil supplies. He proclaimed, "This will not stand."

Then Secretary of Defense Richard Cheney flew to Riyadh, Saudi Arabia, to show King Fahd bin Abdul Aziz al Saud satellite photos of Saddam Hussein's amassed Iraqi Army (the Middle East's largest army at the time) in attack formation along the Saudi border. "After Allah," King Fahd once said, "we can count on the U.S." King Fahd thus agreed to host coalition troops, led by the U.S., to be based in Saudi Arabia to protect his kingdom and prepare for the 1991 liberation of Kuwait, called, "Operation Desert Storm."

The U.S. also signed an agreement in 1991 with Bahrain to base the U.S. 5th Fleet in Manama, Bahrain, where the U.S. naval presence continues to guarantee safe passage of Persian Gulf oil to the U.S., Europe and Japan. By the mid-1990s, with globalization in full swing, demand for oil rose as emerging economies like China and India needed it to fuel their rapid growth.

New oil crises

The year 2004, according to Larry Goldstein, an oil expert at the Energy Policy Research Foundation, marked a turning point in global energy supplies. "What happened in 2004," he

A canopy of black smoke hangs above Kuwaiti oil wells. When Iraq's defeat in the Persian Gulf War was imminent, Saddam Hussein ordered his retreating forces to set fire to the Kuwaiti oil wells. © PETER TURNLEY/CORBIS

argued, "was the world's first demand-led energy shock." That demand came largely from China and its 9.4% GDP growth rate. The 1973 oil price shock came from the Yom Kippur war in the Middle East; the 1979–80 shock came from a revolution in Iran; in 2004, China's growing economy required 6.5 mb/d, almost double earlier demand estimates. China vaulted ahead of Japan into second place behind the U.S. among the world's biggest energy consumers. Since 1990, China's demand for oil has grown at 6%–7% a year, putting it on pace to reach over 8.5 mb/d by 2010.

In 2004, other factors in the global oil industry worked to limit supply. Drilling equipment and skilled petroleum engineers proved scarce, Russia began squeezing out more productive foreign producers from its oil fields and long-standing environmental concerns limited new drilling in the U.S. and the West. Concerns over the political stability of Nigeria and Iraq, hurricanes in the Gulf of Mexico and fears of terrorism all contributed to less confidence, less oil and higher oil prices. On Oct. 15, 2004, prices rose to a record $55 per barrel. A weakening dollar also contributed to price increases, as oil prices are measured in dollars; when the dollar declines in value, producers must raise prices to stabilize their profit margins.

Anthony Cordesman of the Center for Strategic and International Studies (CSIS) outlines several factors that influence the oil market, each involving major uncertainties. They include the long-term factors that impact oil and gas supplies (rates of discovery, development and production costs, oilfield life span, impact of new technology), the rise of new economic powers such as China and India, emerging Asian and Middle Eastern economies (which accounted for as much as 40% of the increase in oil demand in 2004), lack of investment in drilling, refining and maintenance, and the overall health of the global economy. "Sustained high oil prices have a marked negative effect

on economic growth in oil-consuming states and tend to slow global economic growth. In addition, low economic growth in industrialized nations and consuming nations causes a decrease in demand for oil and hence lower oil prices."

Energy initiatives

In response to the events of 2004, increasing public angst and declining economic growth, President Bush signed the Energy Policy Act of 2005 into law to "encourage energy efficien-

A petroleum worker labors at the Laiohe oil field in Panjing, China in February 2007. China stepped up efforts to secure access to foreign energy, adding nine oil- and gas-producing countries to a list of economies where its companies are offered incentives to invest. AP PHOTO

cy and conservation, promote alternative and renewable energy sources, reduce our dependence on foreign sources of energy, increase domestic production, modernize the electricity grid, and encourage the expansion of nuclear energy." In his January 2006 State of the Union Address, he declared the U.S. had become "addicted to oil," outlining his Administration's plan for an "Advanced Energy Initiative to Help Break America's Dependence on Foreign Sources of Energy." The plan set a goal to replace "more than 75% of our oil imports from the Middle East by 2025" with a 22% increase in clean-

energy research at the Department of Energy (DOE). The President argued that Americans could achieve this goal by diversifying energy sources for their homes, businesses and cars.

On Dec. 19, 2007, President Bush signed the Energy Independence and Security Act of 2007, which claims to reduce America's dependence on oil by "increasing the supply of alternative fuel sources by setting a mandatory Renewable Fuel Standard (RFS) requiring fuel producers to use at least 36 billion gallons of biofuel in 2022," and "reducing U.S. fuel demand by setting a national fuel economy standard of 35 miles per gallon by 2020—which increases fuel economy from current levels by 40%. The bill also requires improving energy efficiency in lighting, including in federal buildings and in appliances by 2013.

On Sept. 30, 2008, responding to constituents worried about oil prices, the U.S. Congress allowed the ban on offshore oil drilling to expire, ending a 27-year old prohibition legislated in the wake of a 1969 oil spill off the coast of Santa Barbara, California. President Bush, clearly pleased, remarked, "This act lifts the legislative moratoria on oil and gas leasing on significant portions of the outer continental shelf…which will allow us to reduce our dependence on foreign oil."

Critics of George W. Bush's energy policies have not usually quibbled with the need for energy reform or improving energy efficiency, but rather the amounts of government cash invested (too little or in the wrong direction versus too much government spending when the country cannot afford it, or let the private sector do it), or with the emphases on certain types of energy promotion (drilling for more oil, using more coal and more nuclear versus conservation or developing renewable solar, wind and fuel-cell technology). Interest groups, corporate lobbies and nongovernmental organizations with a particular bent or self-interest try to grease the gears of the energy debate, as well as bend leaders' hearts and minds in their respective directions.

Moreover, to what degree does "energy independence" represent a "national unicorn campaign"—everybody wants one, but does it really exist in a global energy marketplace? Perhaps a better goal is "energy diversification" rather than "energy independence," and even then it will require far more investment in both the government and private sectors.

Research and development

On the government investment side, the Congressional Research Service has noted historically, from 1948 to 2003, nuclear energy received from the U.S. Department of Energy 56% of its total research and development (R&D) budget, fossil fuels (oil, gas, and coal) 24% of its total R&D, renewable energy 11% and energy efficiency 9%. Perhaps now, five years after the turning point of 2004, these numbers may change, but that will depend on political will, as well as the economic circumstances and the mindsets that influence it.

Author and *New York Times* Op-Ed columnist Thomas Friedman thinks those numbers must change. "The reason there's a shortage of [venture capital] investing in green is because

there's been a shortage of federal funding from the Department of Energy in renewable research." He quotes Daniel M. Kammen, an energy policy expert at UC Berkeley, who says all the federal dollars going into energy research altogether—including oil, gas, coal and solar—amount to $3 billion per year, supplemented by $5 billion in private venture-capital funds. Combined, Kammen reminds us, this equals "about nine days of fighting in Iraq." The $8 billion represents 0.8% of the $1 trillion per year energy industry—a paltry amount if the stakes for energy independence are as high as has been heard. The norm for research and development in most industries ranges from 8% to 10%. This might suggest government inertia, competing spending priorities or perhaps inertia caused by competing government spending priorities. On the other hand, alternative energy investments have not yet proven their cumulative worth or potential to either the public or private sectors. However, neither case may prove entirely true.

A 2006 independent Council on Foreign Relations task force study, *The National Security Consequences of U.S. Oil Dependency*, points to another possible approach: "U.S. energy policy has been plagued by myths, such as the feasibility of achieving 'energy independence' through increased drill-

U.S. oil imports*	
CANADA	1,890
SAUDI ARABIA	1,542
MEXICO	1,207
VENEZUELA	1,051
NIGERIA	998
IRAQ	675
ANGOLA	512
ALGERIA	312
BRAZIL	217
ECUADOR	209
KUWAIT	205
COLOMBIA	190
CHAD	106
EQUATORIAL GUINEA	68
AZERBAIJAN	67

*Thousands of barrels per day
YTD 2008, per month average

SOURCE: EIA

ing, or anything else. For the next few decades, the challenge facing the U.S. is to become better equipped to manage its dependencies rather than pursue the chimera of independence." The study argues that most leverage available to the U.S. will come through domestic policy choices, including how to reduce or limit the growth of oil consumption combined with increasing attention on how these domestic choices can be integrated into U.S. foreign policy decisionmaking processes.

Energy incentives

For a long time, the U.S. has taken a toll on world resources with its huge energy consumption and demand. Over time, the U.S. will represent an increasingly smaller percentage of the world's total population while the rest of the world begins to consume a higher percentage of available global energy resources. Globalization of the world economy also means increasing global demand for fossil fuels, the standard energy source that the U.S. has used for so long to leverage its own economic growth.

An important lesson from the 2008 market turndown is the importance of diversifying risk. If the U.S. wants, for either environmental

LOW FUEL

LEGITIMATE EXCUSES ON WHY WE'RE STILL DEPENDENT ON FOSSIL FUELS GAUGE

FUEL DOOR

CAGLECARTOONS.COM/JOHN DARKOW

or economic reasons, to change the equation at home and abroad, it must make economic sense to do so, and the U.S. must create the economic incentives at home and abroad to facilitate change. Energy supplies and foreign policies are intertwined, although not always in obvious ways.

What are the options? Proposals have included greater U.S. diversification, self-sufficiency in producing and refining oil and gas, the development of cleaner coal, additional nuclear power plants, providing more incentives for green-friendlier alternative transportation technologies such as hybrid and fuel-cell cars and using renewable geothermal, solar and wind power to heat and cool buildings. In August 2008, the Congressional Research Service noted "renewable energy sources (except hydropower) continue to offer more potential than actual energy production, although fuel ethanol has become a significant factor in transportation fuel, and wind power has recently grown rapidly."

If T. Boone Pickens has his way, wind power will play a key role in reducing "the largest transfer of wealth in the history of mankind." "In 1970,"

Pickens asserts, "we imported 25% of our oil. Today it is nearly 70% and growing." He estimates at current oil prices, "we will send $700 billion out of the country this year alone—and that's four times the annual cost of the Iraq war." The $700 billion figure also represents the initial estimated cost of President Bush's proposal to Congress for financing the 2008 bailout of banks and financial markets ($830 billion with congressional add-ons). Can the U.S., as Pickens argues, become the Saudi Arabia of wind power? His plan, however, has been put on hold since the drop in the price of natural gas has rendered wind, for the moment, too expensive.

Should the U.S. pursue an "all of the above" private-sector-oriented approach to energy security that Senator John McCain (R-AZ) has proposed? Or should it focus, as Senator Barack Obama (D-IL) offered during his successful presidential campaign, more on renewable energy sources and publicly fund $15 billion per year over the next decade to achieve 10% of self-sufficiency via renewable sources by 2012 and 25% by 2025? Is either plan affordable, especially if the price

of oil continues to fall in the wake of the current economic downturn? President-elect Obama has reminded the U.S. that falling oil prices are no excuse to put off tackling dependence on foreign oil.

Should Americans just consume less and rethink the current reliance on fossil fuels? Thomas Friedman argues in his new book, *Hot, Flat and Crowded*, that America needs to renew itself with government help through a green revolution, retool its and the world's energy economy in that process and use American know-how and technology to make it happen. He argues this renewal will allow the U.S. to stop buying oil and gas from countries without liberal democratic systems such as Saudi Arabia or Venezuela, which he dubs "petro-dictatorships."

Subnational engines of change?

State governments may have begun to pave the way. In September 2006, California Governor Arnold Schwarzenegger signed the "California Global Warming Solutions Act of 2006" into law, announced as "a first in the world comprehensive program of regulatory and market mechanisms to achieve real, quantifiable cost-effective reductions of greenhouse gases."

The Western Climate Initiative, endorsed by seven governors (Arizona, California, Montana, New Mexico, Oregon, Utah and Washington) and four Canadian provinces (British Columbia, Manitoba, Ontario and Quebec) aims to slash regional greenhouse gases by about 15% below 2005 levels by 2020. Friedman also points out how even Germany, in a Central European region not known for its sunny weather, has implemented enough federal incentives to create a huge market for solar energy.

Ultimately the German example demonstrates how a national government, if really serious about diversifying its energy future, must play a more active role in creating economically viable incentives. This runs the

World Crude Oil Reserves, 1973, 1991 & 2005

SOURCE: Energy Information Administration: *International Energy Annual, 1990 and 2005*

LUCIDITY INFORMATION DESIGN

So what has German Technology produced

gamut from R&D investments to tax incentives for consumers beyond those already incorporated in the 2005 Energy Act.

National security priority

In *Newsweek*, Richard Haas, president of the Council on Foreign Relations, wrote a memo to the next U.S. President on the "world that awaits him" and what will be waiting in his in-box. Haas called for a new strategic framework that, among other priorities, recognizes globalization and its implications. "America cannot do this by itself; the challenges of this era have no single national origin and no national solution. Multilateralism is the only realistic way ahead. The operative term is 'integration.' We need to bring other major powers into the design and operation of the world—before the century is overwhelmed by the forces globalization has unleashed." He also emphasized that energy policy "has never received the attention it merits. Energy policy is national security policy."

In the same issue, Michael Bloomberg, mayor of New York City, notes in his memo that the oil-rich Middle East has now begun investing in green power, and that the U.S. should do the same. "Americans can either be the pioneers of green power or the purchasers. If we are the pioneers, we will create tens of thousands of good-paying jobs. If we are the purchasers, we will continue transferring billions of dollars of our wealth overseas—and the high tech jobs that go with them."

Bloomberg's views echo those of T. Boone Pickens and Thomas Friedman. In the book, *America and the World: Conversations on the World and the Future of American Foreign Policy*, David Ignatius, associate editor and columnist for *The Washington Post* interviewed two former national security advisers, Zbigniew Brzezinski, who served under President Carter, and Brent Scowcroft, who served under the first President Bush, about the future President's role in shaping energy policy: "How does presidential leadership get us to do the thing that's hard for any

ARTIZANS.COM/PAUL FELL

people, but I think hardest for Americans, which is to give up some of our fabulous wealth and opportunities for our long-run good and for the good of the world?" Dr. Brzezinski answered, "The President is uniquely positioned to be an educator of the country, a public definer of its long-range interests and how these interests mesh into the larger global context. Only the President can do that. The issue is how we define the good life. Are the unlimited acquisition of material possessions and ever-higher use of energy the ultimate definition of the good life? How is this going to be sustainable on a global basis?... The issue has to be put on the national agenda."

General Scowcroft's response: "First we have to change the mind-set. Throughout development of the industrial age, we have generally behaved as thought the pollutants we produced just disappeared in the environment, and nature has been so capacious that they seemed to go away. We poured them into the ocean, we put them into the air, and they just seemed to go away. Now we've begun to realize that they don't go away. And the quantities that are being produced, with the increase of population and civilization, are beginning to defeat nature's ability to

absorb them. That's the fundamental thing Americans have to grasp."

The globalization of the world economy means that America, as part of that world, cannot separate itself from this reality. The U.S. must review the way it buys and uses energy and it should integrate these concepts into its foreign policy goals.

The example of something called ARPANET (Advanced Research Projects Agency Network), a government-sponsored Department of Defense R&D investment in cost-effective communications that led directly to the creation of the internet, is instructive. That invention helped integrate the world economy through cost-effective global communications. The U.S. now needs another like-minded R&D project to provide an alternative and cost-effective way to fuel the national and global economy. The national security of the U.S. and its allies requires no less. An important question remains: Will the next U.S. Administration have the energy, the vision and political will to accomplish it? ●

OPINION BALLOTS AFTER PAGE 64

QUESTIONS

1. Should the U.S. government involve itself in the U.S. energy market? Should it regulate it to protect consumers, invest in alternatives to fossil fuels, or allow the global marketplace to "take care of business"?

2. To what degree do you believe the U.S. should invest in energy alternatives versus diversify its energy resources. Are they mutually exclusive?

3. What role should individuals, corporations and governments play in reducing national reliance on fossil fuels? What mix of renewable energy versus fossil fuels should the U.S. aim for, over what time period?

4. What role can the U.S. play in convincing China, India, and others to change their policies on carbon emissions? Should the U.S. revisit ratifying or renegotiating the Kyoto Protocol?

5. How can states or regions lead the way for a more sustainable energy future, and at what point must the federal government come into compliance with their wishes? Does the U.S. need a "Green Revolution" that can serve as the next engine of economic growth for the economy? What sort of incentives will work?

6. How does the U.S. balance the expectations and priorities of a new Administration with the host of domestic and international problems that require attention? Can the U.S. integrate energy policy successfully into its future plans? Should American leaders make energy an issue of national security?

NOTES: ....
....
....
....
....
....
....
....
....
....
....
....

READINGS

Brzezinski, Zbigniew, Scrowcroft, Brent, and Ignatius, David, **America and the World: Conversations on the Future of American Foreign Policy.** New York, Basic Books, 2008. 304 pp. $27.50 (hardcover). A written dialogue of unscripted conversations with two former national security advisers explores the unprecedented foreign policy challenges facing the U.S. today and seeks to articulate "the center of responsible opinion on American foreign policy."

Collier, Paul, **The Bottom Billion: Why the Poorest Countries Are Failing and What Can Be Done About It.** New York, Oxford University Press, 2007. 224 pp. $15.95 (paper). A concise, penetrating reassessment of development aid that challenges conventional views.

Cordesman, Anthony H., and Al-Rodhan, Khalid R., **The Global Oil Market: Risks and Uncertainties.** Washington, DC, Center for Strategic and International Studies, 2006. 168 pp. $22.95 (paper). A risk assessment of the global oil market centered on four primary concerns in six major oil-producing regions of the world.

Friedman, Thomas L., **Hot, Flat, and Crowded: Why We Need a Green Revolution—and How it Can Renew America.** New York, Farrar, Straus and Giroux, 2008. 448 pp. $27.95 (hardcover). The well-known *New York Times* columnist and triple Pulitzer Prize winner's engaging case for the U.S. to take a leading role in fighting global warming, population growth and the battle for resources among the world's burgeoning middle class.

"The Future of Nuclear Energy." **Bulletin of the Atomic Scientists,** Sept./Oct. 2008. Entire issue. Experts consider a range of benefits and challenges facing broader adoption of nuclear power for civilian use.

Gingrich, Newt, and Haley, Vince, **Drill Here, Drill Now, Pay Less: A Handbook for Slashing Gas Prices and Solving Our Energy Crisis.** Washington, DC, Regnery Publishing, 2008. 185 pp. $14.95 (paper). An argument for solving America's energy problems by developing its domestic energy resources, by the former speaker of the House of Representatives.

Krupp, Fred, and Horn, Miriam, **Earth: The Sequel: The Race to Reinvent Energy and Stop Global Warming.** New York, Norton, 2008. 256 pp. $24.95 (hardcover). A business-centric proposal for reducing climate change through cap and trade mechanisms, development of new clean-air technologies and adoption of strict federal carbon-emissions standards.

Speth, James Gustave, **The Bridge at the Edge of the World: Capitalism, the Environment, and Crossing from Crisis to Sustainability.** New Haven, CT, Yale University Press, 2008. 320 pp. $28.00 (hardcover). The author, a renowned environmentalist, argues that degradation of the Earth is not simply the result of inconsistent or inattentive national policies; it is "a result of systemic failures of the capitalism that we have today."

Yergin, Daniel, **The Prize: The Epic Quest for Oil, Money, and Power.** New York, Free Press, 1993. 928 pp. $22.00 (paper). A comprehensive history of the energy industry and energy-producing states that provides insights to the roots of many of the U.S. public's stances on big business, antitrust legislation and other crucial issues of the last century.

TO LEARN MORE ABOUT THIS TOPIC AND TO ACCESS WEB LINKS TO RESOURCES GO TO www.greatdecisions.org/topic3

The Arctic age
by Ed Struzik

As rising temperatures alter the landscape of the Arctic, creating new challenges and opportunities, how prepared is the U.S. to deal with these changes?

In 2007, a U.S. Geological Survey study concluded that two thirds of the world's polar bears, including all of those in Alaska and most of Canada's western Arctic, will be gone by 2050. The only ones remaining will be those inhabiting the High Arctic regions of Canada and western Greenland. PHOTO BY ED STRUZIK

In the summer of 2007, the Russian government sent a two-vessel expedition (one icebreaker, one research vessel) to the North Pole on a mission that was supposed to be mainly scientific. Only when the ships got to the top of the world did the geopolitical purpose of the venture become apparent to the rest of the world. Veteran Arctic explorer Artur Chilingarov, a member of Russia's lower house of Parliament, descended 14,000 feet in a deep-sea submersible and deposited a Russian flag, cast in rust-free titanium, on the seafloor.

The entire event was choreographed and filmed in a way that was clearly intended to announce to the world, and to the Russian people back home, that the seabed under the North Pole, the 1,100-mile-long Lomonosov Ridge, was an extension of Russia's continental shelf. Expedition members were treated like heroes when they arrived home. "We were there first and we can claim the entire Arctic, but if our neighbors like Canada want some part of it, then maybe we can negotiate with them," said Vladimir Zhiron-

ovsky, the populist leader of Russia's ultranationalist Liberal Democratic party.

Audacious as it seemed, given the rules and legal regime in place for resolving boundary issues in the Arctic, Zhironovsky's comments reflected in some measure what the Russians were thinking. A few days after the flag planting, strategic bombers were dispatched over the Arctic Ocean for the first time since the cold war ended. "The division of the Arctic," the Russian daily newspaper *Rossiiskaya Gazeta* declared some time later, "is the start of a new redistribution of the world."

Canada was the first, but not the only, country to protest. "This isn't the 15th century," said Peter MacKay, the country's foreign minister. "You can't go around the world and just plant flags and say, 'we're claiming this territory.'" The U.S. was a little slower off the mark. State Department officials appeared to be taken off guard by the theatrical nature of the move. The U.S. was not alone in wondering what to make of it all. Most countries with interests in the Arctic

ED STRUZIK *was the 2006–2007 recipient of the Atkinson Fellowship in Public Policy and a finalist for this year's Grantham Prize. He is author of* The Big Thaw, *which is to be published by John Wiley and Sons in the spring of 2009.*

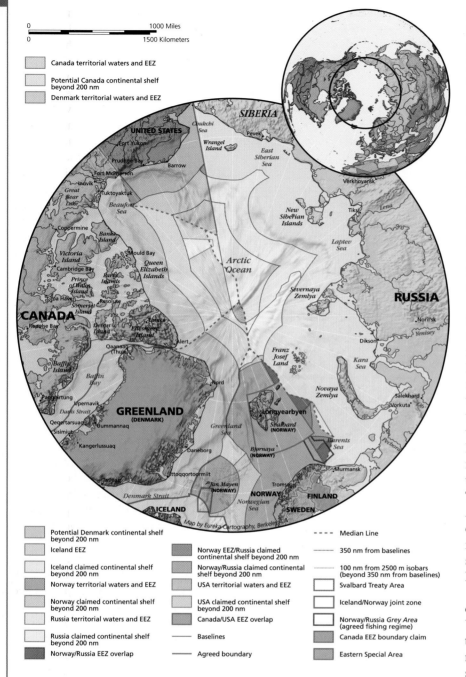

Map legend:

- Canada territorial waters and EEZ
- Potential Canada continental shelf beyond 200 nm
- Denmark territorial waters and EEZ

0   1000 Miles
0   1500 Kilometers

- Potential Denmark continental shelf beyond 200 nm
- Iceland EEZ
- Iceland claimed continental shelf beyond 200 nm
- Norway territorial waters and EEZ
- Norway claimed continental shelf beyond 200 nm
- Russia territorial waters and EEZ
- Russia claimed continental shelf beyond 200 nm
- Norway/Russia EEZ overlap

- Norway EEZ/Russia claimed continental shelf beyond 200 nm
- Norway/Russia claimed continental shelf beyond 200 nm
- USA territorial waters and EEZ
- USA claimed continental shelf beyond 200 nm
- Canada/USA EEZ overlap
- Baselines
- Agreed boundary

- - - - Median Line
·········· 350 nm from baselines
·········· 100 nm from 2500 m isobars (beyond 350 nm from baselines)
- Svalbard Treaty Area
- Iceland/Norway joint zone
- Norway/Russia *Grey Area* (agreed fishing regime)
- Canada EEZ boundary claim
- Eastern Special Area

Map by Eureka Cartography, Berkeley, CA

seemed puzzled by what the Russians were up to.

For more than a century, the Arctic has been dismissed as no-man's land, of interest only to missionaries, military strategists, outdoor adventurers and the aboriginal people who live there. Only eight countries—the U.S., Russia, Canada, Norway, Sweden, Finland, Denmark and Iceland have any legitimate claims to areas within the Arctic Circle. Each controls a 200-nautical-mile economic zone along its coasts.

Only five of these countries—the U.S., Canada, Russia, Norway and Denmark (Greenland)—have given any indication that they will exercise the option of claiming territory that lies beyond these boundaries. Currently, that territory, which is all under water, is supervised by the International Seabed Authority, an autonomous organization that was established under the 1982 United Nations Convention on the Law of the Sea (UNCLOS). By rules of the convention, no country has a right

to extend the boundaries beyond the 200-nautical-mile limit unless they can prove that the zones of expansion are part of an undersea continental shelf connected to their territory.

Most countries have been content to leave it to the 21-member UN technical committee that oversees the Convention on the Law of the Sea to review and recommend which country owns what in this part of the Arctic. The committee does this on the basis of the geological data submitted by each nation. The deadline for doing so depends on when a submitting country ratifies the Convention on the Law of the Sea. Ten years is currently the time a signing country has to make a submission.

Several things have accounted for the Russian drama and for the world's sudden interest in the Arctic. First, and most important, is the Arctic ice that has been melting at a rate that will soon make it possible for ships to pass safely through both the Northern Sea Route that links Western Europe to Asia along the Siberian coast and the more challenging Northwest Passage, which connects the North Atlantic to the Pacific through the archipelago of Canada. This is not unimportant because an Arctic route either from Europe to Asia or from Alaska to the Eastern Seaboard is up to 6,500 nautical miles, or 40% shorter, than a trip through the Suez or Panama canals.

Secondly, the world is rapidly running out of oil and gas and mineral reserves. Up until recently, most of the reserves in the Arctic have been too expensive, too risky or too inaccessible to exploit. The spiking price of oil is taking care of the high costs, new drilling technologies are making Arctic oil more accessible and the melting ice is now quickly taking care of some of the risks.

The development of the Arctic's vast oil, gas and mineral reserves would be a boon to a world economy that is starved for new sources of fossil fuels and metals not threatened by political unrest and terrorist activities. A warmer Arctic, however, also presents some formidable challenges that are beyond the ability of just one nation to resolve. Not only does it open the continent's backdoor to drug smugglers, illegal aliens, terrorists and energy-starved countries like China, which are also in desperate need of finding new sources of fossil fuels, but it also raises the potential for an environmental catastrophe that could make the *Exxon Valdez* accident, the biggest man-made environmental disaster in North American history, look like a minor oil spill.

The impact on fish and wildlife and the aboriginal people who inhabit the Arctic could be just as catastrophic. With sea ice melting, glaciers receding and storms picking up steam in a warming polar environment, many coastal communities in Alaska, the Northwest Territories of Canada and Siberia are becoming increasingly vulnerable to flooding and erosion. A warmer and shorter ice season also means less time for polar bears to hunt seals and more

time for disease and biting flies to take their toll on caribou, musk oxen and tens of millions of migrating birds that nest in the Arctic. Beluga whales and narwhal, which hide under the ice to avoid killer whales, and hover along ice edges to feed on Arctic cod, could also be threatened. Commercial fishing resources could shift and exacerbate boundary disputes that remain unresolved.

Theoretically, a polar meltdown could shut down or disrupt the ocean conveyor belt that brings warm water into the North Atlantic and moderates the climate of Britain, northern Europe and eastern North America. In the longer term, the melting Arctic's contribution to rising sea levels could also displace the 104 million people who live in coastal areas within a meter of the ocean surface.

Those who live on higher ground in more temperate and tropical regions of the world will not escape the changes that are coming. Polar ice is the genesis of cold fronts that bring rain and snow to much of the Northern Hemisphere. If that mass of ice shrinks, winters will not go away, but the problems people in both drought- and wet-weather-stricken regions are now facing could worsen.

The rest of the world will also be vulnerable to boreal forest fires that will inevitably escalate in size and severity in the coming decades as the north heats up. Few people in the eastern U.S. realize it, but part of the suffocating smog that cities there suffered through in the summer of 2003 contained fallout from fires in Alaska and the Yukon that were occurring at the same time. All told, 6% of Alaska and 4% of the Yukon burned that record-hot year. ●

Consequences of melting

Scientists had been issuing warnings about the long-term effects of a warming world even before the Reagan Administration (1981–89) came to power. Most of them suspected then, as they know now, that the effects of this warming would be more pronounced in the polar regions than anywhere else in the world.

The Reagan Administration made headlines by putting a freeze on funding for climate-change research. Decisionmakers and the public, however, did not really start to take serious notice of the implications until the late 1980s and 1990s when heat waves started killing people in alarming numbers. In 1995, there were a record 70 heat waves that scorched cities from the American Midwest to the Eastern Seaboard. The hardest hit was Chicago, where 739 people died.

Even when the heat of the 1990s exceeded the warm, drought-prone decade of the 1980s, not everyone was convinced that this was the work of "greenhouse gases," which trap heat in the atmosphere. Natural variability,

which included changes in the North Atlantic Oscillation, the atmospheric regime that governs climatic conditions in most parts of the Northern Hemisphere, made the period 1920 to 1940 almost as warm as the 1980s and 1990s, without the added input of carbon dioxide, methane and other greenhouse gases trapping the Earth's heat.

Many scientists, including those at the National Snow and Ice Data Center (NSIDC) in Boulder, Colorado, and the Canadian Ice Service, were still sitting on the fence in 2000 trying to determine whether natural variability or greenhouse gases were more responsible for the warming. But they soon came to realize that no amount of natural variability could account for the rapid retreat of ice in the Arctic over the next eight years. In 1980, there was almost as much summer ice in the Arctic as there is land in the U.S. outside of Alaska and Hawaii. By the summer of 2005, that amount of ice was reduced by the amount of land there is east of the Mississippi River. According to

NSIDC climatologist Mark Serreze, it was the least amount of ice recorded since satellites started taking pictures of the Arctic in 1979, and quite likely the least experienced in the last century.

By the end of the summer of 2007, the ice had retreated so far beyond all expectations that most experts were shocked, if not stunned, by what they saw in the satellite imagery. Across the Arctic as a whole, the meltdown was where climatologists expected it would be in 2030. What really made the big melt of 2007 an eye-popping one was the absence of ice in areas where it almost never melts. The so-called "mortuary" of old ice that normally chokes McClintock Channel in the High Arctic was almost all gone. What is more, Viscount Melville Sound, "the birthplace" of a great deal of new Arctic ice, was down to half its normal summer cover. "The ice is no longer growing or getting old," noted John Falkingham, chief forecaster for the Canadian Ice Service. "Ten years from now," he said at the end of that summer, "we may

Climatologists were stunned by the amount of Arctic ice that had melted by the end of the summer of 2007. The retreat was where they had expected it to be in 2030. PHOTO BY ED STRUZIK

look back on 2007 and say that was the year we passed the tipping point."

Navigational possibilities

The notion that the Arctic could become a shortcut between Europe and Asia goes back more than 500 years to when the Italian explorer John Cabot (Giovanni Caboto) first set sail into the northwest Atlantic to find a passage to the Orient. Over the next 350 years, more than 140 vessels tried and failed to find a passage through this icy world. These included American-backed voyages of Elisha Kent Kane, Isaac I. Hayes and George Washington DeLong, all of whom believed that there was a navigable open polar sea at the North Pole suitable for ships to pass through. Not until Norwegian explorer Roald Amundsen's ship *Gjoa* steamed through Lancaster Sound in 1903 and entered the Bering Sea three years later was the Northwest Passage successfully navigated.

Amundsen's voyage, however, did little to persuade other seafaring explorers to follow. The prospects of getting through all that ice was still so daunting and dangerous that over the course of the next 65 years, only 36 full transits of the Northwest Passage were made. Most of those were done for purposes of sovereignty and military strategy and often with the help of powerful icebreakers. Only a handful were designed for commercial purposes.

Theoretically, there are only seven practicable shipping routes through the Northwest Passage. The shortest one of those, the route that goes through Mc-Clure Strait toward Alaskan waters in the western Arctic, was not successfully navigated from west to east until 1993, a record hot year up until that point in time. Since then, the number of vessels sailing through the Northwest Passage has been steadily increasing. Between 2000 and 2004, there were 25 vessels that made the voyage, more than twice as many as in the same period a decade before. In 2007, 86 ships had entered the Arctic waters along the Northwest Passage. Eleven of them made the full transit.

While the northern polar route is now navigable for some of the summer months, experts are still debating when and whether the Northwest Passage will become safe for navigation. There is still a great deal of ice in the North American Arctic because the islands of the archipelago shade and protect it from the disintegrating forces of sun, winds and tides. Predictions for a seasonally ice-free Northwest Passage vary anywhere from eight to 50 years. Even then, there is some doubt about the ability of certain ships to get through multiyear ice that will inevitably calve off the permanent ice pack closer to the North Pole before drifting south. There is, however, no debating that the number of partial and full transits along the northern polar route and

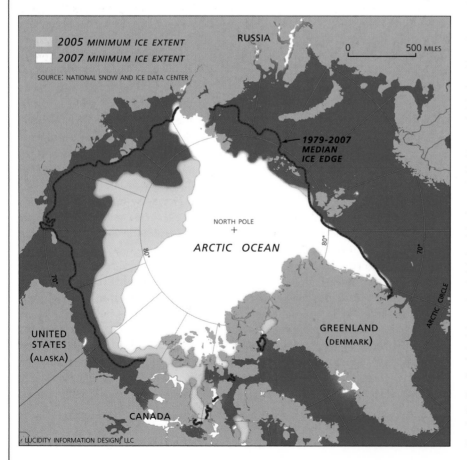

2005 MINIMUM ICE EXTENT
2007 MINIMUM ICE EXTENT

SOURCE: NATIONAL SNOW AND ICE DATA CENTER

RUSSIA

0   500 MILES

1979-2007 MEDIAN ICE EDGE

NORTH POLE
+

ARCTIC OCEAN

80°

80°

70°

70°

ARCTIC CIRCLE

UNITED STATES
(ALASKA)

GREENLAND
(DENMARK)

CANADA

LUCIDITY INFORMATION DESIGN, LLC

through the Northwest Passage will increase exponentially as oil and gas, mining and tourism activities in the Arctic heat up.

The Russians are further ahead than anyone else in planning for this to happen. Part of their foresight arises from experience and the fact that the Northern Sea Route has opened up much more quickly to shipping than the Northwest Passage. The country currently operates 14 icebreakers, more than the rest of the world combined. One of them, the *Kapitan Khlebnikov,* has transited the Northwest Passage 12 times, more than any other ship.

Russia has also been quicker than anyone else in making sure that a new generation of icebreakers, tankers and platforms are built to withstand the hazards of sailing through and operating in these dangerous waters. The country is currently doing this by blending some Communist-era big-spending strategies with free-enterprise principles. Recognizing that its private sector and shipbuilding yards did not have the resources or capacity to revamp the country's aging Arctic fleet, for example, then President Vladimir Putin signed a decree in 2007 establishing the United Shipbuilding Corporation. The government-sponsored project is using the state's financial power to bolster the shipbuilding sector so that it can exploit the hydrocarbons buried beneath the seabed of the Arctic.

In addition to new icebreakers, the Russians plan to build 40 ice-resistant oil platforms and 14 offshore gas platforms by 2030. They are also seeking to acquire 55 ice-resistant tankers and storage tankers, as well as 20 gas carriers that will be capable of delivering fuel to Russia and foreign nations like China that have already agreed in principle to finance some of these endeavors.

The North Pole is not the only area of the Arctic that the Russians are targeting. They are also pushing the concept of an Arctic Bridge that would connect the Russian port of Murmansk with the small Canadian port of Churchill in southern Hudson Bay. The Russians propose to use icebreakers to clear the way for freighters to carry oil, wheat, fertilizer and other goods to and from North America and Europe and Asia

Russian nuclear-powered icebreaker Yamal *travels to the North Pole through the Arctic Ocean, July 3, 2007. The icebreaker is a ship for use in waters continuously covered with ice.* NERY YNCLAN/NBC NEWSWIRE VIA AP IMAGES

via a sea route over the North Pole. This is an idea that has the support of both China and India and the American company that owns and operates the port of Churchill. Canada is also interested, but not yet committed. To prove that it can be done, the Russians used the route to ship a load of fertilizer to the port of Churchill in October 2007. That ship left Canada with a load of wheat.

Icebreakers needed

The situation in North America is very different. The Canadian Navy has not operated an icebreaker in the Arctic since the 1950s and it currently has no capacity to enter any Arctic waters that are significantly covered in ice. Most of the five icebreakers being used by the Canadian Coast Guard in the Arctic are nearing their end of life. The Canadian government has recently taken steps to address this problem. In August 2007, Prime Minister Stephen Harper announced his government's intention to build a new Polar Class icebreaker that would be more powerful than anything currently in the fleet. That icebreaker, however, is not scheduled to come into service until 2017 when the *Louis St. Laurent,* the current flagship of the fleet, is decommissioned.

The Canadian government has also announced that it plans to build six to eight Polar Class 5 patrol boats. These, however, would have only limited icebreaking capabilities and they would only be used in the Arctic on a seasonal basis. There is still no indication who is going to be building these patrol boats and when they might come into service. There is already some concern that recent recessionary pressures might result in delays.

The situation is even more critical in the U.S., where two of the country's three icebreakers, the *Polar Star,* which is out of service, and the *Polar Sea,* have already exceeded their intended 30-year life service. The *Healy* is used primarily for scientific purposes. The ability of the U.S. to operate in Arctic waters is so diminished that Admiral Thad Allen, commandant of the U.S. Coast Guard, recently testified that the "nation is at a crossroads with Coast Guard domestic and international icebreaking capabilities." While touring Alaska in the summer of 2008, Admiral Allen told *The New York Times*: "All I know is, there is water where it didn't used to be, and I'm responsible for dealing with that. Given the 8 or 10 years it would take to build even one icebreaker, I think we're at a crisis point on making a decision."

The Pentagon's Pacific Command, Northern Command and Transportation Command were of the same mind when they strongly recommended in a letter that the Joint Chiefs of Staff do something about Admiral Allen's predicament. Everyone seems sympathetic, but it is not yet clear whether the Coast Guard will get to purchase one or possibly two new icebreakers at a cost of between $800 million to $925 million each. It is also not clear whether one is going to be enough.

Like Canada, the U.S. needs greater icebreaking capability to deal with new developments in the Arctic. But unlike Canada, the U.S. has responsibilities in Antarctica as well. Moreover, the U.S. has yet to sign the UN Convention on the Law of the Sea. Should it do so, as most military and legal experts are urging the government to do, it would need icebreakers to help collect the data required in order to extend its economic zone or counter the claims of other nations like Russia, which are eager to expand their claims to the Arctic undersea resources.

Cornucopia of resources

No one knows exactly how much oil and gas there is in the Arctic. Virtually every expert who has studied the potential agrees that the reserves are enormous. Russia owns the bulk of gas resources in the Barents Sea, including the massive Shtokman field, which is the largest offshore gas reservoir in the world. The region has proven reserves of 3.2–3.7 trillion cubic meters of gas, an amount that could supply all of Europe's needs for seven years.

The Russian Ministry of Natural Resources calculates that the Arctic territory it now controls contains as much as 586 billion barrels of oil. By comparison, all of Saudi Arabia's current proven oil reserves amount to only 260 billion barrels.

This has attracted the interest of international energy companies like BP, which are largely excluded from the oil produced by the 13 members of the Organization of the Petroleum Exporting Countries (OPEC). Many of them are desperate to find new ways of adding to their declining inventories. While recognizing the risks of doing business in a country where corruption and harassment have long dogged the energy industry, BP was still willing to take a gamble and invest billions of dollars to get a share in the Russian developments.

With increasing instability in the Middle East and North Sea oil drying up, Norway has also indicated that the Arctic is now a main strategic priority for the country, which is currently the world's third-largest exporter of oil and gas. It is also the most technologically advanced when it comes to frontier-energy development.

Energy potential

In the summer of 2008, the U.S. Geological Survey (USGS) verified why the Arctic has become the "Holy Grail" for energy interests. After an exhaustive four-year review of all of the geological data available, it estimated that there are in the Arctic 90 billion barrels of undiscovered, technically recoverable oil, 1,670 trillion cubic feet of technically recoverable natural gas and 44 billion barrels of technically recoverable natural gas liquids in 25 geologically defined areas thought to have potential for petroleum.

That would account for about 22% of the undiscovered, technically recoverable resources in the world. Put another way, the Arctic holds about 13% of the undiscovered oil, 30% of the undiscovered natural gas, and 20% of the undiscovered natural gas liquids in the world. About 84% of the estimated resources are expected to occur offshore.

Given the current rate of world consumption of oil, untapped reserves in the Arctic could meet global demand for at least three years. The findings are of particular importance to the U.S. The USGS estimates that a third of the undiscovered oil is located off the coast of Alaska.

The energy potential in the Arctic could be much higher because the estimates do not take into account gas hydrates, bands of highly concentrated methane gas frozen in the permafrost. Gas hydrates—lattice-like ice structures that trap large quantities of methane, the major component of natural gas—are found on both the Atlantic and Pacific coasts of North America and in many others parts of the world. Those located in the Arctic, however, are among the most accessible and potentially the most economical to exploit. In November 2008, an expert panel convened by the Council of Canadian Academies conservatively estimated that the amount of methane hydrates are potentially one or more orders of magni-

CAGLECARTOONS.COM/PATRICK CHAPPATTE

tude larger than conventional reserves.

Like the Russians, energy companies in North America have already recognized the Arctic's energy potential. According to the USGS, energy exploration has resulted in the discovery of more than 400 oil and gas fields north of the Arctic Circle. These fields account for approximately 40 billion barrels of oil, more than 1,100 trillion cubic feet of gas, and 8.5 billion barrels of natural gas liquids.

The real value of energy in the North American Arctic came to light in 2008 when energy companies spent record sums for oil and gas leases.

Royal Dutch Shell, for example, paid $2.1 billion to acquire leases in Alaska's Chukchi Sea. ConocoPhillips spent $506 million in the same lease sale. In the Canadian Arctic, BP Exploration Ltd. spent $1.2 billion for three of five oil and gas leases that the Canadian government auctioned off. The leases cover about 611,000 hectares of the Beaufort seabed. BP's largest bid was $1.18 billion for a 202,380-hectare parcel. The amount BP paid surpasses the record $585 million that Imperial Oil and ExxonMobil Canada paid the year before.

Oil and gas, however, are only part of the wealth that is being exploited in the Arctic. Alaska's commercial fishery is already worth $1 billion annually. The turbot fishery in between Arctic Canada and Greenland is a vibrant one that could grow as the Canadian territory of Nunavut investigates new sources in largely untapped Arctic regions.

The opening of shipping lanes in the Northwest Passage would also be a boon to mining companies that have had their eyes on all the gold, silver, zinc, iron, diamonds and other mineral deposits buried in the more inaccessible areas of the Arctic world. The Slave geologic province, for example, which is located in between Great Bear Lake and Great Slave Lake in northern Canada, is widely regarded as the richest untapped mineral deposit in the world. Currently, three of the world's most productive diamond mines are operating in and around this area. Most experts believe the region's potential has

Russian Marshal Ustinov *missile cruiser leaves for the Barents Sea in August 2004. Russia announced that it was sending warships to patrol Arctic waters for the first time since the breakup of the Soviet Union—the latest move to increase the country's global military presence.* AP PHOTO

barely been tapped because there is no all-weather road or any port connecting it to the outside world. Currently, all three diamond mines are using ice roads in the deepest darkest months of an Arctic winter to get their fuel and supplies in and their unprocessed diamonds out.

New threats emerge

As the value of the Arctic's energy and mineral wealth becomes more apparent to the outside world, and as shipping lanes and polar flyways open up, the threat from smugglers and terrorists will likely rise. In 2008, for example, the Canadian government was warned once again that the diamond industry could be infiltrated by smugglers, drug dealers and terrorists who are looking for high value, highly portable and not easily detectable diamonds that could be sold on the black market in return for arms and drugs. Recent bombings of natural gas pipelines in northern Alberta and northern British Columbia also serve as reminders that the proposed multibillion-dollar gas pipelines that may soon carry gas from Alaska and the Mackenzie and Beaufort sea region of Canada could also be vulnerable. The apprehension of illegal immigrants trying to get into Canada via the port of Churchill, the airport in Iqaluit and the Inuit community of Grise Fiord via Greenland is also troublesome.

Whether or not Canada and the U.S. are prepared to deal with these threats is an issue that is being increasingly debated by military analysts and global security experts. However, weaknesses in the security system started to come to light in the late 1990s.

One of the first and most brazen incidents occurred in the fall of 1998 when a Russian IL-76 flew over the North Pole en route to the port of Churchill on the shores of western Hudson Bay. The Il-76 is a large cargo plane, even bigger than the enormous C-130 Hercules used by the Canadian and U.S. military.

According to intelligence reports, the weather was poor in Churchill that night. Strong winds were blowing snow on the runway, so visibility was marginal at times. That is not unusual for November in this part of the world. What was unusual was the pilot switching off his landing lights the moment he hit the tarmac.

The Russian crew was not an "overfriendly" bunch when they disembarked that night. But that somber mood changed dramatically the next morning when they gathered for beers at a local restaurant.

The Russians did not stay long. Shortly after a Bell 206 helicopter landed at Churchill, the Russian crew drove back to the airport, dropped the plane's cargo doors, loaded the heli-

NOW THAT FOSSIL FUEL USE HAS MELTED THE ICE CAP WE CAN DRILL FOR MORE FOSSIL FUELS!

Mike Keefe The Denver Post 09/18/07

copter and took off. No one was there to ask questions, examine receipts or inspect export documents, if there were any to inspect. Canadian intelligence officials, however, were monitoring the flight of the IL-76, from the moment it landed in Churchill to the point when it touched down in a region of Russia known for organized crime activity. Whether they let the Russians do what they did for intelligence purposes, or whether they were powerless to intervene, remains unclear. What was clear is that the small airport in Churchill had no capacity to deal with a situation like this. There was only one person on duty at the time.

The broader significance of the incident came into sharper focus the following year when a Chinese research ship, ostensibly en route to the North Pole to study climate change, rounded the coast of Alaska before getting trapped in ice. With the help of Canadian and American ice-observing networks and satellite receivers, the ship's captain was shown a way through the ice.

Instead of heading on toward the North Pole, however, the ship showed

up unannounced at the tiny Inuit community of Tuktoyaktuk in the western Arctic. When the Inuit in the small community reported the ship's presence to Canada's Royal Canadian Mounted Police (RCMP) a makeshift team of police officers and civil servants working in the area was assembled to investigate and board the ship. There, they found several machine guns and a passport that was unaccounted for. When questioned, the ship's captain said they were there to meet up with a Chinese tour guide who, intelligence officials later learned, happened to be a Chinese national who had claimed refugee status in 1993. The unlikely presence of a refugee posing as a tour guide in an Inuit community that is infrequently visited by tourists was suspicious at best.

These two incidents, and several others that followed in the ensuing years, got military and security officials seriously wondering about the prospects for the future, especially after 9/11 showed the world that the continent was not safe from terrorists' activities. If the backdoor of the continent was vulnerable to suspicious entries like these, many were asking, what would the situation be like in 20 or 30 years' time when climate change was expected to melt sea ice sufficiently to allow for partial or full passage through its Arctic waterways? Would the Canadian or U.S. military or Coast Guards be able to stop a rogue ship if it took a run through the Northwest Passage to save 6,500 miles or maybe load up on valuable freshwater from an Arctic river or lake? Would transport or environment officials be able to clean up an oil or fuel spill if a tanker like the Exxon Valdez was damaged by ice and spilled its cargo? And what about a ship that might be trying to smuggle in people?

A decade later, military and security

officials are still asking the same questions. But now a rapidly warming Arctic is running out the clock for both the Canadian and the U.S. governments to do something about it. The Center for Naval Analyses, a private consultant to the U.S. government, warned in 2007 that geopolitical upheaval caused by climate change could create new havens for terrorists, trigger waves of illegal immigration and disrupt oil supplies. In a report commissioned by the center, Retired Admiral Donald Pilling, a former vice chief of U.S. naval operations, reiterated the long-standing view that neither Canada nor the U.S. has the military capability to handle future threats in the Northwest Passage.

Retired Canadian Colonel Gary Rice further elaborated on that warning in a 2007 report to the Conference of Defense Associations Institute. In that report, he outlined various scenarios in which things could go horribly wrong in the Arctic. These included a scenario in which the $16 billion Mackenzie Gas pipeline is completed and already pumping natural gas to markets in the U.S. Young aboriginal people, however, have become increasingly militant because land claims and other governance issues have still not been resolved. Nor have their people benefited from the wealth of gas that is being shipped south. So a group of them, unhappy with the status quo, forms the First Nations' Liberation Movement. They acquaint themselves with the art of irregular warfare and start to blow up compressors and pipeline sections.

His final scenario is perhaps the most prescient in light of current events. In this case, the Russian Arctic container vessel Norsk Nova has set sail from Murmansk to Churchill by way of the North Pole route. Three weeks before the departure, a Chechen terrorist cell affiliated with al-Qaeda bribes the poorly paid and drug-addicted commander of a badly secured storage unit at the Sevmorput naval shipyard near Murmansk. He turns a blind eye to a piece of cargo that contains a trunk-sized, man-portable, low-yield nuclear device.

The ship's cargo is then loaded onto railcars destined to go south. The nuclear device, however, spontaneously detonates, inflicting a one-kiloton ground-level explosion. All matter within 150 meters of the fireball is vaporized. In the 500-meter area outside that perimeter, winds of over 150 miles per hour destroy all the buildings in the area. Two ships, including an oil tanker, are badly damaged. Oil spills into the sub-Arctic waters of Hudson Bay.

Everyone within 1,100 meters of the blast is hit with a neutron and gamma-ray dose that will kill them within 30 days. Those living within two square miles of the blast will suffer the same fate if they remain in the area for 48 hours.

In recent years, Canadian military and security officials have taken steps to deal with some of these issues with a series of exercises in the Arctic. Operation Narwhal (the largest and most ambitious Canadian military exercise in the Arctic up until that time) took place in the summer of 2007 off the southwest coast of Baffin Island.

According to one top military official, Operation Narwhal was supposed to "show the world we'll be watching if they trespass on Canada's Arctic." What the world saw, if anyone outside of Canada was watching, was that even when the military staged a scenario in which it intercepts a foreign vessel en route to the Arctic to meet a plane smuggling narcotics in from Mexico, it could not pull it off without serious hitches.

Scenarios such as these are not just Canada's concern. Unlikely as it might seem now, the prospects of a suitcase bomb blowing up at the port of Churchill or a Liberian-based single-hulled oil tanker taking a short cut through the Northwest Passage to save time and fuel is not out of the question in the future.

If such a bomb found its way to Chicago, the results would be even more catastrophic than if it blew up in Churchill. And should that Liberian tanker run into ice and start leaking oil, it might simply carry on into Alaskan waters, where it could potentially threaten the billion-dollar fishery. If that tanker were so severely damaged by ice that it was totally disabled, there would be no feasible way of containing the spill or cleaning it up. With no port in the Arctic, it would be very difficult to get a cleanup crew on site. Unless the accident occurred near an air base like Resolute, helicopter support would be impossible.

Environmental and territorial concerns

If anything was learned from the *Exxon Valdez* oil spill, it is that a cleanup would have to happen very quickly. A rotating workforce would be needed immediately. There would be a need for heavy equipment and a way of handling the oily waste.

Another important lesson learned from the *Exxon Valdez* disaster is that no amount of money can clean up a spill of that size. The best and most effective way of dealing with a catastrophe like that one is to target those areas that are most important.

Not only would an oil spill in the Bering and Chukchi seas and the Northwest Passage have a devastating impact on polar bears, which are already threatened by the loss of ice, but it could also threaten fish populations and other marine life. The possible catastrophic scenarios are numerous. One that stands out, however, is a single-hulled oil tanker that makes a run through the Northwest Passage, claiming, as the U.S. and the European Union do, that this is an international strait. In Lancaster Sound, the tanker runs into a sheet of thick ice that punctures the hull of the tanker. Oil begins to spill out.

Several thousand beluga whales are in the area feeding on Arctic cod that are, in turn, feeding on the krill that thrive along the edges of the ice. At least two dozen polar bears are on this sheet of ice, hunting seals.

Canada's flagship, the *Louis St. Laurent*, has just left the port outside of Halifax and is at least a week away from the scene. The *Henry Larsen*, another Coast Guard icebreaker, is in the Lincoln Sea, helping scientists map the seabed. It is at least four days away. The one U.S. icebreaker still in operation is nowhere near the area.

There are only four helicopters operating out of Resolute, the nearest air base. One, however, is down due to mechanical problems. The other three have all been dispatched by the Polar Continental Shelf Project to serve scientists in the field. Weather issues, which are common in the Arctic, have them grounded for the time being. What little air power the Canadian military has at Eureka, on Ellesmere Island, is not enough.

Down south, both the U.S. and Canada are suffering through one of the worst forest-fire seasons ever. Virtually every nonmilitary plane and helicopter in North America has been commandeered to deal with these infernos. (This actually happened in 2003 when fires in British Columbia, Alberta and Alaska taxed the firefighting system to the maximum.)

The amount of oil spilling out of the tanker is substantial. It flows under the ice and is carried by strong winds and currents to bird-nesting islands and to the turbot fishery in Baffin Bay and Davis Strait. Thick fog and cloud cover make it impossible for either satellites or planes to track the flow of oil. The *Exxon Valdez* is no longer North America's worst man-made disaster.

Geopolitical implications

It has become increasingly clear that the Arctic is no longer an obscure part of the world, of interest to very few. Climate change and the world's insatiable thirst for resources, be it oil, gas, methane hydrates, metals, diamonds or fish, have launched a race that will inevitably result in another redrawing of the map of the world.

In spite of Russia's planting of a flag at the North Pole, the 1982 UN Convention on the Law of the Sea remains the best way of resolving the boundary issues beyond the 200-nautical-mile economic zone. The redrawing of that part of the Arctic map, however, will take some time. Russia has until 2009 to complete its case; Canada and Denmark have until 2013 and 2014 respectively. If the U.S. ratifies the UNCLOS in 2009, it might take until 2019 or 2020 before its boundary issues are resolved.

Russia, of course, is the wild card in this risk scenario. Whether the Russians are willing to wait another decade or more to exploit what they think is rightfully theirs remains to be seen. The U.S. needs to act soon. Since the U.S. has not ratified the UN convention, it cannot legitimately lay claim to those resources off its 200-nautical-mile economic zone. Nor can it counter those competing claims by Russia and Norway. Sitting on the sidelines also means that the U.S. does not have a seat on the UN commission that will eventually make recommendations on those claims. Even if the U.S. were to ratify the convention, as the heads of the U.S. Coast Guard, the U.S. Navy, many in corporate America and environmentalists insist, its ability to support and assert its claims will be handcuffed by the condition of its small fleet of icebreakers. The U.S. Navy, which has the broadest maritime reach of any in the world, is almost incapable of operating in the Arctic Ocean. That must also change.

The U.S., however, is only part of the solution. The redrawing of the map of the Arctic beyond the 200-nautical-mile zone is just one of a number of challenges that Arctic nations face.

Several other boundary disputes still need to be resolved. Denmark has laid claim to Hans Island, a barren outcrop of rock off the coast of Ellesmere Island that Canada claims as its own. In the western Arctic, the U.S. and Canada have yet to agree on a maritime boundary line extending from the Alaska/Yukon border.

The 1,600-mile maritime boundary line between Alaska and Siberia was

Crude oil from the tanker Exxon Valdez, *top, swirls on the surface of Alaska's Prince William Sound, April 9, 1989, 16 days after the tanker ran aground, spilling millions of gallons of oil and causing widespread environmental damage.* AP PHOTO/JOHN GAPS III

supposed to have been resolved in 1990, when, after nine years of negotiations, the U.S. and the Soviet Union signed an agreement to divide the area. The Russian Parliament, however, has refused to ratify it. Parliamentarians claim that the deal robbed them of 30,000 square miles of territory.

And there is Canada, which claims the Northwest Passage as part of its territorial waters. That claim is disputed by both the U.S. and the European Union. As a result, its status remains in a kind of legal limbo.

U.S. involvement needed

Boundary disputes will not be resolved with military force or the planting of flags on the seabed. There is an international legal regime and dispute-resolving mechanism system in place through which many of the issues can be resolved. The fact that circumpolar countries have been meeting to discuss territorial disputes and technical issues that relate to the continental shelf is a positive sign that these disputes can be worked out. So is the decision by Canada and the U.S. last summer to share the *Louis St. Laurent* icebreaker so that scientists could map the contentious seabed of the Beaufort Sea.

The U.S., however, has to get involved in a more meaningful way. The best way for the U.S. to start doing this is by ratifying UNCLOS.

With each year that passes in which it fails to do so, the "grab and run" scenario that seems so unlikely now or in the near future becomes increasingly possible as the energy inventories of the world diminish. Canada and the U.S. were right to shrug off the Russians planting a flag at the North Pole. But what would either country do if the Russians showed up in disputed territory five or ten years from now with a drilling team and a drilling platform?

Russia is not the only potential problem. Canada and the U.S. have to find a way of managing traffic through the Northwest Passage. Agreeing to disagree on whether this is an international strait or territorial waters controlled exclusively by Canada is no longer practicable. Sooner or later, some ship, be it one from Russia or China or one registered in a country of convenience, is going to test this route. Potentially, one of those ships is going to run into trouble. Canada and the U.S. face the decision to set their differences aside and agree on some form of joint management of this maritime route. This would include everything from ensuring that notices of passage are registered and tariffs collected to ensuring that safety and environmental regulations are followed. Canada and the U.S. also need the support of the circumpolar nations to make this work.

The UN Commission on the Limits of the Continental Shelf is not going to necessarily have the final say. The commission is a technical body that can only make recommendations. It cannot rule definitively on territory in which there are overlapping claims. In the event of that happening, the countries involved will have to work it out themselves. If they refuse or fail to do so, they can either take the dispute to the Law of the Sea Tribunal or the International Court of Justice.

Antarctic blueprint

The short history of Antarctica provides lessons on what might be done while these boundary and passage issues are being resolved. In Antarctica, the 12 countries that laid claim to parts of the continent agreed to put their differences aside until the 1959 Antarctica Treaty was signed; 46 countries have now acceded to that treaty. The Antarctica Treaty prohibits military activities, the disposal of radioactive wastes, and any economic exploitation of the continent. It compels participating countries to meet regularly to discuss issues of mutual concern and resolve potential conflicts. While not perfect, it has functioned extremely well.

The stakes and circumstances in the Arctic would require a very different treaty. Unlike Antarctica, there are people living in the Arctic. Nearly 2 million live in Russia, 650,000 in Alaska, 130,000 in Canada and a little over a million in Greenland, Iceland, the Scandinavian countries and the Faeroe Islands. The interests of these people would have to be represented and accounted for.

It is also unrealistic to expect any country to refrain from economic activity in the Arctic given the high stakes

CARTOONISTS & WRITERS SYNDICATE. CARTOONWEB.COM/KAL

and the investments that have been made so far. At the very least, rules and regulations governing shipping, drilling, disposal of wastes, safety and impacts on aboriginal people and wildlife could be addressed in a more meaningful and coordinated way through the treaty process.

There is already a body in place that could facilitate a treaty like this. The Arctic Council was formally established in 1996, five years after the eight Arctic nations had signed the Arctic Environmental Protection Strategy (AEPS). In addition to the eight member nations, sanctioned observers include six non-Arctic nations—Britain, France, Germany, the Netherlands, Poland and Spain—and several international organizations, including the International Union for Conservation of Nature, the International Red Cross Federation, the Nordic Council, the Northern Forum and a handful of nongovernmental organizations such as the Association of World Reindeer Herders.

The council has done tremendous work over the years, but there is evidence to suggest that its influence has

been waning at high levels of government. A treaty would raise the political profile of Arctic issues and compel circumpolar nations to act on issues that have traditionally been ignored or put on the back burner.

Skeptics who think there is plenty of time to adjust and respond to the changing circumstances in the Arctic are mistaken. So far, the climate models projecting future climate change in the Arctic regions have not been wrong, but they have severely underestimated how quickly the changes that have happened already would occur.

"It's not so much what we know that's a problem," according to Mark Serreze, NSIDC senior research scientist. "It's what we don't know. The paleoclimate record tells us that the system can change very, very quickly, on the order of just 10 years. I suspect that there are surprises ahead that we won't be ready for." •

OPINION BALLOTS AFTER PAGE 64

QUESTIONS

1. Why has the U.S. been so slow to react to the growing changes in the Arctic region?

2. Will the U.S. be able to balance resource extraction interests with the need to protect the delicate environmental systems of the Arctic? What about the other countries bordering the Arctic?

3. How would you propose dividing up the potential resources in the Arctic? Should parcels be sold to the highest bidder, as is the current system? Should considerations be given to the local people who inhabit specific regions of the Arctic? Should companies be required to submit environmental protection plans in addition to development proposals?

4. Given the differences between the Arctic and Antarctic, most notably that people live in the Arctic, will an international consensus be achievable for governing the Arctic region? What do you consider the most important problems a treaty should be drafted to deal with?

5. The author raises the point that if Russia installed a drilling platform in the far north 10 years from now, there would be little the U.S. could do. What would be the likely U.S. reaction? What do you think the U.S. could do to challenge such a move? How could a race for the Arctic exacerbate great- and rising-power tensions?

6. Do you think Russia's move to claim part of the Arctic should be a wake-up call for the U.S.? Should it overcome its objections and ratify UNCLOS, so it can fully participate in the framework for dealing with boundary disputes, which are going to be ever-more prevalent with the rapid melting taking place in the Arctic region?

7. The increased melting of the Arctic ice is opening up shorter polar shipping routes and the ability to exploit vast oil, gas and mineral reserves, but it is also presenting many formidable new challenges that will have to be dealt with internationally. What do you consider to be the most difficult problems arising out of these new circumstances?

8. Russian President Dmitry Medvedev said in September 2008 that his country's task "is to turn the Arctic into Russia's resource base of the 21st century." Do you think the U.S. should take this "challenge" seriously and try to act quickly to help ensure that all the concerned nations get their fair share of the abounding resources that have recently been uncovered? What would be the best way to do that?

NOTES: ....
....
....
....
....
....
....
....

READINGS

Bader, Jeffrey, Yergin, Daniel, et. al., **The Global Politics of Energy.** Washington, D.C., The Aspen Institute, 2008. 249 pp. $19.95 (paper). Featuring some of the most prominent energy experts to date, this collection of papers focuses on how recent developments in energy markets, including climate change and soaring prices, will impact the future of energy and foreign policy.

Blum, Douglas W., ed., **Russia and Globalization: Identity, Security, and Society in an Era of Change.** Baltimore, MD, John Hopkins University Press, 2008. 408 pp. $48.00 (hardcover). A scholarly compilation of research covering the themes of identity and security as part of Russia's globalization.

Borgerson, Scott G., "Arctic Meltdown: The Economic and Security Implications of Global Warming." **Foreign Affairs,** March/ April, 2008, pp. 63–77. A concise, instructive view of how the melting Arctic icecap presents political challenges as well as eco-

nomic opportunities, and why the U.S. must lead the way toward a multilateral diplomatic solution.

"The High North: The Arctic Contest Heats Up." **The Economist** (London), Oct. 11, 2008, p. 70. A concise view of Russia's recent maneuvering in the "High North" heightens concerns among its neighbors.

Osherenko, Gail, and Young, Oran R., **The Age of the Arctic: Hot Conflicts and Cold Realities,** Studies in Polar Research. New York, Cambridge University Press, 2005. 336 pp. $65.00 (paper). A comprehensive primer on conflicts of interest in the Arctic, U.S. policy options and possible solutions to these global controversies.

Sale, Richard, **The Arctic: The Complete Story.** London, Great Britain, Frances Lincoln Publishers, 2008. 640 pp. $42.00 (hardcover). A written and pictorial view of a lifetime's work in the Arctic by a leading scholar and glaciologist.

TO LEARN MORE ABOUT THIS TOPIC AND TO ACCESS WEB LINKS TO RESOURCES GO TO www.greatdecisions.org/topic4

Egypt: key ally in the Middle East
by Bruce K. Rutherford

Egypt has long been an important U.S. ally in the Middle East. How will the relationship change when Mubarak passes from the scene?

Pyramids are faintly visible through the air pollution over Cairo. Egypt has the Arab world's largest population and largest military, as well as its second-largest economy. BILL FOLEY/LANDOV

With the media's attention focused so tightly on Iraq, it is easy to forget the essential role that Egypt plays in Middle Eastern politics. It has the Arab world's largest population (80 million in 2007) and largest military, as well as its second-largest economy. It commands an exceptionally strategic location astride the Suez Canal, which serves as the conduit for roughly 10% of the world's seaborne trade and virtually all of the oil that flows from the Persian Gulf to Europe. It is the Arab world's most prolific source of art, film and literature, and is also an important center for Sunni Islamic thought and tradition. Accordingly, the country serves as a model for political development in other Arab states. Its political and legal institutions have been emulated to varying degrees in Kuwait, the United Arab Emirates, Jordan, Iraq and Syria. All of these factors make Egypt one of the most influential countries in the region, or as a popular adage puts it, "as Egypt goes, so go the Arabs."

Governance challenges

Egypt's importance as a regional power is partly the legacy of its larger-than-life revolutionary leader, Gamal Abdel Nasser (President from 1956 to 1970). The coup that he led in 1952 overthrew a corrupt monarchy and set in motion the transformation of Egypt's political and economic life. Nasser established a tightly centralized regime based on state dominance of the economy and society. A vast welfare system was created in which the government was tasked with providing food, education, medical care, transportation and a host of other services at heavily subsidized prices. Political competition was banned and replaced by a single party

BRUCE K. RUTHERFORD *is assistant professor of political science at Colgate University. He is the author of* Egypt after Mubarak: Liberalism, Islam, and Democracy in the Arab World *(Princeton, 2008). Parts of this article utilize material from this book and are used with permission from Princeton University Press.*

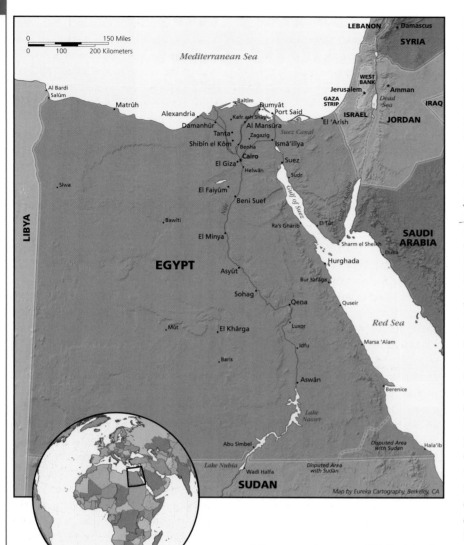

Map by Eureka Cartography, Berkeley, CA

(the Arab Socialist Union), whose power was reinforced by a large and ruthless intelligence apparatus.

Anwar Sadat, who succeeded Nasser in 1970, made some minor changes to this regime. Reforms adopted in the mid-1970s enabled a small private sector to emerge. A multiparty political system also developed, but it was still dominated by the president's party (now called the National Democratic party).

The current president, Hosni Mubarak, inherited this system in 1981. A cautious man by nature, he refrained from any dramatic economic or political reforms, although the economic contradictions of the Nasser-era regime became increasingly apparent. The

public-sector firms established in the 1960s had created many jobs, but they also lost vast sums of money while producing shoddy goods. Nasser's welfare state promised generous subsidies on virtually all the essentials of life, but the public budget was unable to sustain this assistance in the face of rising prices and a steadily expanding population. These conflicting pressures brought the economy to a virtual standstill in 1990, with unemployement reaching 18%, the inflation rate above 20% and external debt exceeding 115% of gross domestic product (GDP). The GDP per capita had fallen from $750 in 1985–86 to $640 in 1989–90.

The first Persian Gulf war, which began with Iraq's invasion of Kuwait in August 1990, only worsened this situation. Over 400,000 Egyptian laborers returned from jobs in Iraq and Kuwait, dramatically reducing remit-

tances from overseas workers (a key source of income for many families) and aggravating unemployment. Tourism receipts fell sharply due to the war, as did Suez Canal revenues. However, Egypt assumed a leadership role in opposing the Iraqi invasion by sending 35,000 troops to help liberate Kuwait.

This decision produced a bonanza of economic rewards. The international community, led by the U.S., forgave roughly 50% of the country's foreign debt and granted a sharp increase in economic assistance. Much of this debt forgiveness and aid was conditioned on Egypt undertaking significant economic reforms. Under the auspices of the International Monetary Fund, Egypt's leaders developed a plan to transform the country into a competitive market economy that is fully integrated into the global economic system. The plan called for reducing the government's chronic budget deficits by cutting government services and subsidies. It also included an ambitious privatization program that aimed to sell off much of the public sector. As these measures were gradually implemented over the next 17 years, they led to a sharp reduction in the government's role in the economy. The number of subsidized items fell from 18 to 4 (bread, wheat flour, sugar and cooking oil). The size of the public sector shrank from 39% of GDP in 1992 to 28% in 2000. New laws governing labor relations, property rights, formation of companies, capital markets and banking began to shift the country toward a more competitive and market-oriented economy. Egypt joined the World Trade Organization in 1995 and announced plans to participate in the Euro-Mediterranean free-trade zone.

These steps sparked a resurgence in the Egyptian economy. By 1996, inflation, the budget deficit and unemployment were down and economic growth averaged 5% per year. This positive growth trend continued over the next decade, reaching 7% in 2006, with exports rising at 21% a year and foreign direct investment reaching a record high of almost $10 billion (9% of GDP, versus 2% in 1990). In essence,

The leader of the Egyptian revolution, Colonel Gamal Abdel Nasser, explains his decision to buy arms and munitions from Czechoslovakia in 1955. © BETTMANN/ CORBIS

Egypt is well on its way to dismantling the state-dominated economic order created in the 1960s and it has reaped dramatic economic benefits from this change of direction.

However, the country still suffers from an inefficient and corrupt bureaucracy that touches virtually every aspect of life. Indeed, the Egyptian state has deteriorated to the point that it is unable to meet many of the demands of daily governance. This erosion of state capability affects the daily lives of Egyptians in myriad ways—severe air pollution has rendered Cairo one of the most polluted cities on earth, and has damaged the health of millions of citizens; ever-worsening traffic problems make a simple trip across town an all-day affair; crowded and decrepit mass-transit systems are dangerous and unreliable; the quality of public education has declined sharply, with primary school classes often exceeding 50 students and university lectures packed to the rafters with 800 or more students; and most of the population receives woefully inadequate medical care. These weaknesses become particularly apparent during national disasters, such as a recent rock slide near Cairo that wiped out an entire neighborhood and produced heart-wrenching images of women and children buried in their homes after the

government's rescue efforts failed. Or, the sinking of an unsafe and overloaded ferry in the Red Sea in 2006, in which over 1,000 people drowned. Or, a fire that erupted in a public train in upper Egypt in 2002 that killed over 400 passengers. These events received extensive coverage in the media and served to underscore the sense that Egypt's government is failing at many of the challenges it confronts.

Coping with economic change

The cornerstone of the government's effort to chart a more promising future is its plan for economic reform, which has produced dramatic improvements in economic growth, but the privatization of many public-sector firms has aggravated unemployment and increased inequality. A broad array of programs are in place to address these problems, such as retraining redundant workers, granting loans to help displaced workers establish their own businesses and allowing dismissed workers to retain access to subsidized housing and medical care while they look for new jobs. However, the implementation of these programs has been—at best—uneven. Many average Egyptians remain uncertain about their personal economic future in an economy where competi-

tion for jobs has increased, but their skills have remained stagnant. This uncertainty has been reinforced by recent increases in the price of basic commodities such as bread and meat, driven by rising global food prices and a decline in the value of the Egyptian currency. These pressures have sparked sporadic demonstrations protesting increased prices, as well as some wildcat labor actions against the privatization process and the resulting decline in job security. By some accounts, there were over 220 actions by independent labor groups during 2006, despite the fact that these actions are prohibited by law. The government has responded with a pay increase for workers in the public sector. However, it lacks the resources to dramatically broaden its subsidy programs or to increase opportunities for government employment, both of which are also at odds with the long-term goal of reducing the government's role in the economy.

This mixture of economic growth, erosion of state institutions and growing public anxiety about the future could have led to a more vibrant political life. Under this scenario, the country's increased wealth might have supported political parties and civil society groups that would try to improve public policy and strength-

Egypt's President Hosni Mubarak gives the keynote address at the annual convention of the National Democratic party in Cairo, Nov. 1, 2008. NASSER NURI/REUTERS /LANDOV

A polling place in the Garden City district of Cairo during the parliamentary elections in November/December 2005. The ruling National Democratic party scored a large victory, winning 311 of the 454 seats in Parliament (68% of the total). Opposition parties won 9 seats, while the Muslim Brotherhood (which ran its candidates as independents) took 88. The government estimated that 26% of eligible voters participated in the election. Independent observers put the figure closer to 10% or less. PHOTO BY BRUCE K. RUTHERFORD

en the provision of state services.

Unfortunately, this has not been the case. The opening of the economy has not been matched by an opening of the political system. President Mubarak has allowed numerous political parties to emerge (24, at last count). However, the regime places many restrictions on their capacity to raise money and to organize. As a consequence, the ruling National Democratic party continues to dominate political life (it won all but 1,000 of the 52,000 seats contested in recent municipal elections). Elections are marred by wide-ranging fraud that includes doctored voter registration lists, manipulation of vote counts and intimidation of opposition candidates and their supporters. Civil society groups are tightly constrained. Independent human rights groups, which began to emerge in the 1980s and 1990s, have been thoroughly hounded by the regime and effectively silenced. Labor unions are organized and controlled by the government, and have proven largely unable to protect workers from the dramatic changes caused by privatization. The media is dominated by state-controlled newspapers and television stations that rarely criticize the government. The regime also has a

long record of human rights abuses, particularly against prisoners in detention.

Yet, the picture is not entirely bleak. An independent labor movement has taken root in recent years and has begun to organize some isolated labor actions. Satellite television is widely available and has introduced programming and news beyond the reach of state control. And, a small but bold group of private newspapers offers good quality reporting that challenges many abuses of state power. But these papers must operate under a press law that places sharp limits on their freedom to investigate state officials (especially at the senior level). This same law also threatens onerous punishments for articles deemed insulting to state officials.

Supporters of democracy were particularly discouraged by several constitutional amendments adopted in March 2007. A few of these amendments provided a glimmer of hope. For example, they broadened Parliament's authority to review the budget and guaranteed its right to question ministers. However, these gains were offset by other amendments that expanded the government's capacity to suppress its political opponents, particularly if their actions could be construed as contributing to terror-

ism. Indeed, anyone suspected of involvement in terrorism in any way can have his/her constitutional rights suspended indefinitely. The government retains the authority to define what actions are supportive of terrorism, without any mechanism of independent judicial appeal. It also continues to operate with broad powers granted by the emergency law, which was renewed for two more years in 2008. This law gives the executive branch wide latitude to arrest and detain citizens with little effective judicial oversight. Egypt has been under emergency rule for Mubarak's entire 28 years in office.

Political alternatives?

Under these difficult conditions, three types of critics of state power have emerged.

THE SECULAR OPPOSITION. The regime dominates virtually every aspect of political life. Through a combination of patronage and graft, it achieves overwhelming victories in electoral contests at both the local and national levels. It also wields a vast array of laws that regulate the formation and actions of political parties, civil society

An Egyptian woman, wearing the hijab, carries a lantern at a market in Cairo. The lantern is a traditional decoration for the Muslim holy month of Ramadan. AP PHOTO/ AMR NABIL

An Orthodox Coptic monk makes the Coptic sign of the cross at Dayr Abu Maqar, in the Wadi el Natrun, Egypt. © BETTMANN/CORBIS

groups and the press. For example, all political parties must be approved by the Political Parties Committee of the Shura Council (the upper chamber of Parliament), which remains under the control of the ruling party. The government can also withhold licensing from any political or social group, monitor (and suspend) its funding and restrict its activities. If these legal tools prove inadequate, the regime can always invoke emergency powers to arrest any individual or suppress any organization that it deems threatening. The political groups that emerge in this environment are weak and fragmented. The country has 23 opposition political parties, but none has developed a significant national following. The largest, the New Wafd, managed to win only six seats in the 2005 parliamentary election (out of 454).

On occasion, political organizations have emerged around specific issues and have briefly commanded a public following. The most recent example is the Kifaya ("enough" in Arabic) movement, which arose in 2004 initially to oppose Mubarak's bid for a fifth term as president. It organized several large demonstrations and, for a short time, brought together critics of the regime

from all corners of the political spectrum. It spearheaded additional demonstrations in 2005 in favor of constitutional and political reform, but then gradually disintegrated amid regime harassment, ideological differences and disputes over leadership.

THE JUDICIARY. Egypt's judiciary has a long and proud history of challenging the executive branch and protecting citizens' rights. It has issued rulings that limit the president's powers under the emergency law, improve the fairness of elections and strengthen freedom of speech and assembly. The professional association for judges—the judges' club—has also been an important advocate for improving the rule of law and judicial independence. It was particularly active in 2005. In accordance with Egyptian law at the time, the judges' club played a central role in monitoring the presidential and parliamentary elections. Its reports were highly critical of electoral fraud and created substantial pressure to improve the electoral process. The judges' club then began calling for broader changes in the legal and political system that would lead to greater respect for democracy and the rule of law. The regime responded by withdrawing financial support from the club, creating a new administrative

body to supervise the judiciary and changing the constitution to reduce the judges' role in the electoral process (and, thus, their political leverage). Despite these steps, the judiciary remains the only institutional constraint on executive power and the most effective proponent of a more liberal political and legal order.

THE MUSLIM BROTHERHOOD. Founded in 1928 as a discussion group and charitable organization, the Muslim Brotherhood (MB) grew within a decade into the largest and best-organized social movement in Egypt. It undertook attacks against the Egyptian government in the 1930s and 1940s, including the assassinations of a judge and a prime minister and the bombings of several government buildings. It initially cooperated with the coup in 1952, but soon fell out with Nasser over his unwillingness to grant it a more prominent political role. The organization was linked to an assassination attempt on Nasser in 1954, which led the regime to ruthlessly suppress it for the remainder of the 1950s and 1960s. However, the MB underwent a revival during the 1970s. The new president, Sadat, released its leadership and many of its members in the early 1970s as part of a general amnesty designed to

Supporters of the Muslim Brotherhood hold banners that read, "We Demand Justice." They are protesting the trials of 40 leading members of the MB before a military court in Cairo, Feb. 26, 2008. The court found 25 of the defendants guilty of membership in an illegal organization and sentenced them to lengthy prison terms. AP PHOTO/NASSER NASSER

show the tolerance and openness of his regime. He also encouraged the MB to organize on university campuses in order to offset the growing influence of leftist and Nasserist groups. Its efforts included offering "training programs" in which prominent members of the movement would explain their views and mobilize students. It also provided numerous services for students, including cheap copies of expensive textbooks, financial aid for needy students and Islamic dress for women. These grassroots initiatives paid off: by 1977 the MB controlled the student associations at most of Egypt's universities. In 1978, it won control of the nationwide General Union of Egyptian Students. Its influence grew further in the 1980s and 1990s, as its supporters won elections for leadership of many professional syndicates, including the associations for lawyers, doctors and engineers. The MB used these syndicates as a base for advocating a greater role for Islam in politics, law and society. It also ran candidates for Parliament in alliance with several secular parties, winning a small number of seats in 1984 and 1987. However, the organization remained vague regarding the specific type of political order that it hoped to create. It often claimed that "Islam is the solution" and that it sought to "implement *Shari'a*," but it carefully avoided spelling out what

these slogans would mean in practice.

In the mid-1990s, a younger generation of more pragmatic MB leaders began to develop a detailed political agenda for the organization that was surprisingly moderate. They supported unrestricted political competition, broad rights for women and political and legal equality for Egypt's Coptic Christian minority. This attempt to chart a moderate path for the MB slowed in the late 1990s, as the regime imprisoned most of the leaders who initiated it.

A new era for the MB?

When these leaders were released in the early 2000s, they revived their plan to develop a comprehensive political platform that would enable the organization to participate more fully in the political process. This effort coincided with the regime's decision (under American pressure) to allow relatively free parliamentary elections in 2005. In preparation for these elections, the MB issued a "reform initiative" and a campaign platform that called for increased respect for the rule of law, constraints on state power, greater protection of civil and political rights and strengthening of democratic procedures, including freer elections and a more prominent role for Parliament in drafting legislation. This agenda, combined with a well-developed grassroots political machine, enabled the MB to win roughly

20% of the seats in Parliament and become the largest opposition bloc.

However, not all observers are convinced that the Brotherhood is a moderate organization. Egypt's Coptic community remains deeply skeptical of the MB and fears that a greater role for it in political life would lead to a reduction in the rights and freedoms of Copts. Brotherhood leaders have attempted to assuage these fears through public statements and meetings with Coptic officials, but to little avail. In addition, advocates of women's rights remain concerned that the MB will reduce opportunities for women. They observe that many of the MB's documents assert the principles that women should enjoy full economic and political rights and that these rights are compatible with Shari'a. However, these progressive statements are always followed by the claim that any change in women's roles in society should conform to public values and traditions. This is widely seen as a caveat that allows the Brotherhood to delay implementing its calls for reform indefinitely and, as a result, makes it a de facto proponent of a very traditional view of women's rights.

Some of these concerns were reinforced in 2007, when the MB issued a preliminary party platform that opposed allowing women or Copts to hold the posts of president or prime minister. The Brotherhood emphasized the narrowness of these constraints and stressed that women and Copts should have full and equal rights in every other aspect of law and society. Critics, on the other hand, argued that this stance reveals the deeply conservative social values of the Brotherhood that would come to the fore if the organization gained a greater share of power. They also pointed to another feature of the draft party platform that called for the creation of a "council of religious scholars" that would advise the Parliament on draft legislation. The MB's leaders asserted that this body would offer nonbinding advice on whether proposed legislation conformed to the ethical precepts of Islam. Critics claimed that this feature of the platform might allow an unelected group

of religious scholars to exercise veto power over proposed legislation.

Regardless of the MB's true intentions, the regime concluded that its strong showing in the 2005 election meant that it was a growing threat. Many of its leaders and activists—including its third-most-senior official—have been arrested and imprisoned. Many of the businesses and investments that supply its working capital have been closed. The regime also adopted several constitutional amendments in 2007 designed to limit the MB's political opportunities. The new amendments prevent the establishment of any religiously based political parties and make it more difficult for the MB to run its candidates for office as independents. But, more importantly, the amendments include a prohibition on "any political activity…based on any religious ideology or foundation." This ban is cast in remarkably broad language—it not only shuts down the Brotherhood as a political organization, it prevents *any* political group from utilizing Islamic principles in its electoral platform or campaign materials. It is clearly an effort to sharply narrow the scope of groups that can participate in Egyptian politics, regardless of their level of popular support.

It remains to be seen how the Brotherhood will respond to this new constraint. It could seek out alliances with secular parties—a tactic that it employed in the 1980s with limited success, due to the reluctance of secular political leaders to subordinate their parties to the MB. It could cease its involvement in politics and focus, instead, on social and cultural activities. Or, it could pursue political change through violent means.　　●

Egypt's relations with the U.S.?

Egypt's strategic location in the eastern Mediterranean at the intersection of Africa and the Middle East has made it the focus of international attention for centuries. For example, France played a central role in building the Suez Canal in the 1860s. It was then replaced by the British, who invaded the country in 1882 and made it a de facto protectorate. Britain remained the most important external player in Egyptian politics through the end of World War II. However, the extraordinary financial and military costs of the war left Britain unable to sustain its influence. Nasser's coup in 1952 further reduced Britain's role, which finally came to an end when its forces withdrew in the mid-1950s. The decline of British power created an opportunity for the newly ascendant U.S. to expand its influence, particularly as it became clear that Egypt would be a strategic battleground in the cold war between the U.S. and the Soviet Union during the second half of the 20th century. Egypt under Nasser initially tried to avoid taking sides and helped to establish the "nonaligned movement" among developing countries. However, a hasty arms deal with Czechoslovakia in 1955 moved the country into the Soviet camp. The U.S. ceased virtually all economic aid for the remainder of Nasser's rule. When Sadat came to power in 1970, he explored the possibility of improving relations with Washington. Sadat was guided by two concerns: he was convinced that the Soviet Union supported his domestic enemies and sought his overthrow; and he believed that only the U.S. had sufficient influence over Israel to bring about the return of Egyptian territory lost to the Israelis in the June 1967 War.

These considerations led Sadat to take the dramatic step of expelling all Soviet military advisers from Egypt in 1972. Surprisingly, he took this step without any prior commitments from the U.S. to provide military advisers or assistance to replace the departing Soviets—and none were forthcoming. Egypt embarked on the 1973 war against Israel relying entirely on its Soviet-equipped military. The outcome of this war was sufficiently ambiguous that the Egyptians could declare a partial victory, and Sadat could claim to have restored the country's honor on the field of battle. The war ended in a cease-fire between Israel and Egypt that left each country's military deployed throughout the Sinai Peninsula. Both countries were eager to carry out an orderly withdrawal of their troops that would avoid unintended clashes that might reignite the war. This diplomatic/military challenge created an opening for the U.S. An American delegation, led by Secretary of State Henry A. Kissinger, mediated the negotiations and facilitated what became known as the Sinai Disengagement Agreements. These negotiations also developed the relationships among political and military leaders on all three sides that eventually led to the Camp David peace process and the adoption of a peace treaty between Egypt and Israel in 1979.

As U.S. ties to Egypt improved in the mid-1970s, Washington resumed its economic assistance with a $370 million aid package in 1975. By 1978, this figure had risen to $943 million. It rose to $1.1 billion in 1979, as a result of the peace agreement with Israel, and a whopping $1.5 billion in military assistance was added. Throughout the 1980s and 1990s, U.S. military and economic aid averaged roughly $2.2 billion per year. Economic aid has been reduced in recent years in an effort to shift the U.S.-Egyptian relationship from "aid to trade," but military assistance remains at its earlier level of roughly $1.3 billion annually. By the end of 2007, the U.S. had sent over $64 billion in eco-

Egypt's Foreign Minister Ahmed Aboul Gheit, left, answers a question as his Iraqi counterpart Hoshyar Zebari looks on during a press conference in Baghdad, Iraq, Oct. 5, 2008. It was the first visit by an Egyptian foreign minister to Iraq since 1990. AP PHOTO/HADI MIZBAN

nomic and military assistance to Egypt over the previous 32 years (in dollars unadjusted for inflation). In constant 2007 dollars, the total figure is roughly $108 billion. The U.S. has announced that the current level of military assistance will be maintained for at least the next 10 years.

In regional politics, the U.S. relationship with Egypt is dominated by three issues: Iraq, Iran and the Arab-Israeli conflict.

Egypt on Iraq

While Egypt was often critical of Saddam Hussein's Iraq, it opposed the U.S. invasion in March 2003. It argued that the invasion would destabilize Iraq and provide an opportunity for the expansion of Iranian influence. It also feared that the invasion would spark widespread public anger throughout the Arab world that would threaten the stability of Egypt and other countries. It further believed that a large American military intervention would confirm and strengthen the ideological claims of radical Islamists, who preach that the U.S. is bent on dominating the Islamic world. Thus, the invasion would broaden the appeal of radical groups such as al-Qaeda that seek to overthrow

the moderate regimes of the Middle East (including Egypt). Egyptian officials continue to express these concerns, even while the security situation in Iraq has improved. Their stated position calls for an American withdrawal at the earliest opportunity, but not a precipitous departure that would leave Iraq in chaos and bring surrounding countries into the Iraqi conflict.

Cairo on Tehran

Both the U.S. and Egypt are concerned by the rise of Iran as a regional power. The U.S. is worried that Iran opposes American goals and allies in the region, and that it wants to spread its influence by supporting violent radical movements such as Hezbollah in Lebanon and Hamas in Gaza. Egypt holds similar concerns and also fears that Shi'a Iran seeks to spread a form of Islam that is at odds with the Sunni orthodoxy espoused by Egyptians. Thus, the U.S. and Egypt both want to limit Iran's influence, but they differ over whether to directly challenge Iran. Under President George W. Bush (2001–2009), the U.S. indicated that it might use military force to limit Iran's ambitions and, particularly, to block its development of nuclear weapons. Egypt has op-

posed this idea and insists on working through diplomatic means (particularly the United Nations) to contain the Iranian challenge. In its view, additional American military action in the region would further weaken the stature of the U.S. and strengthen radical Islamists in Iran and the Arab world.

Arab-Israeli conflict

Ever since the 1979 Egypt-Israel peace treaty, the U.S. has viewed Egypt as an essential ally in efforts to resolve the Arab-Israeli conflict. However, relations between Israel and Egypt have remained cool. The Egyptians saw the Camp David process as a first step toward the establishment of a Palestinian state and a just solution to the plight of Palestinian refugees. Unfortunately, the political status of Palestine remains unresolved. As long as this problem continues to fester, most Egyptians are unwilling to fully embrace Israel and will resist building the economic and cultural ties needed for warmer relations.

Nonetheless, Egypt has played an important role in mediating between Israel and the Palestinian leadership. Throughout the Oslo peace process in the 1990s, Egypt was a regular participant in negotiations and offered to provide practical assistance that would facilitate peace (such as training Palestinian security forces). It has continued this role, although deep internal divisions among Israelis and Palestinians have hampered negotiations. Among the Palestinians, a sharp and violent split has emerged between Hamas (a Palestinian Islamist movement that opposes negotiations with Israel) and Fatah (a more secular movement that has accepted the principle of negotiations). This rivalry peaked in the summer of 2007, when Hamas forces expelled Fatah from Gaza with substantial loss of life. Egypt has attempted to mediate among the Hamas leadership in Gaza, its leadership in Damascus, Syria and the Fatah leadership based in the West Bank. It has tried to facilitate the emergence of a broad-based Palestinian political movement that can participate effectively in negotiations with Israel, and has called on Hamas to accept previous Palestinian peace commitments, recognize Israel's right to exist and renounce the use of violence. These efforts are essential for moving the U.S.-sponsored "Road Map for Peace" forward.

However, the U.S. and Israel allege that Egypt has allowed the smuggling of weapons across its border with Gaza, which, in turn, has strengthened Hamas. Egypt rejects this charge and has substantially increased its presence along the border in order to improve security and reduce smuggling. Nevertheless, Egypt's situation on the Gazan border is complex. In response to Hamas's consolidation of power in Gaza in 2007, Israel imposed a partial blockade on shipments of many items (including fuel and medical supplies) into the territory. As the situation became more desperate, Gazans looked increasingly to the Egyptian border as the only place to acquire essential goods. In January 2008, these pressures led Hamas militants to dynamite the barrier between Gaza and Egypt, thereby enabling thousands of Gazans to rush into Egypt. While the border was eventually resealed and most of the

Egyptian students hold a demonstration outside Cairo University, Jan. 23, 2008. They are protesting Israeli policies in the Gaza Strip and the West Bank. AP PHOTO/AMR SHARAF

Gazans returned home, the event underscored the delicate balance that Egypt must maintain: it needs to patrol the border in accordance with international law and its agreements with Israel; but it cannot ignore the deprivations of the

1.4 million Palestinians living in Gaza, whom it regards as fellow Arabs suffering under a harsh blockade that inflicts needless pain and suffering.

The executive branch in the U.S. seems aware of this delicate balance, but Congress is less sympathetic. In 2007, Congress passed a bill that partly tied $100 million in U.S. military aid to an improvement in security on the Egypt-Gaza border (it also called for increased respect for human rights and judicial independence in Egypt). President Bush blocked this effort, but prominent members of Congress continue to demand greater U.S. pressure on Egypt to tighten security at its border. For its part, Egypt calls on the U.S. to adopt a more evenhanded approach to the conflict that recognizes the shortcomings of Israeli policy. It claims that the U.S. has been indifferent to Palestinian suffering caused by the Israeli blockade of Gaza and by Israeli policies in the West Bank. It also notes that Israel continues to build new settlements in the West Bank in violation of the commitments that it made to President Bush in the "Road Map for Peace" and at the Annapolis peace conference in November 2007, convened by President Bush and

Secretary of State Condoleezza Rice (2005–2009). Egypt argues that these Israeli policies are impediments to peace, but that the U.S. has taken no steps to alter Israel's behavior.

Domestic affairs

In addition to these regional issues, Egypt's internal affairs are an important component of its relationship with the U.S. The U.S. has a long record of supporting the government's economic reform plan, which has been backed by a generous American aid program. However, the question of political reform is a continuing point of tension. Since the 9/11 attacks, leaders of both political parties in the U.S. have argued that terrorism by radical Islamists is partially a result of the repression and stagnation in Arab dictatorships. These suffocating conditions produce a large pool of frustrated, hopeless and angry young

Gamal Mubarak, the son of Egyptian President Hosni Mubarak, is assistant secretary general of the ruling National Democratic party (NDP) and chairman of the party's policies committee. He spoke at a press conference at the fifth annual convention of the NDP in Cairo, Nov. 2, 2008. Arabic reads, "New Thinking for the Future." AP PHOTO/ NASSER NASSER

men and women who yearn for greater dignity and purpose in their lives. They become easy recruits for terrorist ideologues promising honor and martyrdom in a struggle against injustice. For proponents of this view, the key to defeating terrorism lies in ending repression and poor governance in the Arab world. In a speech in Cairo in June 2005, Secretary Rice asserted that "for 60 years the U.S. pursued stability at the expense of democracy... in the Middle East—and we achieved neither. Now, we are taking a different course. We are supporting the democratic aspirations of all people." In his State of the Union address in February 2005, President Bush declared, "The great and proud nation of Egypt, which showed the way toward peace in the Middle East, can now show the way toward democracy in the Middle East." U.S. officials at all levels have called on Egypt to improve its human rights record, increase the independence of the judiciary, allow the emergence of vibrant opposition parties and permit free and fair elections. These efforts have produced some gestures by the Egyptian government, but little substantive change. For example, President Mubarak agreed to amend the Egyptian constitution in 2005 to allow for competitive presidential elections (previously, the president was nominated by Parliament and then confirmed by the people in a referendum). However, the details of the amendment and the supporting laws made it virtually impossible for an opposition candidate to mount a viable challenge.

Mubarak also allowed a relatively free parliamentary election campaign in the fall of 2005, but then reverted to the old tricks of rigging and fraud when it appeared that an opposition

group (the Muslim Brotherhood) was doing well. Following the election, Mubarak embarked on a widespread campaign to weaken the MB by arresting its leaders and confiscating its financial assets. He also initiated a crackdown on opposition journalists, which led to large fines and imprisonment for some critics of the regime. However, as Mubarak undertook these measures that were clearly at odds with America's goal of building democracy, the U.S. remained largely silent. Rice visited Egypt again in 2007 and adopted a tone sharply different from her 2005 visit. She made little mention of political reform in either her public appearances or her press releases. The reason for this shift was simple: the U.S. needed Egypt's help on pressing regional matters, particularly growing instability in Gaza, the deteriorating situation in Iraq and the expansion of Iranian influence. U.S. officials feared that a continued emphasis on political reform would anger the Egyptians and lead to less cooperation on these vital issues. The Egyptian government reinforced this fear by denouncing U.S. statements that criticized Egyptian politics, claiming that they constituted unacceptable interference in Egypt's internal affairs.

As the U.S. contemplates its future policy toward Egypt, it will need to decide on the importance of democracy promotion. Is democratization essential to Egyptian stability and regional security and, if so, should it be at the center of the U.S.-Egyptian relationship? Or, is it a relatively peripheral concern that can be set aside when pressing regional issues are on the agenda?

What of Egypt's future?

Egypt's ambitious plans for economic reform are likely to continue apace. The government appears convinced that market-oriented economic restructuring is the only way to produce sufficient growth in jobs and income to maintain the country's social stability. This trajectory of economic change raises several questions.

Can Egypt successfully manage

the challenges produced by market reform? The government has established several programs to compensate and retrain workers displaced by the reform process. These programs must be administered with much greater skill and effectiveness. In addition, Egypt also needs political structures (fair elections, effective political parties, a strong Parliament and an accountable presidency) that can peacefully manage the social tensions produced by market reform. Currently, these political structures are not in place.

Will economic reform lead to political reform? Some political scientists argue that market-oriented economic restructuring can aid democratization by decentralizing economic power and creating a larger private sphere that supports independent civil society groups, political parties and media outlets. Alternatively, others argue that market-oriented reform creates higher levels of social tension, as public-sector workers lose their jobs and inequality rises. In this environment, autocratic regimes often restrict public freedoms in order to limit strikes and political demonstrations that might slow the pace of economic change. These steps make a democratic transition less likely.

There are examples that support each of these arguments. Taiwan and South Korea followed the first path, in which market-based economic reforms provided the foundation for later democratization. China, in contrast, has followed the second path of rapid economic reform with little or no expansion in political freedoms. The constitutional amendments of 2007 provide some indication of where the Egyptian government is headed. These amendments swept away features of the constitution that impeded market reform and, thereby, cleared the path for building a market economy. However, they made no effort to broaden political rights. Indeed, the amendments expanded the government's power to infringe on the rights of citizens, particularly if their activities could be construed as aiding terrorism. President Mubarak appears

BUILDING DEMOCRACY IN EGYPT

intent on separating economic and political reform, moving quickly on the former while avoiding the latter. In this regard, Egypt seems inclined to follow the example of China. During the recent Olympics in Beijing, several Op-Eds in government-related newspapers applauded China's success at achieving great prosperity while preserving social stability. The Op-Eds expressed particular admiration for China's decision to concentrate on the well-being of the community rather than individual rights. In their view, this development model avoids the selfishness and greed that characterize the American style of capitalism and democracy.

After Mubarak?

However, Mubarak, who turned 80 in May 2008, reportedly suffers from some health issues. When he passes from the political scene, his successor will have the opportunity to reexamine the relationship between economic and political reform. At this point, Mubarak's likely successor is unclear. Some believe that his son, Gamal, is the probable heir, in light of his growing importance within the ruling party and the support that he enjoys within the business community. Others think that he lacks the "common touch" needed to gain the public's affection, and that he does not have strong backing from

the military and security apparatus. Another possibility is Omar Suleiman, the head of Egyptian intelligence, who has the security credentials needed to satisfy the military but has little experience with the ruling party or with economic matters. Still others believe that the successor may be a political unknown who is, nonetheless, supported by the powerful leaders at the ministries of interior and defense. If Mubarak has chosen a successor, he is keeping quiet about it and has allowed speculation to continue unabated.

As Egypt enters a political transition upon Mubarak's passing, the U.S. will need to make decisions on several key issues that will shape the future of this relationship. What steps can the U.S. take to further aid the development of a market economy and mitigate the social tensions that such reforms produce? What priority should be assigned to democracy promotion and improvement in human rights? Should the U.S. condition its economic and military aid on the adoption of specific political reforms? And, how can the U.S. gain broader cooperation from Egypt on key regional issues such as the Arab-Israeli conflict, the reconstruction of Iraq and the containment of Iran?

OPINION BALLOTS AFTER PAGE 64

QUESTIONS

1. Is a close U.S. relationship with Egypt important? If yes, how important is it relative to the U.S. relationship with other nations in the region (such as Israel, Saudi Arabia, Iraq, Iran and Turkey)?

2. The U.S. sent $108 billion in military and economic aid (in 2007 dollars) to Egypt from 1975 through 2007. Do you think this was a good use of American money? Should the U.S. continue to send military and economic assistance to Egypt?

3. Should the U.S. condition its economic and military aid on the adoption of specific political reforms in Egypt? Is this a good idea in principle? Is it likely to succeed in practice?

4. What steps can the U.S. take to facilitate the development of a market economy in Egypt? What policies could mitigate the social tensions that economic restructuring produces?

5. Does market-oriented economic reform provide the foundations for democratization? Or does it reinforce authoritarianism?

6. What priority should the U.S. assign to democracy promotion and human rights? Should they be at the center of its foreign policy toward Egypt and the Middle East? Or, should they take a backseat to more traditional U.S. interests, such as access to oil, protection of Israel and security of the Suez Canal?

7. What are the sources of radical Islamic terrorism? Will democratization address them and reduce the threat posed by terrorism?

8. Should the U.S. try to strengthen the secular opposition in Egypt? Or the judiciary? If yes, how can this be accomplished?

9. Should the U.S. engage in a dialogue with the Muslim Brotherhood, even though the organization is banned in Egypt? If yes, what should be discussed? Do you think the Muslim Brotherhood is a moderate organization that the U.S. should support? Or is it a threat to American interests and values?

10. How can the U.S. gain broader cooperation from Egypt on key regional issues such as the Arab-Israeli conflict, the reconstruction of Iraq and the containment of Iran?

11. What are America's interests in Egypt and the Middle East? How would you prioritize them?

NOTES: ....
....
....
....
....
....
....
....
....
....
....

READINGS

Baker, Raymond William, **Islam without Fear: Egypt and the New Islamists.** Cambridge, MA, Harvard University Press, 2006. 320 pp. $19.00 (paper). Examines the ideas and strategies of Egypt's moderate Islamists.

Goldschmidt Jr., Arthur, **Modern Egypt: The Formation of a Nation-State,** 2nd ed. Boulder, CO, Westview Press, 2004. 256 pp. $34.00 (paper). A thoughtful and succinct study of Egypt's history from the mid-18th century to the present.

Ikram, Khalid, **The Egyptian Economy, 1952–2000: Performance, Policies, and Issues.** New York, Routledge, 2005. 320 pp. $180.00 (hardcover). Extensive analysis of the Egyptian economy and the challenges of economic reform by a former World Bank economist.

Kassem, Maye, **Egyptian Politics: The Dynamics of Authoritarian Rule.** Boulder, CO, LynneRienner Publishers, 2004. 213 pp. $19.95 (paper). Analyzes the foundations of Egyptian authoritarianism and the reasons for its longevity.

Kepel, Gilles, **Muslim Extremism in Egypt: The Prophet and the Pharaoh,** 2nd ed. University of California Press, 2003. 290 pp. $21.95 (paper). A study of the origins and development of radical Islam in Egypt by a prominent French scholar and leading expert on Islamic movements.

Mitchell, Richard P., **The Society of the Muslim Brothers.** New York, Oxford University Press, 1993. 392 pp. $35.00 (paper). Originally published in 1969, this is the classic work on the origins and early development of the Muslim Brotherhood.

Rosefsky Wickham, Carrie, **Mobilizing Islam: Religion, Activism, and Political Change in Egypt.** New York, Columbia University Press, 2002. 300 pp. $29.50 (paper). Examination of the rise of political Islam in the 1990s, utilizing extensive interviews with Islamic thinkers and activists, by an associate professor of political science at Emory University.

Rutherford, Bruce K., **Egypt after Mubarak: Liberalism, Islam, and Democracy in the Arab World.** Princeton, NJ, Princeton University Press, 2008. 304 pp. $35.00 (hardcover). Assesses the current prospects for political and economic reform.

al-Sayyid Marsot, Afaf Lutfi, **A History of Egypt: From the Arab Conquest to the Present,** 2nd ed. New York, Cambridge University Press, 2007. 196 pp. $24.99 (paper). A concise and insightful overview of Egyptian history since the 7th century, by the first Egyptian woman to obtain a Ph.D from Oxford.

TO LEARN MORE ABOUT THIS TOPIC AND TO ACCESS WEB LINKS TO RESOURCES GO TO www.greatdecisions.org/topic5

1 RISING POWERS

ISSUE A. Which of the following rising or dominant powers do you feel is most effecting change in the global system? (Rank from 1 to 10)
___ Brazil
___ China
___ EU
___ India
___ Japan
___ Russia
___ South Africa
___ South Korea
___ Turkey
___ Other _____

ISSUE B. Which of the following issues do you think will pose the greatest challenge to the global system? (Rank from 1 to 6)
___ Climate change
___ Competing or clashing ideologies
___ Limited energy resources
___ Nuclear proliferation
___ Terrorism by nonstate actors
___ Other _____

Your zip code: ....
Date: /   /2009   *Ballot continues on reverse side.*

2 AFGHANISTAN/PAKISTAN

ISSUE A. In order to secure Afghanistan, the U.S. should (rank from 1 to 4, with one being most important)
___ Increase current U.S. troop levels operating in Afghanistan, regardless of other NATO contributions.
___ Negotiate with regional players such as India, Russia and China for diplomatic and economic or even military assistance in Afghanistan and Pakistan.
___ Continue training and stabilization operations, but let Afghanistan directly target insurgents.
___ Other _____

ISSUE B. To control or limit Afghan poppy production, the U.S. should (rank from one to four, with one being most important)
___ Pursue a stringent policy featuring crop eradication.
___ Target those at the top of the value chain, whether or not they are members of the Afghan government.
___ Promote and aid in the economic development and trade of other products.
___ Reform the judicial and legal branches of the Afghan government, especially at the local level.

Your zip code: ....
Date: /   /2009   *Ballot continues on reverse side.*

3 ENERGY

ISSUE A. The most effective steps for the U.S. to take with regard to energy in the *short-term* are to (rank in priority from 1 to 5, with one being the most effective):
___ Begin switching from coal-generated electricity to natural gas, which is cleaner burning.
___ Expand drilling in the Arctic National Wildlife Refuge (ANWR) and all possible domestic areas, including the Rockies and reserves off the coast of Alaska in the Arctic.
___ Impose higher gasoline taxes regardless of market price to encourage less car use.
___ Immediately raise fuel-efficiency standards for automobiles.
___ Expand refinement capacity (which is currently in short supply).

ISSUE B. Regardless of the cost of oil, the U.S. should continue to expand its strategic petroleum reserve, which at the current rate of consumption would supply the U.S. with about 33 days worth of oil.
❑ Agree
❑ Disagree

Your zip code: ....
Date: /   /2009   *Ballot continues on reverse side.*

4 ARCTIC

ISSUE A. Do you agree or disagree with the following statements?:

	AGREE	DISAGREE
1. The U.S. should immediately ratify the 1982 United Nations Convention on the Law of the Sea (UNCLOS).	❑	❑
2. The U.S. must develop a plan for its Navy based upon the premise that the Arctic region will be open for exploration, transport and trade in the next 10 years.	❑	❑
3. The U.S. should acquire enough icebreakers to handle operations in both Antarctica and the Arctic.	❑	❑
4. The U.S. must do whatever is necessary to actively compete for resources in the Arctic.	❑	❑
5. The U.S. must ensure all parties in the region take adequate environmental measures.	❑	❑

Comment: _____
_____

Your zip code: ....
Date: /   /2009   *Ballot continues on reverse side.*

Please submit only one ballot per person, per topic. Ballots must be received by June 30, 2009.
Mail ballots to: **FOREIGN POLICY ASSOCIATION, 470 Park Avenue South, New York, NY 10016-6819**

ISSUE C. Aid to Afghanistan should be:
- ❏ Channeled through the central government in Kabul, conditioned on specific benchmarks.
- ❏ Divided between Kabul and tribal groups, on condition that they fight against relevant insurgency groups.
- ❏ Handled by the UN and other specific NGOs.

ISSUE D. Given the political and cultural history of Afghanistan, incorporating in the government tribal leaders and Taliban who have given up terrorism is an important step toward the stabilization of the country.
- ❏ Agree
- ❏ Disagree

ISSUE E. Specific U.S. military policy for Afghanistan should:
- ❏ Increase troop levels in Afghanistan by expanding the U.S. defense budget.
- ❏ Reduce troop levels in Iraq to send more troops to Afghanistan.
- ❏ Maintain current levels of troops in Afghanistan.
- ❏ Begin withdrawing troops from Afghanistan.

Comment: _____

2

ISSUE C. As a matter of policy, do you believe the U.S. should:

	YES	NO
1. Lead the creation of a new global agreement on climate change to replace the Kyoto Protocol?	❏	❏
2. Protect its own interests in energy and natural resources first and foremost?	❏	❏
3. Pursue terrorists or other nonstate actors that threaten national security?	❏	❏
4. Work through the United Nations to solve global challenges?	❏	❏
5. Take any action necessary to keep nations that currently don't have them from developing nuclear weapons?	❏	❏
6. Change its "soft power" strategy and how it interacts with the citizens of rising powers?	❏	❏

Comment: _____

1

ISSUE B. The region above the Arctic Circle should be (select one):
- ❏ Opened up to territorial claims by sovereign states, as ultimately decided by UNCLOS.
- ❏ Governed under treaty as an international region, like the Antarctic.
- ❏ A combination of the two approaches.

ISSUE C. With respect to the Northwest Passage, the U.S. should:
- ❏ Consider it an international waterway and work with Canada and the EU to jointly manage and patrol it.
- ❏ Continue to "agree to disagree" over the sovereignty of the NW Passage.
- ❏ Relinquish this claim to Canada.

ISSUE D. As of November 2008, the EU, which has no direct coastline on the Arctic Ocean, was describing the polar region as part of Europe's "immediate vicinity" and proposing "binding international standards" to govern offshore oil exploitation. Should the EU nations be involved in setting the guidelines for the non-EU states (Canada, the U.S., Norway and Russia) preparing to exploit the regions's rich petroleum reserves?
- ❏ Yes
- ❏ No

4

ISSUE C. As a multilateral approach, improving energy efficiency and reducing dependence on fossil fuels should be an explicit (with specific mandates for countries) requirement of any international climate-change agreement, such as the upcoming post-Kyoto treaty to be adopted in Copenhagen in 2009.
- ❏ Agree
- ❏ Disagree

ISSUE D. In order to achieve energy independence (or diversification), the U.S. should (rank in order of priority, with one being most important):
- __ Spend money on research in viable alternative sources.
- __ Develop domestic initiatives to cut energy consumption, such as raising efficiency standards on appliances and machinery.
- __ Invest in infrastructure that work towards the goal of reducing energy consumption, such as mass transit projects.
- __ Plan for and begin energy exploration and extraction in U.S.-claimed regions in the Arctic.

Comment: _____

3

5 EGYPT

ISSUE A. Rank the following issues for the U.S. vis-à-vis Egypt, with 1 being most important and 4 being least important:

___ Increasing Egypt's role in the Middle East peace process.

___ Reforming the Egyptian economy.

___ Pushing for domestic political reforms, such as greater freedom of the press and judicial independence, among others.

___ Gaining greater cooperation from Egypt on its policies toward Iraq and Iran.

ISSUE B. Should the Muslim Brotherhood play a role in Egyptian politics?

❏ Yes
❏ No

Comment: _____
_____
_____
_____
_____
_____

Your zip code: _____
Date: /   /2009   *Ballot continues on reverse side.*

6 FOOD

ISSUE A. How significant for the long term was the latest food price crisis?

❏ Very important. It could signify a structural shift in supply-demand patterns.

❏ Somewhat important. With all the other foreign policy issues the U.S. confronts, food prices should be an important, but secondary issue.

❏ Not very important. The recent food crisis was part of the traditional cyclical pattern of prices.

❏ Other _____
_____
_____

ISSUE B. A new Green Revolution is needed to alleviate the global food crisis. Do you think that genetic modification of crops is the answer?

❏ Yes. There is no reason not to go ahead with this technology.

❏ Yes, with reservations. More testing needs to be done to determine the possible repercussions.

❏ No. There is no way of knowing that genetic modification of crops will not set off a chain reaction, creating an environmental disaster.

Your zip code: _____
Date: /   /2009   *Ballot continues on reverse side.*

7 CUBA

ISSUE A. In light of the historic leadership change that took place in Cuba in 2008, and the fact that the Cuban economy is starting to play a significant role in the global economy, do you think it would be in the best interests of the U.S. to: (select one)

___ Drop the current U.S. embargo against trade with Cuba?

___ Develop trade relations with Cuba that go beyond the current "cash only" agricultural sales, but stop short of lifting the embargo?

___ Maintain the trade embargo with Cuba until there is a real change in its government's philosophy.

ISSUE B. With Raúl Castro at the helm as president, pursuing a path of limited economic opening, Cuba is on the verge of a huge political transition. Do you think Raul's leadership will:

❏ Breathe new life into the Cuban Revolution?

❏ Sow the seeds for Cuba to evolve into a different kind of society altogether?

Comment: _____
_____

Your zip code: _____
Date: /   /2009   *Ballot continues on reverse side.*

8 HUMAN RIGHTS

ISSUE A. The most essential criteria for putting U.S. troops in harm's way and committing U.S. tax dollars to a foreign conflict are: (Rank in order of significance, with 1 being the most significant and 7 the least.)

___ Immediate threat of attack or invasion.

___ Anticipated future threat, e.g., Iranian nuclear weaponry.

___ Ally threatened by common foe, e.g., cold-war scenario.

___ Fulfillment of treaty obligations, e.g., UN mandate.

___ Securing vital natural resources, e.g., oil or water.

___ Regime change, e.g. overthrowing Iraq's Hussein.

___ Stopping "crimes against humanity," e.g., Rwanda.

ISSUE B. The "Responsibility to Protect" concept should be actively endorsed and implemented.

___ Yes
___ No

Comment: _____
_____

Your zip code: _____
Date: /   /2009   *Ballot continues on reverse side.*

ISSUE C. What should the U.S. focus on to reform its global food policies? (Rank in order of priority)

___ Conclude the Doha Round by lowering the subsidies that the EU and the U.S. provide.

___ Change the way U.S. food aid is purchased vis-à-vis the CSIS report.

___ Develop an international standard for GM crops.

___ Reverse its ethanol mandates for corn.

___ Expand its current food aid programs while keeping basic policies the same.

___ Expand aid in the form of agricultural infrastructure investment.

___ Nothing, reserve U.S. political capital for more important issues.

ISSUE D. Ensuring adequate global food supply is an important component of U.S. global security.

❑ Agree
❑ Disagree
❑ Other _____
_____

Comment: _____
_____
_____
_____
_____

6

ISSUE C. What would be the most effective way for the Muslim Brotherhood to facilitate political change? (choose one)

❑ Expand its social service and education programs.
❑ Increase its efforts to take part in elections and Parliament, despite the arrests of its members.
❑ Adopt a more-pragmatic approach to ideology and politics that places less emphasis on Islam.
❑ Form alliances with secular parties.
❑ Other _____
_____
_____
_____
_____

ISSUE D. How important to U.S. Middle East policy is Egypt's support? (choose one)

❑ Crucial
❑ Important, but not crucial
❑ The U.S. could do without it

Comment: _____
_____
_____
_____
_____

5

ISSUE C. Would you have recommended armed intervention to stop abuses in the following conflicts?

	YES	NO	MAYBE
Bosnia (Serbian-Muslim ethnic cleansing)	❑	❑	❑
Burma/Myanmar (rejection of typhoon relief)	❑	❑	❑
Cambodia (massive Khmer Rouge genocide)	❑	❑	❑
Darfur (Sudanese ethnic cleansing)	❑	❑	❑
Germany (prewar Nazi killings and oppression)	❑	❑	❑
Iraq (at any time under Saddam Hussein)	❑	❑	❑
Kosovo (threatened Serbian-Armenian atrocities)	❑	❑	❑
Rwanda (Tutsi extermination)	❑	❑	❑
Somalia (political chaos and famine)	❑	❑	❑
Uganda (Idi Amin's murderous regime)	❑	❑	❑
United States (Japanese internment in World War II)	❑	❑	❑
Zimbabwe (stolen elections, mass political murder)	❑	❑	❑

8

A. *How many years have you participated in the* GREAT DECISIONS *program (that is, attended one or more discussion sessions)?*
❑ This is the first year I have participated.
❑ I participated in one previous year.
❑ I participated in more than one previous year.

B. *What is your age?*
❑ 17 or under ❑ 18 to 30 ❑ 31 to 45
❑ 46 to 60 ❑ 61 or over

C. *Your sex?* ❑ Female ❑ Male

D. *Have you been abroad during the last two years?*
❑ Yes ❑ No

E. *Do you know, or are you learning, a foreign language?*
❑ Yes ❑ No

F. *What is the highest level of formal education you have completed?*
❑ Some high school ❑ High school degree
❑ Some college ❑ College graduate
❑ Advanced degree

G. *How often are you asked for your opinion on foreign policy?*
❑ Often ❑ Sometimes ❑ Hardly ever

H. *How many **hours**, on average, do you spend reading one* GREAT DECISIONS *chapter?*
❑ Less than 1 hr. ❑ 1–2 hrs.
❑ 3–4 hrs. ❑ More than 4 hrs.

I. *Do you have access to the internet (check all that apply)?*
❑ Yes, at home. ❑ Yes, at work. ❑ Yes, at school.
❑ Yes, at the library or internet café. ❑ No.

J. *Would you say you have or have not changed your opinion in a fairly significant way as a result of taking part in the* GREAT DECISIONS *program?*
❑ Have ❑ Have not ❑ Uncertain

7

Global food crisis
by Elaine Monaghan

Higher food prices triggered riots around the globe. What caused the price spike, and what can be done to ensure the world's food security?

Women wait to buy rice at a mobile government shop selling at subsidized rates in Dhaka, Bangladesh, April 4, 2008. The government has increased its food relief through free food distribution, food-for-work programs and subsidized food sales to tackle the situation. AP PHOTO/PAVEL RAHMAN

Until recently, the topic of food in the U.S. conjured up contrasting images of a burger-and-fries-fueled obesity epidemic, relatively expensive fresh fruits and vegetables and the rise of organic produce. The narrative ran that while millions of Americans overeat, risking diseases that are rare in less-developed parts of the world, whole populations elsewhere face hunger, malnourishment and even starvation. It was a view that any modern Westerner can remember being pointedly reinforced by a parent or grandparent as he or she picked over ice-cold peas.

But beginning in 2006, that picture grew far murkier. Riots erupted across the globe in early 2008 as food prices headed skyward, fueled by a complex myriad of influences. Corn, wheat and soybean stocks hit historic lows, with wheat reserves at their lowest level in three decades. Major producers suffered a number of climactic shocks, notably drought in Australia, Eastern Europe and Ukraine (once known as the bread-basket of the Soviet Union), and flooding in the U.S. Midwest. Rising energy costs delivered an additional blow, raising transportation costs and the price of fertilizer, which requires natural gas to produce. Corn was increasingly used not to feed hungry mouths, but to fuel vehicles, the consequence of what many argue was a short-sighted effort to tackle climate change, though commentators disagree over the extent of its impact. The understandable knee-jerk reactions of affected countries were to reduce or stop food exports, which simultaneously stimulated hoarding and pushed prices even higher. Some argued that market speculators betting on higher future food costs also inflated prices, though many economists dispute that this had any major influence.

In the second half of 2008, prices began to fall, and with the onset of a global recession toward the end of the year, looked set to stay lower. However, they still remained considerably higher than before the crisis began, prompting suspicions that a structural shift in the global food supply had taken place, resulting in forecasts that

ELAINE MONAGHAN *is a Washington, D.C.-based freelance journalist and author specializing in foreign policy. She has worked for* The Times *(London) and Reuters, in Ireland, Great Britain and Russia.*

prices would simply rise again once economies began to recover.

Critics of the meat industry were happy to give their view a fresh airing—people should eat more plants, especially given that the production of beef and dairy require resources that far outstrip their value as a fuel for humans. It is a point that environmentalists have been making for years. In her 2000 title, *Stolen Harvest,* Indian physicist turned environmental-activist Vandana Shiva argued that the commercialization of the food supply system and pressure from the World Trade Organization (WTO) had robbed the globe of a sustainable food supply, noting at the same time that 70% of U.S. grain production goes to feeding cows. Prominent author and food writer Mark Bittman, a critic of overconsumption of processed foods and meat, noted in a late 2007 presentation that while world population had only doubled between 1950 and 2000, meat consumption had increased fivefold. Of significance was the rise in demand for meat among the growing middle classes of China and India, one key factor in last year's price increases. Bittman puts the percentage of ozone-depleting gases attributable to livestock at 18%, with farm animals occupying an estimated 70% of the world's agricultural land.

While mainstream economists and advocates of feeding the hungry might not devote the same energy to tackling agribusiness, they do all agree on one

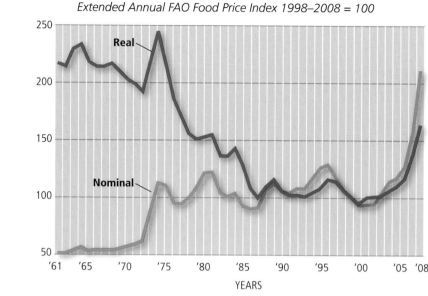

Nominal and Real Food Prices: 1961 – 2008
Extended Annual FAO Food Price Index 1998–2008 = 100

SOURCE: United Nations FAO and Orden

LUCIDITY INFORMATION DESIGN

This graph shows the decline and growth in food prices over recent decades. The blue line, which is adjusted for inflation, demonstrates that prices in real terms, despite the recent shocks, remain significantly lower than they were before the Green Revolution, putting the crisis of 2008 in a wider historical context.

point—the impact price spikes had on the world's poor; and the subsequent need for a comprehensive approach to the problem of a stable global supply of food in the face of increasing demand.

'Silent tsunami'

The price increases in the early months of 2008 took such a path that the executive director of the United Nations World Food Program (WFP), Josette Sheeran, spoke of a "silent tsunami

that respects no borders," invoking the maxim that there are "only seven meals between civilization and anarchy." As noted by the charity Oxfam (which has played a leading role in pushing international institutions and governments to adopt policies that will address the underlying infrastructural problem of a lack of investment in farming in poor countries), by June of 2008, global food prices had risen 83% in just three years. A look at statistics from the U.S. Department of Agriculture for one key commodity in many developing countries—rice—tells the story. In Vietnam, rice export prices rose from an average of $184 per metric ton for the 2002–2003 crop to about $300 in the spring of 2007, before exploding to $390 in January last year and rocketing to a peak of $1,088 in May 2008. By September 2008, the price had leveled off to $566, but even that was more than twice what it had been two years earlier.

In the U.S., the cry of "You better eat what's on your plate" took on a new meaning for many American households as the cost of food, as measured by the Bureau of Labor Statistics, was

Demonstrators form a barricade during a protest in the town of Les Cayes, Haiti, April 7, 2008. A man was killed by gunfire as demonstrators took to the streets, raising the death toll to five in protests against rising food prices. EDUARDO MUNOZ/REUTERS /LANDOV

6.2% higher in September 2008 compared to a year earlier, partly because weakness in the U.S. dollar encouraged exports. Beef was up 6.1% and dairy had risen 4.9% over September 2007. Vegetables were up 10.3% and fruit, 9.2%. For most Americans, that necessitated a rejiggering of the family budget. For some, it translated into a spike in food stamp enrollment. But for inhabitants of the developing world living on 50 cents a day, according to Sheeran, the inflation in food prices represented a "catastrophe": what choices can a family make when most of their income goes to feeding the family?

Riots spread, according to the International Food Policy Research Institute (IFPRI) in Washington, one of 15 centers promoting modern science for poor farmers, supported by an alliance of 64 governments, private foundations and international and regional organizations called the Consultative Group on International Agricultural Research (CGIAR). They became violent in a to-

tal of 21 countries and food insecurity burst into the American consciousness simultaneously as a domestic poverty issue and as a national security problem. In March 2008, the WFP found that half the population of Pakistan—most likely a partial refuge for Osama bin Laden as well as a breeding ground for anti-American militancy—was "food insecure"—that is, at risk for hunger. While this does not necessarily raise the specter of a French Revolution, as Sheeran reminded her audience, a hungry man is an angry man, and in Haiti, that truism indeed made itself felt last year. On April 12, 2008, the government, barely emerging from decades of economic collapse, fell under the weight of spiraling prices for basic staples like rice and beans after 10 days of riots that pitted stone-throwing protesters against UN peacekeepers and national police. In oil-rich Russia, in scenes that would have been reminiscent of food-deprived Soviet times had protests been allowed, thousands took

CAGLECARTOONS.COM/FREDERICK DELIGNE

to the streets in anger at spiraling grocery costs. In Egypt, where food prices had risen by 16.8% in 2007, dozens were hospitalized following clashes surrounding a textile mill on the Nile Delta, amid fury at low wages and high prices. Even Naples, Italy, birthplace of the pizza Margherita, felt the shock of price increases. In late August 2008, pizza chefs gave away 5,000 traditional thin-crust Neapolitan pizzas to protest restaurants unfairly overcharging. In a microcosm of the larger problem, there was pressure in Italy for price controls as pasta and bread became dramatically more expensive.

A structural shift?

In the midst of the crisis, many governments responded to desperate WFP calls for increased aid as the value of their existing pledges and donations plummeted by more than half. As of Oct. 26, 2008, the U.S. was way ahead in terms of donations for 2008, at $1.9 billion (Saudi Arabia, in second place, was at $500 million). Critics countered that this short-term generosity stood in stark contrast to other U.S. food aid policies. Major complaints concerned the inefficient way the U.S. handles its deliveries of food aid, its apparent inability or unwillingness to reduce the amount of corn-based ethanol used to power vehicles and its refusal to tackle the thorny question of subsidies to U.S. farmers.

The global food crisis proved that a radical solution was required. Many experts and organizations, including the WFP, called for a new Green Revolution—a reference to a mid-20th century movement that boosted crop yields by

Ratios of Per Capita Consumption: 2005 / 1990

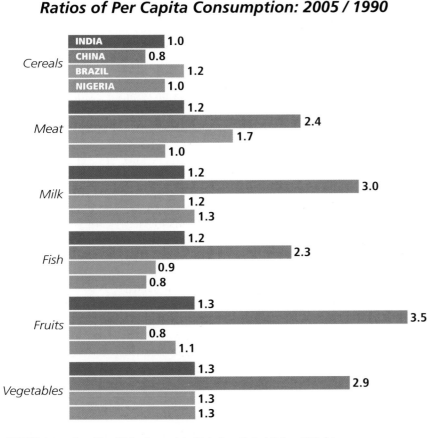

Cereals	INDIA	1.0
	CHINA	0.8
	BRAZIL	1.2
	NIGERIA	1.0
Meat		1.2
		2.4
		1.7
		1.0
Milk		1.2
		3.0
		1.2
		1.3
Fish		1.2
		2.3
		0.9
		0.8
Fruits		1.3
		3.5
		0.8
		1.1
Vegetables		1.3
		2.9
		1.3
		1.3

SOURCE: International Food Policy Research Institute from United Nations FAO data

LUCIDITY INFORMATION DESIGN

Cows are fed grain at Hunter Haven Farm in Pearl City, Illinois, July 24, 2008. With 70% of U.S. grain production going to feeding cows, critics of the meat industry advise people to eat more plants, since the production of beef and dairy require resources that far outstrip their value as a fuel for humans. TERRY HARRIS/MCT /LANDOV

taking advantage of innovations in seed sharing, irrigation and pesticides. This approach—deemed at the time to have silenced doomsday scenarios of population growth inevitably outstripping food supply—helped crop output to grow by 117% while the world's population grew by only 90% (1962–96). Without another generation of innovators, such as Norman Ernest Borlaug, U.S. Nobel laureate in 1970 and father of the Green Revolution, many argue the world cannot hope to find the key to a challenge that anticipates a growth in world population to 10 billion by 2050 (from the current 6.7 billion).

As the food-price crisis began to subside in late 2008, food experts, fearing a loss of attention to the problem, sustained their calls for a global resolution. Alex Evans, who is leading a project on rising food prices, based at Chatham House (London) and New York University, laid out the parameters of the challenge in an April 2008 essay. According to the World Bank, by 2030, demand for meat will have grown by 85% and for food overall by 50%. At the same time, climate-change forecasts suggest agriculture will suffer, particularly in Africa, with the Intergovernmental Panel on Climate Change anticipating an increase of between 40 million and 170 million undernourished people in this

time frame. Additional price pressure will come from energy costs, which are also broadly expected to continue to increase. While the range of estimates of remaining available arable land varies, the UN Food and Agriculture Organization (FAO) says the world can only count on another 12%. Moreover, irrigation will not be the panacea it was during the Green Revolution, given the tripling over the last 50 years in demand for fresh water, while forecasts say the number of people chronically short of water will have risen to more than

4 billion from half a billion by 2050.

However, perhaps the hardest thing to deal with, Evans argued, will be the temptation by some to resort to hyperbole. Using spiraling food prices to revive the pre–Green Revolution fear of population growth as a way of demanding quick solutions to a highly complex problem risks a self-fulfilling prophecy. He points in particular to environmental groups who supported the conversion of corn into ethanol before realizing it could increase world hunger. In any event, Evans notes, such talk harks back to the 18th century English philosopher Thomas Malthus, who saw hunger as a necessary evil and force of nature that no government could hope to control. Apropos of which "[p]eople rarely make better decisions for being in a fearful frame of mind," Evans commented.

Evans also cautioned against adopting an approach that relies too heavily on the promise of technological advances, particularly given the new complications of rising fuel costs and global warming. In a message echoed by many participants in the debate, he saw in the 2007–2008 food-price shock an opportunity to tackle the underlying problems of inadequate investment in agriculture and government policies that had yet to catch up with the realities of the age. The emergence of food as a top-ranking political issue, he wrote, provides de-

velopment advocates with a chance to form "new alliances, new coalitions and new drivers for change."

The array of possible policy fixes is wide, and a global consensus is far from clear on some key points—notably genetic engineering—which some see as the key to a second Green Revolution. Similarly, the question of whether free trade helps or hurts is a hot-button issue, as well as how the U.S. handles its food-aid deliveries. No less complex are the questions of whether corn should continue to be converted to ethanol to help fill gas tanks and if market forces can be harnessed to address the crisis, or whether individual behavior must change. Can the international commu-nity hope to make progress when even the President of the U.S. cannot per-suade Congress to devote one quarter of its spending on international food aid to purchases in recipient countries rather than in the U.S.? Or should the world just leave it to market forces to fix, accepting, perhaps rather like Mal-thus did, that hunger is a fact of life? ●

Global strains

While calls for emergency food aid fell on fertile ground last year, the crisis dragged the interna-tional community further away from achieving the hunger-eradication tar-get enshrined in the UN Millennium Development Goals, agreed upon by the largest gathering of world leaders in history in September 2000. Halfway to the 2015 deadline for goal number one—to halve the world's desperately poor and malnourished compared to 1990 levels—only poverty reduction was broadly on target. According to a monitoring report in September 2008, the number of people living in extreme poverty fell from 42%, or 1.8 billion, in 1990 to 26%, or 1.4 billion, in 2005. However, the percentage of undernour-ished people had only declined from 20% in 1992 to 16% in 2004. Worse, the report added: "The recent hike in food prices is eroding the limited gains in reducing hunger." The report found that many countries in Sub-Saharan Africa, the Middle East and North Africa were "seriously off track." As Evans, who has advised the British government, Oxfam and the WFP on how to tackle the crisis puts it, there's something seriously wrong when the Earth's food supply averages out at 2,700 calories a day, yet half the world is starving.

Moreover, critics have noted a sin-gular lack of concrete action emanating from a trio of global gatherings—an FAO summit in Rome, Italy, the annual meeting of the Group of Eight (G-8) leading industrial countries in Toya-ko, Japan, and trade talks in Geneva, Switzerland—despite the fact that the world was facing the biggest spike in food prices in decades.

Joachim von Braun, director general of IFPRI, said that it was encouraging that the G-8 had put global food secu-rity on its agenda. He praised its efforts to increase food production, accelerate development of "second generation" biofuels—broadly speaking, the kind that do not use edible foodstuffs—and its commitments to invest $10 billion in food aid, nutrition interventions and social protection. However he and oth-ers expressed disappointment at a lack of specifics. The G-8 could have frozen biofuel production, cut it or introduced a moratorium instead of just promis-ing to work with other stakeholders "to develop science-based benchmarks and indicators for biofuel production and use." He added that the $10 billion was all well and good, but it needed to be released in a "timely" manner and it was "disappointing that no clear commitments were made to specific amounts." With the G-8's talk of a "global network of high-level experts" and other new groupings, it was "not enough to simply add an unclear set of actors and yet more meetings...without a clear understanding and delineation of the mechanisms for coordination." Lacking too, added von Braun, was a sufficient connection on the part of the G-8 between the food-security and climate-change agendas.

There was little sign that any glob-ally unifying incentive had been forged even in the midst of the crisis. The World Bank noted that 26 countries that are net food exporters had intro-duced bans or restrictions that contrib-uted to the price spikes. Between April and May of 2008, India, Egypt, Viet-nam, Brazil, Cambodia and Indonesia banned, suspended or restricted rice exports in an attempt to gain control of spiraling prices. Some countries, such as the Philippines, which decided to strive for rice independence, took the crisis as a hint that they should become self-sufficient.

The Economist (London), in May 2008, noted the folly of this tactic, invoking the specter of North Korea, whose isolationist approach has ren-dered it unable to survive without food aid. But even *The Economist* acknowl-edged the complications inherent in developing a trade reform process that helps. It cited one study that showed poverty would fall in 13 countries if all subsidies and tariffs were removed, a theory, it said, to which the World Bank had once adhered. But under the leadership of Robert Zoellick, former U.S. trade negotiator, that philosophy has changed—mainly due to an analy-sis that found that higher food prices led to more poverty. The article noted Zoellick's cry that 100 million people were being plunged below the poverty line and said the bank and others should "beware of sweeping generalizations about the impact of food prices on the poor," given that higher prices can bring benefits to rural farmers. The tensions between these different argu-ments showed how important it was to get trade reform *right*. Many have suggested that the question of cutting subsidies to farmers in rich countries, a major bone of contention in the Doha Round of trade talks which entered their seventh, unresolved year in 2008, was potentially less helpful overall than cutting tariffs would be.

Doha's role

While many economists argued that concluding Doha could help, Oxfam urged caution, recalling the case of Haiti, when in 1995, a World Bank/International Monetary Fund program that called for rapid liberalization cut rice import tariffs from 50% to 3%, unleashing a flood of cheap U.S. imports. Haiti consequently had to import 80% of its rice needs at a time of skyrocketing prices—a situation that helped bring the government to its knees. "Unfortunately, there is a temptation for trade negotiators to ignore such nuances and use the food-price crisis in order to whip up momentum for a quick deal," Oxfam wrote in June 2008. It said proposals on the table at the WTO failed to protect developing countries' needs to ensure food security and protect rural livelihoods, yet allowed the U.S. and European Union (EU) to maintain high levels of agricultural spending and "a license to continue dumping" commodities in developing countries in times of surplus. Many development experts refer to the practice of exporting food from rich to poor countries as "dumping" because flows have tended to increase at times of low prices and decrease at times of high prices. The word is also used as a weapon to criticize U.S. agricultural subsidies, which have been so high that exports are priced below the cost of their production, creating an unfair playing field for farmers in developing countries.) The following month, negotiations on resuming the trade talks collapsed, largely due to the failure of the U.S. and India to agree on New Delhi's demand for safeguards for its farmers.

Doha was intended to boost the world economy, particularly in developing countries. The outline of a deal had emerged in July 2007, shortly before the collapse, with a draft that would have led the EU to cut subsidies above $60 billion by 75% to 85%.

The U.S., whose subsidies fell into a lower category of between $10 billion and $60 billion, would have had to cut its ceiling by 66% to 73%—a level exceeded by the $289 billion farm bill Congress approved over President George W. Bush's (2001–2009) veto in May. Part of the anger of developing countries was directed against the U.S. seeking to maintain a subsidies ceiling—between $13 billion and $16.4 billion—that was approximately twice the level of its actual subsidies—$7 billion—which were depressed by the higher prices that farmers were receiving on the market. "When and if food prices go down, subsidies will go way up again, and that does have an impact on the markets," says Gawain Kripke, director of policy and research at Oxfam America. "Saying trade is important is different from saying that free trade is important. Trade is often not free at all, rather it is very consciously directed and strategic."

Food-for-fuel challenge

This picture of clashing interests grows even more complicated when consid-

Guatemalan message

FACED WITH THE THREAT that rich countries might merely heave a sigh of relief that the immediate food-price shock had passed, nutrition experts fought to keep the world's attention on the future. They argue that improving the health of the living has the long-term effect of decreasing population growth—one of the key stresses on food supply.

One sharp knife in the arsenal of John Hoddinott, a senior research fellow at IFPRI, is data from a nutrition-intervention study among poor, rural Guatemalans between 1969 and 1977. Anyone under the age of seven was eligible to participate, so the length of involvement in the study varied. In papers he coauthored, the benefits of feeding children under three well rather than leaving them to weather the impact of market-driven shifts was demonstrated.

The purpose was to show that nutritional deficiencies in early life have a lasting effect into adulthood and consequently do not necessarily subside when an immediate crisis passes. The nutritional intervention consisted of randomly supplying some villagers with a drink high in energy and vegetable proteins and supplying a less-nutritious supplement to other villagers, on a voluntary basis. Between 2002 and 2004, the researchers returned to Guatemala and tracked down most of the original participants. They learned that the men who had received the nutritious supplement during the first two years of life earned on average 46% more, or 37% higher if they received it during the first three years. Interventions after that had no measurable impact. Women, who are less engaged in the labor market in Guatemala, did not demonstrate an improvement in wages. However, in a subsequent analysis, Hoddinott and his colleagues discovered that women who received the drink remained in school for the equivalent of an additional 1.2 grades, achieved higher reading comprehension scores and demonstrated higher nonverbal cognitive ability. To Hoddinott, these findings carried a dramatic message for people living in developed economies who might doubt the value of supplying food to the less fortunate.

Another dire consequence in such times of stress is for people to take children out of school so they can work—a step that is rarely reversed, Hoddinott said. Taken along with the results of the Guatemalan study, he concluded: "The argument that we don't have to worry about this because prices are likely to go down doesn't hold." He added: "People can have very short attention spans. These are problems that really require people to stick with the solutions for a long time. Sometimes what we need is less blah blah blah and more real action on the ground."

ering the potential impact of biofuels, given a huge boost by a U.S. energy law passed in 2007 calling for an approximately 500% increase in their output by 2022, mainly from corn and soybeans. As Kripke explained, 40% of the world's corn is produced in the U.S. and one third of it was set to be converted to ethanol to fuel cars in 2008. "That's a pretty big displacement of global food products away from corn," on which he said about 2 billion people rely upon as their chief staple.

Oxfam and other development advocates blame congressionally mandated production targets in particular for boosting food prices. However, estimates of the impact that food-into-fuel production will have on prices range from about 3% (the White House) to 75% (unpublished estimates by the World Bank, according to Oxfam). Many take as their guide IFPRI's estimate (30%), which falls below the middle of that range. But according to Kripke, it's a moot point. "What we know is that the conversion of food

A grain transport truck is loaded up with corn, harvested in the fall of 2007, in Curran, Illinois. An informal coalition of oil refiners, environmentalists and food processors aims to convince lawmakers that rising output of corn-based fuel is making food more expensive worldwide by siphoning off livestock feed supplies and discouraging U.S. farmers from planting other critical crops, such as wheat and soybeans. AP PHOTO/SETH PERLMAN

into fuel is driving prices up. Period."

Also, Benjamin Senauer, a professor of applied economics at the University of Minnesota, has been quoted as blaming biofuel production for 390,000 additional deaths among children under five, with the number rising to 475,000 by 2010 if the congressional mandate of 15 billion gallons of corn-based ethanol and 1 billion gallons of biodiesel by 2015, and 36 billion gallons by 2022, holds true. C. Ford Runge and Senauer, writing in an online supplement to *Foreign Affairs* in May 2008, warned against the "green" virtues of biofuels. They cited an article by Nobel laureate Paul Crutzen, a pioneer

of ozone-depletion science, as saying that the heavy use of nitrogen fertilizer on corn and European rapeseed for vegetable-oil diesel would have a net negative effect on greenhouse gases because they would produce such high levels of nitrous oxide, which is 296 times more damaging than carbon dioxide. "It is now time for governments to respond, not with trade distortions and subsidies, but by ending the failed policies that have created an artificial industry that is emptying the stomachs and purses of the world's poor," they concluded.

The academics have also turned their guns on hedge funds, which they said had contributed to the crisis by "making huge bets on corn and the bull market unleashed by ethanol." Others have been more cautious about assigning blame. Laurie A. Garrett, science and health fellow, in a working paper for the Council on Foreign Relations (CFR) in May 2008, claimed that nervousness over stock and real estate investment had prompted shifts to commodities, but their impact on food prices was yet to be determined, and a subject of review by government regulators.

The Grocery Manufacturers Association, seeing the impact on food prices hurting its business, joined forces

WE'RE ON THE WAY TO SOLVING AMERICA'S OBESITY PROBLEM!

CAGLECARTOONS.COM/BOB ENGLEHART

with development advocates in raising concerns before Congress. Scott Faber, the association's vice president for federal affairs, in testimony before a May 2008 congressional hearing, listed the various factors influencing food prices before declaring "the most significant new factor and the *only* factor affecting food and feed prices that is *under the control of Congress,* is the sudden and significant increase in food-to-fuel production."

Many experts note the availability of sugar as an alternative to corn, since it burns far more efficiently, but they also note the long-term impact of using arable land to grow anything other than food for people. Still, sugar-into-ethanol producer Brazil, second only to the U.S. in ethanol production, announced in September 2008 that it would collaborate with Washington in promoting biofuels. In another strange twist of this complex set of trade relations, Brazil still plans to sue the U.S. at the WTO over its ethanol import tariff.

Killing with kindness?

The food-price crisis in 2008 focused attention on the question of U.S. food aid, how it is delivered and who really benefits.

Many economists and development advocates argue that while actual food aid might be necessary in times of acute

shortages, it tends to skew markets in the recipient country and should be used only in an emergency. Using cash to generate local or regional purchases, they argue, is far more effective in the long term. However, the Cargo Preference Act of 1954, which mandated that half of all civilian agency cargoes be shipped on U.S.-flagged vessels, and was updated in 1985 to cover 75% of some agricultural loads, stands in the way of change.

Critics of U.S. food aid welcomed attempts by President Bush to cut the percentage that goes in the form of food surpluses from nearly 100% to 75%—though Congress ultimately approved only a $60 million pilot program over four years, which requires the agriculture secretary to establish projects using locally purchased food.

Garrett described Bush's proposal as a "nice start," but urged further cuts to 50% by fiscal year 2009 and additional reductions over the next five years. Instead of food, poor farmers in developing countries need tools like tractors and seed stock. "Congress must stop pitting the financial interests of large agricultural companies against the food security of hundreds of millions of people over the coming decade," she wrote. "Protecting crop production in Iowa or California through such distorting mechanisms of mandatory crop

'aid' dumping is little more than a cynical grab for votes—*by both parties*."

In July 2008, an important series of recommendations emerged along similar lines from a task force in which Garrett participated under the auspices of the Center for Strategic and International Studies (CSIS). It received particular attention because it was co-chaired by respected Sen. Richard G. Lugar (R-IN), the corn and soybean farmer who has headed the agriculture committee and instigated free-market policies that were later overturned under pressure from fellow farmers. The CSIS report slammed the U.S. aid system as a "broken, expensive, $1.6-billion-per-year program that is yielding declining returns at the very moment when performance to meet urgent new needs is most acute." It noted it can take up to six months for U.S.-procured commodities—which make up more than 40% of WFP supplies—to reach recipients with shipping, handling and management costs gobbling up 65% of the budget in 2007. This figure is expected to head upward. Garrett also noted that the Government Accountability Office found that transportation and business costs had fueled a 52% drop in food aid sent overseas because freight rates had risen dramatically from 2002 to 2006. "This shameful misuse of aid dollars must come to an immediate end," she pleaded.

The report of the CSIS task force, cochaired by Sen. Robert Casey (D-PA), called for a doubling of emergency food relief funds to $3.2 billion and big improvements in efficiency and speed of delivery. It also said that 75% of emergency funds should be used to buy locally and regionally, leaving only 25% of the pie for U.S.-origin food shipped on U.S. carriers. It called for $1 billion in development assistance per year for infrastructural improvements abroad, including seeds, fertilizers, rural credit, new technologies, an acceleration of efforts to reduce dependence on corn and aggressive pursuit of a conclusion to the Doha Round.

Christopher B. Barrett, international professor of agriculture at Cornell University, places much of the blame for the lingering preferred cargo system on the shipping industry and its supporters, who, he says, had understandably seen no benefit in advertising their role in a system that creates a 45–85% markup on the cost of deliveries. He accused the shipping and agribusiness lobbies of getting the language on the local-purchase pilot study "rigged" so as to render it "most likely to fail."

However, Gloria Tosi, a maritime consultant who has long represented the aid shippers, disagrees. She says the true price differential between shipping aid on a U.S.-versus a foreign-flagged vessel was 15% or 16%, most of which was reimbursed. She also said that month-to-month, there were

"no offers" from foreign shipowners 40% of the time, adding that the industry had never opposed the idea of local purchases. Rather, there was concern that decoupling the law that governs food aid deliveries from U.S.-produced commodities and shipping would dilute congressional support for the dollar amount required to help feed the world's poor—even more so in a time of economic crisis. "We have American-flagged vessels that were built specifically for this trade and they're very competitive," she said.

However, Barrett believes the pilot study will prove what he and other experts have argued for years about the inefficiency of the system, especially since two thirds of non-U.S. food aid is

already procured in developing countries. "People know how to do this and do it right," he said. "It saves money, ensures cultural appropriateness and reduces delays in getting food into the hands of hungry people." He added, "So even though opponents have tried to stack the deck, they ultimately will fail. It's just we'll have to wait another five years."

Maybe in a few years, U.S. lawmakers will have created a more equitable system of food aid, Doha will be settled under an arrangement that favors farmers the world over and scientists will have spawned the next Green Revolution, right? Perhaps, but first there is another giant thorn in the side of the food security crisis. •

Frankenfoods or loaves and fishes?

Much of the international debate over how to recreate the Green Revolution has focused on the question of improving crop yields through genetic modification geared for a time of changing climates. Major producers, including Australia, Canada and the U.S., have significant doubts about growing genetically modified (GM) crops, recognizing consumer fears about the creation of unnatural products, which some, particularly in Europe, have dubbed Frankenfoods. Yet, as Lugar said at the unveiling of the CSIS report, virtually all 23 countries that grow GM crops are food exporters and the nearly 40 states threatened by the food-price crisis at that time were not. Since 2000, many countries, particularly in Africa, have rejected or limited GM imports, including food aid, for fear of having their own exports blocked by Europe. "The governments and people of Europe must understand that their opposition to safe GM technology contributes to hunger in Africa," Lugar said.

The World Bank agrees. According to Katherine Sierra, vice president for sustainable development, many GM

crop varieties are showing promise at a time when "climate-ready" crops are critical. Australian Agriculture Minister Tony Burke, experiencing his country's worst drought in over a century, has remarked that GM technology would be required on a massive scale and that it would be a "mistake" for anyone to think that simply reversing biofuel policies would resolve the problem.

Opposed to GM

GM crops also have some powerful and famous opponents, from Friends of the Earth to Prince Charles, the heir to the British throne. He made something of a splash by saying in an interview in August 2008 that the adoption of GM crops had set the world up for "the biggest disaster, environmentally, of all time." He accused agribusiness of carrying out a "gigantic experiment with nature" and talked of a "nightmare vision" in which millions of small farmers were driven from their land into unsustainable conurbations of "unmentionable" awfulness. "Count me out," he said, if you think the food security challenge can be met with "one form of clever

genetic engineering after another."

Hoddinott says the collective view at IFPRI is that people should keep an open mind. He noted for example "golden rice," a GM crop created using genes from daffodils and a soil bacterium that accumulates betacarotene in the grain, which would theoretically fuel vitamin A production in humans. Despite having the potential to prevent future generations in poor countries from going blind, development of this crop has been stymied by the lack of an international system to overcome patent restrictions for technology that would allow the crop to be grown. Hoddinott says developing countries should be allowed to make their own choices. "It seems completely inappropriate that I, as a middle-aged white guy, should tell people in developing countries what they should and shouldn't eat." But the science is still patchy. The International Assessment of Agricultural Science and Technology for Development, a UN- and World Bank body, found in a report endorsed by 60 countries in April 2008 that some GM crops demonstrated yield increases of

CAGLECARTOONS.COM/ARCADIO ESQUIVEL

between 10% and 33% in some places, but yield declines in others. Environmental groups often portray genetic engineering of the food supply as a profit-driven misallocation of resources when the promotion of a healthy diet would be more constructive. "This technology is virtually impossible to contain," the Friends of the Earth's "GMO Activist Toolkit" says, adding that GM organisms can cross-pollinate quickly

and "alter all of life as we know it."

At one of the scientific homes of the original Green Revolution, Borlaug's former academic base in Mexico, the International Maize and Wheat Improvement Center, biotechnology is said to have "an important role" in promoting more stable crops "while preserving the environment." The center's head, Thomas Lumpkin, has said that governments have a responsibility to explain the impact of high food prices on the poor and the ability of GM crops to help. "By denying them this technology, you are keeping them hungry, they are dying," he added.

Mulling over Malthus

Senator Lugar, a strong proponent of the responsible use of GM technology, is certain Malthus will again be proven wrong, as he was most recently by the Green Revolution. However it remains unclear whether technology will be the panacea it was during the Green Revolution, whose benefits are now being questioned by environmentalists who blame it, in part, for the emergence of food-supply inequity.

Some observers of these trends hear a touch of false alarm in the dire predictions coming from, among others, Lester Brown, a prominent economist

and global environmentalist whose concerns about population growth are clear from the title of one of his books, *Outgrowing the Earth*. He believes the latest food-price crisis was unlike anything that came before it. In April 2008, he wrote that unless food security was quickly restored, the number of failing states would increase dramatically, "threatening the very stability of civilization itself."

Warren Belasco, professor of American Studies at the University of Maryland (Baltimore County) and author of *Meals to Come*, says it is not the first time Brown and others have raised the specter of doomsday scenarios, recalling a book that Brown wrote as a young economist arguing that the gap between grain supply and demand could only be met through 1984. "I have the feeling that some adjustments are probably going to be made in the market and we'll probably muddle through again and food prices will stabilize," Belasco says.

His view seems to be reinforced by the 2008–2017 outlook of the Organization for Economic Cooperation and Development (OECD) and the FAO, which found that for cereals at least, "the downside risk for prices in the future seems to be increasing." It also noted, as demonstrated by the graph (see p.66) supplied by IFPRI's Hoddinott, that once adjusted for inflation, prices had not risen as high as they did in 1972–74, when supply shortfalls and major Soviet grain purchases doubled and tripled grain prices. In fact, according to the same analysis by IFPRI experts in October 2001, grain prices at the end of the last century were at a 100-year low in real terms.

Evans, in remarks to the author and in a speech at a WFP meeting in October 2008, strongly disputed the OECD-FAO outlook, saying that while its analysis concluded that prices had tailed off—and in fact fallen further since the outlook was published (courtesy of the financial crisis that sent markets plummeting in September and October)—it nonetheless failed to take into account the impact of climate change, water scarcity and

Indian model and actor Milind Soman poses during a campaign against genetically modified food in New Delhi, India, Oct. 16, 2008. The "I am No Lab Rat" campaign, coinciding with World Food Day, was launched by Greenpeace against genetically modified food being allegedly tested on Indians. AP PHOTO/GURINDER OSAN

oil prices, which it assumed would stay between $90 and $105 a barrel for the next decade. "Supply fundamentals really aren't shifting," Evans told me, noting that oil output has been stuck at 85 million barrels a day despite soaring demand. "I think the downturn is creating a delay, and as soon as the economy picks up again, we'll be straight back, looking at the same issues."

Evans says any new Green Revolution will have to be considerably "smarter" than the last one, which succeeded primarily by increasing crop yields. The next one will simultaneously have to make the system much more sustainable, requiring industry to become a "good steward"; it will also have to be more resilient and elastic to withstand coming turbulence; and it must be more equitable. "The whole history of humanity is a story of how population has risen and in tandem with that, generated tremendous clusters of innovation. We've done it before and we can do it again, but we have to get on with it."

Menu of options

From the individual to the institution, it seems there are as many potential answers to the food-security crisis as there are types of rice. Some see the need for a manifesto for responsible eating on an individual level; others see solutions in trade agreements or the promise of new technology. Ultimately, most experts agree that an all-of-the-above approach will be required, and in particular, that investment in agricultural infrastructure and institutions in developing countries is essential.

Ray Offenheiser, a prominent voice in the debate in the U.S. and head of Oxfam America, says this is as true in the U.S. as in the rest of the world. "When the food crisis hit, what federal agency was responsible for evaluating whether there was in fact a global food crisis?" he said in an interview. "The answer is, there was none. So they send food aid in the short term, but there's no one there to think about the long-term issue." When Andrew

A Romanian farmer shows genetically modified soybeans in the village of Varasti, north of Bucharest, May 2004. Romania, Europe's biggest soya grower until 1989, is the sole producer of GM soybeans on the continent, with about 35,000 hectares under cultivation. Environmentalists accuse U.S. biotech firms pioneering genetically modified organisms (GMOs) of using poorer Eastern European countries as a backdoor to a reluctant EU. BOGDAN CRISTEL/REUTERS /LANDOV

Natsios took over the U.S. Agency for International Development (USAID) in 2001, Offenheiser recalled, he complained there had been 48 agricultural economists there a decade before and by 2001, they were down to six. A similar tale of waning support for investment and infrastructure is told by members of CGIAR, the worldwide alliance. Emile Frison, head of Biodiversity International, another CGIAR research center, said in June 2008 that the knowledge required to create higher-yield harvests had been hobbled by a collapse in funding for research as donors had been lulled into complacency by the depressed food prices during the 1980s and 1990s, and rich countries had cut support for agriculture from $6 billion to $2.8 billion between 1980 and 2006 in inflation-adjusted terms. "That's one of the reasons we're facing a food crisis now," he said.

Offenheiser sees hope in the fact that the international community is now tackling the problem head on, notably through the World Bank and the project announced by Bill Gates and Howard Buffett, Warren Buffett's

eldest son, at the UN General Assembly in September 2008. Through their foundations, they plan on giving $75 million to small farmers in Africa and Latin America so they can sell food aid to the WFP, a move described as a "revolution" by the WFP's Sheeran. Much of the money will go into better farming methods, high-yield seeds and other infrastructure areas that development advocates say are in dire need of help.

However the international community chooses to move forward, few would dispute that food security is now inextricably linked to the questions of climate change, resource demand and sustainability. For Pulitzer Prize–winning author Thomas L. Friedman, writing of the need for a new Green Revolution in *Hot, Flat and Crowded*, the change will have to come fast. "We are all Pilgrims again. We are all sailing on the *Mayflower* anew," he wrote. "This is not about the whales anymore. It's about us." ●

OPINION BALLOTS AFTER PAGE 64

QUESTIONS

1. What distinguishes the 2007–2008 food-price shocks from prior food-price increases?

2. How has the increased worldwide demand for resources such as oil affected food prices? Do you think climate change has affected food prices?

3. Should the U.S. move forward with CSIS report recommendations, which stipulate that 75% of food aid should be purchased locally or regionally? What are the benefits or problems with such policies?

4. When food prices spiked, riots broke out in many poor countries. Do you think "food insecurity" in other countries poses a threat to U.S. national security?

5. Why have some countries been so reluctant to embrace GM crop technology? Is this a sustainable approach?

How does this affect the policies of developing countries?

6. How large a role do you believe the corn-into-ethanol production in the U.S. played in the recent rise in food prices? Do you believe that the current ethanol mandates are a practical policy? If yes, why? If no, what would possible alternatives look like?

NOTES: ....

READINGS

INDIA- SUPPORT PRICE- GUARANTEED FLOOR PRICE

Belasco, Warren, **Meals to Come: A History of the Future of Food.** University of California Press, 2006. 393 pp. $21.95 (paper). Belasco, a professor at the University of Maryland Baltimore County, gives an entertaining and detailed account of the culture and history behind the debate.

Friedman, Thomas L., **Hot, Flat, and Crowded: Why We Need a Green Revolution—and How it Can Renew America.** New York, Farrar, Straus and Giroux, 2008. 448 pp. $27.95 (hardcover). The well-known *New York Times* columnist and triple Pulitzer Prize winner's engaging case for the U.S. to take a leading role in fighting global warming, population growth and the battle for resources among the world's burgeoning middle class.

Hunnicutt, Susan C., ed., **World Hunger.** Farmington Hills, MI, Greenhaven Press, 2006. 90 pp. $21.20 (paper). From the "At Issue" series aimed at juvenile readers, this series of articles give a brief and educational flavor of the various arguments.

Lappé Frances M., and Lappé, Anna, **Hope's Edge: The Next Diet For A Small Planet.** New York, Tarcher, 2003. 464 pp. $15.95 (paper). Prolific food and democracy activist Frances Lappé and her daughter present a manifesto for vegetarianism that is peppered with tales of individual success stories from Wisconsin to sustainable agriculture activists in France.

Paarlberg, Robert, **Starved for Science: How Biotechnology Is Being Kept Out of Africa.** Cambridge, MA, Harvard University Press, 2008. 256 pp. $24.95 (hardcover). With a foreword by Jimmy Carter and Nobel laureate Norman E. Borlaug, Paarlberg argues that rich countries are keeping agricultural science out of the hands of poor Africans, having already benefited from it themselves.

Patel, Raj, **Stuffed and Starved: Markets, Power and the Hidden Battle for the World Food System.** London, Portobello Books, 2007. 438 pp. $29.95 (hardcover). This former World Bank, World Trade Organization and UN employee investigates the global food market and argues it works only for corporate executives.

Shiva, Vandana, **Stolen Harvest: The Hijacking of the Global Food Supply.** Cambridge, MA, South End Press, 2000. 150 pp. $14.00 (paper). Formerly one of India's leading physicists, this winner of the Alternative Nobel Peace Prize delivers a tough case against the impact of globalization on farming and the environment that portrays the World Trade Organization as tyrannical and firmly opposed to genetic engineering.

338.19. PAT

TO LEARN MORE ABOUT THIS TOPIC AND TO ACCESS WEB LINKS TO RESOURCES GO TO www.greatdecisions.org/topic6

Cuba on the verge

by Daniel P. Erikson

People carry a giant flag with a photograph of Cuba's retired leader, Fidel Castro, during the May Day parade on Havana's Revolution Square, May 1, 2008. Hundreds of thousands of Cubans marched through the square in a red-splashed May Day celebration that urged economic gains and increased productivity from workers. REUTERS /LANDOV

On Jan. 1, 2009, the Cuban Revolution marked its 50th anniversary—and the Communist regime in Cuba, founded and created by Fidel Castro, commemorated its 50th year in power. A half century ago, Castro and his band of young guerrilla leaders entered Havana to popular acclaim, having successfully seized power from the unpopular dictatorship of Fulgencio Batista, the U.S.-backed strongman who fled into exile. Cuba, an island of 11 million people located just 90 miles south of Florida, has fascinated, irritated and vexed American policymakers ever since. In the early 1960s, the Castro government appalled Washington by striking up an alliance with the Soviet Union in the midst of the cold war. The U.S. government responded by imposing economic sanctions and then breaking off diplomatic relations in January 1961. The early episodes of conflict between the U.S. and Cuba have become the fodder of legend. In April 1961, President John F. Kennedy (1961–63) authorized the Cuban-exile-led Bay of Pigs invasion, which Castro's forces eas-

ily repelled, prompting Kennedy to declare that "victory has a thousand fathers, but defeat is an orphan." In October 1962, the discovery by U.S. spy planes that the Soviet Union had secretly installed nuclear weapons in Cuba prompted the Cuban Missile Crisis, which remains the closest the world has ever come to nuclear war. The diplomatic fallout from these events provoked the U.S. to implement an ever-tightening series of economic sanctions on Cuba, including prohibitions on trade and investment and a ban on Americans' ability to engage in tourist travel to the island. The current clash between the U.S. and Cuba was forged in the cauldron of the cold war and has only deepened in the years since the collapse of the Soviet Union in 1991, as Washington took further moves to strengthen the U.S. embargo and isolate the Castro government.

George W. Bush (2001–2009) was the 10th U.S. President to spar with Fidel Castro and he vowed to hold a tough line against the Cuban government and bring democracy to the island while maintaining the embargo. Like

7

Cuba today is torn between socialism and capitalism. With the Castro era coming to an end, what is the next step for Cuba? Will U.S. policy change any time soon?

DANIEL P. ERIKSON *is senior associate for U.S. policy and director of Caribbean programs at the Inter-American Dialogue, the Washington-based center for policy analysis and exchange on Western Hemisphere Affairs, and author of* The Cuba Wars: Fidel Castro, the United States, and the Next Revolution.

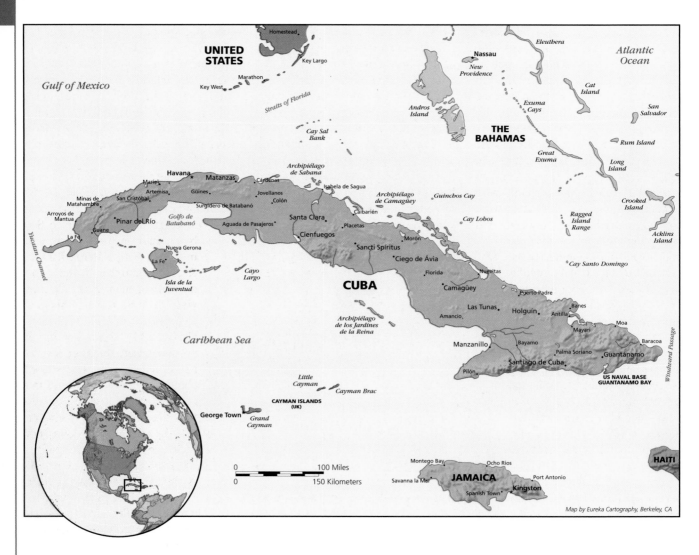

Map by Eureka Cartography, Berkeley, CA

many of his predecessors, however, President Bush's initial plans for Cuba were largely based on waiting for Fidel Castro to die, but it soon became clear that his important allies in South Florida's Cuban-American community demanded a more proactive approach. The Bush Administration responded to these pressures by setting into motion an extensive array of planning exercises to prepare the U.S. to hasten democracy in a post-Castro Cuba. These included two high-level reports from a "Commission for Assistance to a Free Cuba" that were released in May 2004 and July 2006, tighter regulations on U.S. travel to Cuba, the establishment of a Central Intelligence Agency (CIA) "mission manager" to collect intelligence on Cuba and Venezuela and increased foreign aid to internal dissident groups within Cuba. Meanwhile, the prospects for Cuban

democracy remained as remote as ever.

Today, even though significant changes are occurring in both Cuba and the U.S., it remains an open question whether the two countries will be able to escape the long shadow of the cold war and forge a new relationship. There is little doubt, however, that historic leadership transitions have occurred in both countries over the past year. In February 2008, Fidel Castro formally ended his long rule after 49 years in power and handed the reins of government over to his younger brother and longtime minister of defense, Raúl Castro. Last November, Democratic presidential nominee Senator Barack Obama (IL) triumphed over his Republican opponent Senator John McCain (AZ) to become the first African-American President of the U.S., while promoting a new foreign policy approach of engagement with Amer-

ica's adversaries. The U.S. and Cuba remain very far apart from truly reconciling their estranged relationship, but the political transitions occurring in both countries may offer some hope for positive change. Still, it will not be easy to overcome the burdens of history and the legacies of the past.

The rise of Raúl

Fidel Castro has been Cuba's indispensable man for nearly 50 years, but rumors of his eternal life were greatly exaggerated. It is true that he has survived a remarkable number of assassination attempts (over 600 by one count), with the U.S. itself planning several of the most audacious. His impressive stamina, hours-long speeches, exacting memory and workaholic tendencies added to the overall perception that he was a force of nature. According to one popular tale, Castro once declined to accept a long-lived Galápagos tortoise as a pet, explaining that "the problem is that just when you get attached to them, they die on you." In recent years, however, it had become increasingly apparent that his health was beginning to fade. In the summer of 2001, Castro fainted in the middle of a speech, and in the fall of 2004, he fell off a stage and broke an arm and a leg. The top Cuban officials who worked most closely with Castro were well aware that his legendary vigor was fading, and they began to voice concerns about planning for the next phase of the Cuban Revolution. Ricardo Alarcón, president of Cuba's National Assembly, wondered aloud about the topic of succession. "The fact is that the generation that took power 45 years ago is retiring and dying off. People like Fidel, Raúl, and myself are getting older every year," he told an American interviewer in 2004. "Unfortunately, I haven't found a way out of that one yet."

Still, Fidel caught nearly everyone by surprise when, on July 31, 2006, he announced that a severe health crisis would force him to give up power. It was only weeks before his 80th birthday when his young executive assistant appeared on television to read a note from Castro saying that the health of Cuba's supreme leader was "ruined" and named a series of ministers to take over the responsibilities of government in his absence. Raúl Castro became the provisional president of Cuba, a position he held for 19 months until he was formally ratified as the island's new leader in February 2008. As Fidel's younger brother, Raúl had served as the head of Cuba's powerful military since the government's earliest days, earning the peculiar honor of being the world's longest-serving minister of defense. The now 77-year-old heir to the throne has since attained an expansive new set of responsibilities previously reserved for Fidel, including the presidencies of

the Council of States and Council of Ministers and the commander in chief of the Cuban armed forces.

At the time of his initial illness, Fidel named a team of six other ministers to take on new responsibilities in his absence. All of the men chosen by Castro were part of his inner circle, but nearly three decades separated their ages, and they came from diverse backgrounds. They included health minister José Ramón Balaguer and vice president José Ramón Machado

Cuba's President Raúl Castro addresses a crowd in front of a banner depicting Cuba's retired leader, Fidel Castro, in Santiago de Cuba, Cuba, July 26, 2008. That date marked the 55th anniversary of the attack by a rebel group led by Fidel Castro on the Moncada army barracks, which is widely accepted as the beginning of the Cuban Revolution. AP PHOTO/ JAVIER GALEANO

Ventura, the 78-year-old Communist party apparatchik who was later appointed as the new number-two man in the Cuban power structure under Raúl. Esteban Lazo, another vice president, chief of ideology for the Communist party and the highest-ranking black man in the Cuban government, was also tasked as a chief promoter of edu-

cation. Carlos Lage, a physician in his 50s who served as vice president and economic czar, was charged with managing the island's energy programs and overseeing "cooperation with other countries in this field," thereby elevating him as the key point man in managing Cuba's crucial relationship with Hugo Chávez in oil-rich Venezuela. In addition, Castro named a troika of individuals to oversee state funds, including Lage as well as the president of the Central Bank, Francisco Soberón, and the younger foreign minister, Felipe Pérez Roque. Ricardo Alarcón, Cuba's top official for managing relations with the U.S., retained his post as president of Cuba's National Assembly. Since becoming president, Raúl has made several additional important personnel changes, including promoting minister of government Ricardo Cabrisas to become the seventh vice president of the Council of State and sacking the long-serving minister of education Luis Ignacio Gómez. Cuba's planned Sixth Party Congress in the second half of 2009 is likely to herald other significant leadership changes.

Raúl Castro has long been an enigmatic figure within Cuba, but few doubt that he has provided the tactical and managerial underpinnings to his brother's long stay in power. Raúl had supervised the Cuban military as it began to manage important sectors of the Cuban economy through its state-owned enterprises. As the individual responsible for developing the institutions of the Communist party, Raúl was committed to its political primacy, declaring that "Only the Communist party—as the institution that brings together the revolutionary vanguard and will always guarantee the unity of Cuba—can be the worthy heir of the trust deposited by the people in their leader." During the provisional period of his presidency, Raúl authorized few concrete changes,

Cubans look at cell phones in a store window as they line up outside a phone center to buy cell phone service in Havana, April 14, 2008. The government of new President Raúl Castro has begun selling cellular service to all citizens for the first time. AP PHOTO/RAMON ESPINOSA

but he repeatedly hinted that economic reform was on the agenda. He urged Cubans to debate economic reforms "fearlessly" and, in July 2007, he acknowledged that "wages today are clearly insufficient to satisfy all needs and have thus ceased to play a role in ensuring the socialist principle that each should contribute according to their capacity and receive according to their work."

Raúl Castro's formal ascension to Cuba's presidency occurred on Feb. 24, 2008, at a long-scheduled meeting of the National Assembly. During his first public address as Cuba's president, he asked the assembly for per-

mission to continue to consult Fidel on decisions related to "defense, foreign policy, and the socioeconomic development of the country." But it was his economic plans, not his exhortations of Fidel, that most sparked people's interest. Raúl outlined a plan for the Cuban government that sounded suspiciously like the American business practice of "downsizing," calling for "a more compact and operational structure," "a lower number of institutions under the central administration of the state" and an effort "to reduce the enormous amount of meetings, coordination, permissions, conciliations, provisions, rules and regulations."

Moreover, he explicitly emphasized that "the country's priority will be to meet the basic needs of the population...based on the sustained strengthening of the national economy and its productive basis."

In his inaugural speech, Raúl also referred to "the excess of prohibitions and regulations" and declared, "In the next few weeks we shall start removing the most simple of them." This was the first time that the Cuban people had heard an estimated time frame for the implementation of reforms, and it was measured in weeks, not months or years. Raúl Castro's first effort to deliver on the expectations he had raised came in mid-March 2008. Citing the "improved availability of electricity," the government lifted a ban on the ability of ordinary Cubans to buy consumer electronic goods like DVD players, computers, 24-inch televisions and microwaves—all goods that were previously only legally available to foreigners and companies in Cuba. Soon thereafter, Cuba legalized the private use of cell phones and dropped the widely disliked ban that prohibited Cubans from staying in the country's top tourist hotels. While the Cuban government stopped short of promoting more wide-ranging economic reforms to allow room for greater entrepreneurship and more flexibility for foreign direct investment, the vast majority of Cuban people who were struggling for economic relief embraced this new streak of economic pragmatism. ●

Cuba's economic challenge

Reinvigorating Cuba's economic performance is perhaps the central challenge facing the island's government, and the scope of the task is enormous. Even before Cuba was struck by three major hurricanes last fall—Gustav, Ike and Paloma—that were estimated to cause up to $10 billion in damages, the Cuban economy was still crawling out of the crisis that engulfed the country following the collapse of

the Soviet Union in 1991. Cuba's dependence on billions of dollars of annual subsidies from its cold-war ally had left it extremely vulnerable to the changes that swept across Eastern Europe and the former Soviet Union in the late 1980s and early 1990s. The Berlin Wall fell in 1989, and the following year Fidel Castro declared that the collapse of the socialist bloc meant that Cuba was entering "a special period in

a time of peace" that would bring profound economic repercussions to the island. In December 1991, the breakup of the Soviet Union and the resulting loss of about $4 billion in Soviet subsidies dealt a severe economic blow to Cuba, from which it has yet to fully recover.

Cut adrift from its main sponsor, Cuba descended into one of the most crippling economic crises experienced by any country in the modern era. Its trading patterns collapsed, its gross domestic product (GDP) plunged by a third between 1991 and 1994, the incidence of malnutrition and disease surged and virtually all motorized transportation in the country ground to a halt. Almost overnight, even members of the Cuban middle class were forced to confront the stark deprivations of poverty: persistent hunger and the lack of electricity, clean water and lifesaving medicines. Cars virtually vanished from the streets as Cubans began to travel on thousands of bicycles purchased at discounted rates from China. Doctors' offices disposed of old height-weight charts used to measure a child's physical progress, because in this harsh new era, Cuban children could no longer be expected to grow as tall or weigh as much as their predecessors.

In 1992, the U.S. Congress tightened the embargo in an effort to provoke the demise of the Castro government—and two years later more than 30,000 Cubans tried to escape the island's crushing poverty in a refugee wave called the *balsero* crisis. By the mid-1990s, however, the Cuban economy had begun to turn the corner. An early decision to allow foreign direct investment in the form of joint ventures started to bear fruit as investors from Canada, Spain,

Mexico and other European and Latin American countries established a foothold in the Cuban market. Long opposed to tourism, Fidel Castro turned to embrace the tourist trade and hundreds of thousands of visitors from First World countries were soon spending millions of dollars annually sunning themselves on Cuba's beaches or exploring historic Havana. The U.S. dollar was legalized and allowed to trade on a one-to-one basis with a local currency called the "convertible peso," although Cubans' state wages were still paid in Cuban pesos that traded at about 25 to the dollar. The first glimmers of legal private enterprise materialized

when the Cuban government issued new regulations permitting a host of self-employment activities, including barbershops, auto mechanics, bed-and-breakfasts and the famous private restaurants known as *paladares*. The reforms went furthest in the agricultural sector, where semiprivate cooperatives and farmers' markets were allowed to

take shape with minimum state intervention. Cuba's new capitalist class was small and weak, but for the first time a substantial number of Cubans could provide for themselves without depending solely on the state for their livelihoods.

In recent years, Cuba has experienced sustained economic growth, but deep problems remained. Citizens still received ration cards for food, but the subsidies were vastly reduced so that it was impossible to feed a family solely with state provisions. The government had slashed defense spending while maintaining spending on health and education, but the quality of these services had become increasingly threadbare. More crucially, the multiple-exchange-rate system created enormous distortions. The average wage in Cuban pesos is equivalent to $17 a month, but basic items like soap, clothing and food were mainly sold in dollar stores at prices that were close to their U.S. equivalent. Peso stores still existed, but they were poorly stocked and sold goods of extremely low quality. This meant that access to the U.S. dollar was the single greatest factor in determining quality of life, a fact that remained true even af-

Tourists travel in a carriage in the old city of Havana, capital of Cuba, Sept. 9, 2006. As an important part of the national economy, Cuba's tourism has witnessed rapid development in recent years, with more than 2 million tourists visiting the country each year. XINHUA / LANDOV

Cuban customs officials inspect a cargo shipment of livestock which was flown into Havana Sept. 21, 2002 from Miami, Florida. Despite his country's traditionally hostile relations with the U.S., then Cuban President Fidel Castro said he welcomed U.S. companies to the inaugural U.S. food and agribusiness trade fair. The event was held nearly a year after Cuba made its first food purchases from the U.S. in four decades. REUTERS/STR /LANDOV

ter the Cuban government formally removed the U.S. dollar from circulation in 2004. The tips collected each month by busboys and taxi drivers working in the tourist sector could overwhelm the $30 monthly wage of a Cuban brain surgeon or even a government minister. Virtually every strata of Cuban society now had to trade goods and services in the black market to survive. Cuba's historic urban middle class began to work as waiters, tour guides, taxi drivers or even prostitutes, completely upending the socialist values of the Cuban Revolution.

Having survived the 1990s, Cuba entered the 21st century facing a profoundly different set of circumstances, both domestically and internationally. Tourism was now a mainstay of the country's economy and small-scale private entrepreneurship was thriving on a limited basis. Hundreds of joint ventures had been signed with foreign companies in sectors including tourism, nickel, biotechnology and petroleum. The 1998 election of Hugo Chávez in nearby Venezuela meant that Cuba once again had an oil-rich ally, a fact that proved especially crucial as petroleum prices began to surge. The U.S. had created several chinks in the armor

of its embargo, allowing more legal visitors to Cuba, authorizing Cuban-Americans to send remittances totaling nearly half-a-billion dollars annually and even legalizing one-way agricultural sales to Cuba. Canadian and European investment remained stable while China leapfrogged ahead to become Cuba's second-largest trading partner after Venezuela. With the economic winds at its back, Cuba posted official growth rates of 11.8% in 2005, rising to 12.5% in 2006, before dropping to around 10% in 2007. While the accuracy of Cuba's data was clouded by a new formula that included the value of social services in its accounting, even the CIA grudgingly acknowledged the island is growing more than 6.5% annually. (Due to hurricane-related destruction and a sharp rise in the price of food imports, Cuba's growth rate for 2008 was expected to be sharply lower.) However, perhaps no factor looms as heavily over Cuba's economic future as the question of what role the U.S. will play.

Trading with the enemy

The U.S. embargo began as a presidential directive issued by President Kennedy in 1962 in the wake of the Cuban

Missile Crisis. Today, the power to repeal the embargo lies with the U.S. Congress. Of course, the White House can still set the tone for the U.S.-Cuba relationship, issue or remove certain trade and travel sanctions and encourage or forbid U.S. diplomats from meeting their Cuban counterparts. But in the 1990s, the U.S. Congress launched a successful assault on the President's ability to reshape the Cuba sanctions and codified many of the embargo's provisions into U.S. law. The results of these efforts have transformed Cuba policy into a complicated legal thicket that neither isolates nor engages the country effectively. In the process, the U.S. Congress has put itself in the driver's seat of U.S.-Cuba policy.

When the collapse of the Soviet Union deprived Cuba of billions of dollars in annual subsidies, Cuba's teetering economy prompted congressional hard-liners—with support from Cuban Miami—to tighten the screws even further. Throughout much of the 1990s,

A worker walks past an oil rig in Havana, Oct. 16, 2008. Cuban oil officials said that Cuba may have more than 20 billion barrels of recoverable oil in its offshore fields, which they hope to start tapping soon. REUTERS/ENRIQUE DE LA OSA /LANDOV

the U.S. congressional debate was polarized between anti-Castro hardliners, who advocated tightening sanctions to hasten the collapse of Cuban communism, and "normalizers," who believed that the U.S. could best help encourage positive change in Cuba by establishing economic and diplomatic ties with the island. At first, the hardliners held sway, as illustrated by the two main pieces of legislation dealing with U.S.-Cuba policy enacted after the cold war: the Cuban Democracy Act of 1992 and the Helms-Burton Act of 1996. The latter bill was signed by President Bill Clinton (1993–2001), who certainly had no love for Castro, whom he partially blamed for his loss of the Arkansas governorship in 1980 after only one term in office (the state reluctantly hosted thousands of Cuban refugees that later rioted and left Clinton with a political black eye). At the time of its passage, the law was chiefly criticized for its extraterritorial provisions that allowed Cuban exiles to sue in U.S. courts for properties they had lost in Cuba and measures that targeted European companies for "trafficking" in expropriated properties and denied U.S. visas to their executives. Today, it is perhaps more relevant that Helms-Burton conditions ending the American embargo on the existence of a transitional government in Cuba that meets more than a dozen specific criteria, including legalizing political activity, releasing political prisoners and organizing free elections. Most pertinently, the law mandates that the President can only consider a government in Cuba to be transitional if it "does not include Fidel Castro or Raúl Castro."

Even as Cuba hovers on the verge of the post-Castro era, American businesses have been reluctant to abandon their traditional position on Cuba: missing in action. European and Canadian companies have been quietly expanding their investments in Cuba while China, and especially Venezuela, have been galloping into the Cuban market. U.S. businesses, by contrast, have been content to sit on the sidelines with few having actively pushed for a more flexible economic policy toward Cuba.

CAGLECARTOONS.COM/CHRISTO KOMARNITSKI

GRiSToon.com

The one exception is the billion-dollar U.S. agribusiness industry, which won an important concession in 2000 when its support helped pass a bill legalizing U.S. food exports to Cuba. Known as the Nethercutt Amendment for its main sponsor, the former Republican congressman from Washington state, George Nethercutt, this bill authorized the sale of U.S. agricultural products to Cuba on a cash-only basis. (It also opened a loophole allowing certain medical exports to Cuba, but a complicated monitoring requirement scared off U.S. companies from using it.) President Clinton signed the bill into law during his last few months in office, and Fidel Castro initially vowed that Cuba would not purchase "even a single grain of rice" under the new legislation.

The dam burst in November 2001 when Hurricane Michelle, the most powerful storm to strike the island since the 1950s, devastated central Cuba. The U.S. offered a token amount of food aid, but Cuba responded by buying the products instead. Within a month, several American companies had consummated a deal with Cuba valued at nearly $30 million—marking the first direct trade between the two countries in 38 years. This new trade relationship

suddenly gave Cuba political relevance that extended far beyond Miami and Washington, D.C., and turned it into a local bread-and-butter issue that has motivated seven sitting U.S. governors to travel to Cuba. Governor George Ryan (R) of Illinois first broke the long-standing taboo in 1999, and Minnesota's Jesse Ventura (I) was the star attraction at the first U.S.-Cuba trade fair in 2002. Top state officials from Idaho, Louisiana, Maine, Nebraska and North Dakota all followed suit. Since 2001, more than $2 billion in trade deals have been signed with American companies, enabling Cuba to leapfrog over nearly 200 other countries to become the 25th-largest export market for U.S. agricultural products. In 2007, the U.S. ranked for the first time as a top-five trading partner of Cuba.

Furthermore, the day when U.S. tourists are allowed to flock to Cuban beaches has the potential to revitalize the Cuban economy. Like its neighbors in the Caribbean, Cuba views tourism as the central pillar in its economic strategy, and the number of foreign visitors to Cuba has grown steadily over the past decade. Today, Cuban tourism represents a $2 billion-a-year industry that brings in about 40% of the island's hard currency reserves. Cuba now has 11 international airports and receives more than 2 million visitors annually. Sensing the economic potential, U.S. travel agents have begun to lobby more intensively for easing the travel ban. Cuba expects that American tourism, which currently sags below 100,000 visitors a year (mainly academics, church groups and Cuban-Americans traveling with U.S. government permission, along with several thousand adventure travelers in violation of the embargo), could surge to several million visitors annually if the travel ban were lifted.

Cuba's hunt for oil has the potential to dramatically reshape the Cuban economy and its relationship to the U.S. With oil prices rising at a record-breaking pace in recent years, Cuba intensified efforts to convert its oil deposits into a powerful source of income. Cuba today produces about 60,000 barrels of oil per day from a geological belt

located about a mile off of its northern coast. The island receives another 100,000 barrels daily from Venezuela, allowing Cuba to fulfill its domestic energy needs. In addition, the two countries have collaborated to build a major refinery in the Cuban province of Cienfuegos, which represents a major new strategic asset for the Castro government. The crucial future test lies thousands of feet below sea level off the Cuban coast, where the U.S. Geological Survey has estimated that Cuba may possess 4.6 billion barrels of offshore oil reserves.

If this figure proves correct and the reserves are commercially viable, then Cuba would surpass half-a-dozen countries to become the fourth-largest oil-producing nation in Latin America, behind only the three giants of Venezuela, Brazil and Mexico. Major companies from Spain, Norway, India, Malaysia

and Canada have purchased exploration rights for blocs of this reserve, and China is also in serious discussions with Cuba. A major oil find would electrify Texas-based U.S. oil companies and potentially transform the U.S. domestic debate on the embargo. In December 2003, Cuba's official news bulletin, *Granma,* published a statement encouraging U.S. oil firms to participate in offshore exploration: "The government of Cuba wishes to say it has no objection whatsoever to the involvement of American oil companies in exploration and drilling in our exclusive economic zone on mutually beneficial terms." In October 2008, the state-owned oil company Cubapetróleo upped the ante by claiming that Cuba may actually have reserves of more than 20 billion barrels of oil in its offshore fields, which would make its reserves comparable to those of the U.S.   ●

The American politics of Cuba

While it remains to be seen whether a major oil find by Cuba would upend the American politics of the U.S. embargo, the consistent White House support for the sanctions reflects the fact that Florida has emerged in recent years as a tightly contested swing state in presidential elections. Despite differing on the details, all major presidential candidates since 1992—George H.W. Bush, Bill Clinton, Bob Dole, Al Gore, John Kerry, George W. Bush, John McCain and Barack Obama—have supported continuing the sanctions regime against Cuba. Moreover, although the Democrats seized control of both houses of Congress for the first time in 12 years in 2006, the new Democratic leadership appears no more eager than its Republican predecessor to lead a major overhaul of Cuba policy. This is due in part to a reinvigorated lobbying campaign by pro-embargo Cuban-Americans, who created a special political action committee to pump hundreds of thousands

of dollars into dozens of congressional races since 2003. But it also reflects the fact that hard-line Cuban exiles, far from fading from the scene, remain an important factor.

The Cuban population in the U.S. is less than 2 million people, but it punches far above its weight in national affairs. This considerable influence emerged from a potent cocktail of factors that have shaped the Cuban exile experience: the relative affluence of the first wave of émigrés in the 1960s; the fast track to legal residency afforded to subsequent Cuban migrants under the provisions of the 1966 Cuban Adjustment Act; their successful efforts at political organization beginning in the 1980s; and, of course, the fact that the hatred that founding generations had for Fidel Castro dovetailed with the top U.S. foreign policy goal of containing communism during the cold war. However, perhaps none of this would have mattered so much, or proven so endur-

ing, if they had settled anywhere in the country besides Florida.

There is little question that the U.S. Electoral College has magnified the Cubans' influence far beyond what would have otherwise been possible. More than 1 million Cuban exiles have settled in southern Florida, representing about 800,000 voters that account for 5% of the state's voting population. Florida's 27 electoral votes make it the fourth-largest vote haul in U.S. presidential elections, behind only California, Texas and New York. More important is the fact that Florida is the only state in the top four that remains competitive between Republicans and Democrats—demonstrated most famously in the 2000 election when the standoff between George Bush and Al Gore resulted in a frantic recounting of hanging chads and butterfly ballots to determine the presidency.

It is true that the internal dynamics of Florida's Cuban population are rapidly evolving even though their dominance at the top of Miami's political and business community remains unchallenged. The founding wave of exiles that arrived in the 1960s is undergoing a leadership transition as many of the dominant figures have passed away. Cubans who escaped the island as children and teenagers are now in their 50s and 60s, and the younger generations are U.S. citizens with weaker ties to the island of their parents' youth. Successive waves of immigration have also changed the community. In 1980, 125,000 Cubans arrived during a migration crisis known as the Mariel Boatlift. In 1994, another 35,000 boat people came during the balsero crisis, prompting President Clinton to implement two huge changes in immigration policy: establishing the "wet foot-dry foot" policy that allowed Cubans who arrive in the U.S. to stay but required those picked up at sea to be returned to Cuba, and the immigration accords with the Cuban government to provide 20,000 U.S. immigrant visas to Cubans each year.

Cuba is, paradoxically, the only country in the world that has signed an immigration agreement with the U.S., and since the mid-1990s about 250,000 Cubans have migrated legally to America. Recently, as many as 15,000 have been arriving each year without authorization, traveling on rustic rafts, smuggled on high-tech go-fast boats or traveling to Mexico and then sneaking across the border. Unlike the political exile forced on the founding generation of Cuban migrants, the profile of these new arrivals corresponds more closely to other Latin American immigrants who leave their countries for economic reasons, in search of a better life. South Florida today is filled with Cubans who have grown up under communism and maintain deep links with their families back home, unlike the city's founding generation of exiles who fled to the U.S. with most of their families and cut many of their ties to Cubans on the island.

2008 U.S. elections

In this context, the U.S. elections in 2008 shaped up to be a major litmus test of both the political leanings of the Cuban-American community as well as the political clout that it carried in deciding U.S. presidential elections. The subtle but significant differences that emerged between John McCain and Barack Obama on Cuba policy helped to sharpen the question. While both candidates pledged to uphold the U.S. embargo (and backed away from prior statements criticizing its effectiveness),

Obama broke with his Republican opponent in two consequential areas. First, he pledged to immediately grant Cuban-Americans the unrestricted right to travel to Cuba to visit family members, as well as to lift the cap on sending remittances back to Cuba. Second, Obama vowed to engage in dialogue with the Cuban government, saying that, "After eight years of the disastrous policies of George Bush, it is time to pursue direct diplomacy, with friend and foe alike, without preconditions. There will be careful preparation. We will set a clear agenda. And as President, I would be willing to lead that diplomacy at a time and place of my choosing, but only when we have an opportunity to advance the interests of the U.S., and to advance the cause of freedom for the Cuban people." Obama's call for dialogue, together with his stated interest in removing barriers to Cuban-American travel and exchange, suggested a likely departure from the policies of isolation advocated by the Bush Administration. Still, Obama did have one important applause line tucked up his sleeve for his Miami audience. "I will maintain the embargo," he said, describing it as "leverage" over the Cuban regime.

The November 2008 election results delivered a mixed verdict on Obama's efforts to finesse the contentious politics of the Cuba issue. Cuban-American voters overwhelmingly rejected his candidacy, with exit polls showing that 65% voted for his opponent John McCain, with Obama winning only 35% support—a whopping 30-point margin of defeat in this segment of the electorate in a contest that was otherwise a landslide for Obama. However, Obama did win a slight majority of Cuban-American voters under the age of 30, although more than 80% of those over the age of 65 voted against him— a fact that demonstrates a process of generational change is unfolding, albeit slowly, in Miami. In three closely watched congressional races featuring new challenges to the Cuban-American incumbents, Representatives Lincoln and Mario Diaz-Balart and Ileana Ros-Lehtinen, the anti-Castro legislators,

The National Capitol building, originally the seat of Cuba's Congress before the Cuban Revolution led by Fidel Castro, is seen through an open window during sunset in Havana, August 3, 2008. REUTERS/CLAUDIA DAUT /LANDOV

A U.S. truck travels along a road that runs parallel to the fence line dividing the Guantánamo Bay Naval Base from the rest of Cuba, Jan. 17, 2006. At right is a U.S. Marine lookout tower. REUTERS/JOE SKIPPER /LANDOV

cruised to surprisingly easy victories in an impressive show of strength. Yet in the end, the strong opposition to Obama among conservative Cuban-Americans had little impact on the state or national elections, as Obama handily won Miami-Dade County, earned a 51%–48% victory in Florida, and did not need Florida's 27 electoral votes to seal his sweeping 365–173 win in the Electoral College. During the campaign, Obama carefully hedged his policy positions on Cuba and voiced support for the U.S. embargo to help make his candidacy more palatable to Cuban-American voters, but the fact that this constituency had little to do with his electoral triumph may give his Administration greater flexibility once he occupies the White House. However, the hard fact remains that political shifts toward favoring greater engagement with Cuba simply have not reached critical mass at the political level in South Florida. On Capitol Hill, the Cuban-Americans who support the sanctions have spent the last

several years building a political fire wall to prevent the embargo from being eroded. Despite the momentous leadership changes unfolding in Cuba and the U.S., the forces for continuity remain very strong on both sides of the Florida Straits.

Still, one of Obama's earliest decisions may generate a great deal of goodwill between the U.S. and Cuba, even though it is only tangentially related to Cuba policy. Obama made closing the U.S. detention facilities at Guantánamo Bay one of the central platforms of his candidacy, and it is a decision that Cuba would welcome. The U.S. Naval Station at Guantánamo Bay has been a land apart from Cuba for more than a century. The current lease agreement dates back to 1903 and has given the notoriously profligate U.S. military one of its few great bargains. The yearly leasing fees for Guantánamo were initially set at 2,000 gold coins, and renegotiated in the 1930s for a nominal annual sum of $4,085. When Fidel Castro seized control of Cuba in 1959, he

declared the base illegal and demanded that the U.S. leave the island. However, the lease stipulates that the agreement can only be dissolved if both parties concur or if the U.S. abandons the base. Thus, Washington's continued interest in Guantánamo Bay has sustained the lease despite Castro's frequent denunciations and his refusal to cash the yearly lease checks.

Beginning in January 2002, when the Bush Administration decided to transfer hundreds of suspected al-Qaeda terrorists to the base in the aftermath of its invasion of Afghanistan in 2001—a process that continued following the Iraq War of 2003—the Guantánamo Bay detention facilities have tarnished U.S. credibility and undermined its efforts to advocate for democracy and human rights in Cuba. While there is little discussion of closing the Guantánamo Bay Naval Station as a whole, progress on ending the practice of holding terrorists suspects there would be welcomed by many Americans and Cubans alike and potentially lay the groundwork for a more far-ranging discussion on the future of Guantánamo.

A global view

Even if the Obama Administration dithers over whether and how to start a constructive dialogue with Cuba, the Castro government will have no shortage of conversation partners and economic allies on the world stage. While the Cuban government remains banned from several important international organizations at Washington's behest—including the Organization of American States, the Inter-American Development Bank, the International Monetary Fund and the World Bank—Cuba remains an active player at the United Nations and has placed thousands of doctors in poor countries overseas, helping to win hearts and minds across the world. For decades, Havana was the Latin American city with the most foreign embassies and diplomatic missions (although Brasília recently surpassed it). Upon taking power in July 2006, Raúl Castro ushered in subtle but important changes in Cuba's foreign policy while benefiting from a widely shared desire on the part of many foreign countries to reach out to Cuba during its moment of transition away from the historic rule of Fidel Castro. By the fall of 2008, Cuba's international strategy appeared to be reaping substantial dividends. The European Union (EU) decided to lift punitive measures that had been implemented in response to Cuba's crackdown on dissidents several years earlier and an ambitious new dialogue was initiated between Havana and Brussels, the EU's de facto capital. Raúl Castro played host to a succession of visiting leaders from the newly empowered developing world, including Brazilian President Luiz Inácio Lula da Silva and Chinese President Hu Jintao, who made his second visit to Cuba last November. Raúl Castro announced plans to visit Venezuela, which is now by far the island's largest trading partner, due to the shipment of 100,000 barrels per day of discounted oil to Cuba in exchange for tens of thousands of Cuban doctors who work in poor Venezuelan barrios. In October 2008, Cuba succeeded in persuading the UN to pass a resolution condemning the U.S. embargo for the 17th straight year by a vote of 185 to 3, with the U.S. joined only by Israel and Palau in opposing the measure.

Cuba's warming diplomatic ties are already yielding economic payoffs. Trade with Mexico has increased with the improvement of relations under President Felipe Calderón. Brazil expressed the desire to become Cuba's top regional trading partner and Cuba has a number of allies it can call upon for investment capital and expertise as it explores for oil off its northern coast. Cuba will continue to hedge its resources from Venezuela through increased engagement with China. Since 2006, Raúl Castro has continued to lay the diplomatic groundwork to allow for greater diversification of Cuba's economic resources in the future. This progress has been aided by the desire of European and Latin American countries to better position themselves to play a role in Cuba's post-Fidel future, as well as the rising economic power of the Asian giants, which has given them

Venezuela's President Hugo Chávez (R) is welcomed by his Cuban counterpart Raúl Castro after arriving at Havana's airport, Sept. 21, 2008. REUTERS/MIRAFLORES PALACE /LANDOV

the resources to deepen ties with Latin America as a whole, and Cuba in particular. While Raúl Castro will never be able to rival the international stature of his brother Fidel, his foreign policy is benefiting from the range of actors in Latin America, Asia and elsewhere that seek to lessen the island's international isolation at the same moment that his government is attempting to build a broader base of political and economic ties with the world.

Even Russia has reemerged as a formidable ally of Cuba. Cuba is reported to be deeply in debt to Russia (to the tune of $20 billion owed to the old Soviet Union), but Russia continues to trade and grant credit to the Cuban government. In September 2006, Russian Prime Minister Mikhail Fradlov visited Havana and signed an agreement opening up a $355 million line of credit over 10 years. The Russian government has recently stated that its objective is to work with Havana "to restore traditional relations in all areas of cooperation," which will breathe new life into an alliance that sustained Cuba for much of the cold war. Russian President Dmitry Medvedev's visit to Cuba in November 2008 highlighted the degree to which Moscow seeks to reestablish ties with its erstwhile ally.

Meanwhile, Fidel Castro's Cuba remains on the verge of one of the most anticipated and dramatic political transitions of our time. During his nearly 50 years at the helm of Cuba, Fidel Castro used the U.S. as a foil to help preserve

his grip on power. Now Raúl Castro is pursuing a path of limited economic opening that may breathe new life into the Cuban Revolution or sow the seeds for Cuba to evolve into a different kind of society entirely. By both instinct and design, the U.S. still perceives itself as having a major role to play in Cuba's future, but Cuba's fate will ultimately be left with the people who remain on the island.

Yet even as Fidel Castro has rallied the populace behind his vision of a nation that must band together to repel the imperialist threat, he has admitted that the U.S. does not pose the only challenge. "The Yankees cannot destroy the revolutionary process," Castro mused in an interview not long ago. But if Cubans turned away from socialism, then "this country can self-destruct. We ourselves could destroy it, and it would be our fault." Fifty years after the Cuban Revolution of 1959, Cuba is torn between socialism and capitalism, hovering on the verge of ending its isolation from the U.S. and showing glimmers of openness that could lead to market reform and perhaps even a future path toward democracy. After a half century of estrangement between their two countries, it is difficult to envision Barack Obama and Raúl Castro sitting down for a meeting—but not for lack of items to discuss. ●

OPINION BALLOTS
AFTER PAGE 64

QUESTIONS

1. The author says that "after a half century of estrangement between their two countries, it is difficult to envision Barack Obama and Raúl Castro sitting down for a meeting—but not for lack of items to discuss." If they were to sit down together, what do you think would be the three most crucial items for discussion?

2. The Cuban Revolution of 1959, followed by the U.S. imposition of economic sanctions and the breaking off of diplomatic relations in January 1961, led to a standoff in U.S.-Cuba relations that has persisted until today. However, with the transfer of power from the ailing Fidel Castro to his brother Raúl and the election of Barack Obama as the next U.S. President, do you think that there exists an opportunity for a new U.S.-Cuba relationship to be forged? Why, or why not?

3. "Reinvigorating Cuba's economic performance is perhaps the central challenge facing the island's government," according to the author. What were the main causes of the severe economic ills? Do you believe that in the 21st century, real signs of improvement in the economy are already being seen?

4. The U.S. Geological Survey has estimated Cuba may possess some 4.6 billion barrels of offshore oil reserves. If this figure is correct and the reserves become commercially viable, Cuba could become the fourth-largest oil-producing nation in Latin America. What effect do you think this would have on the U.S. embargo on Cuba?

5. Upon officially taking office as president, Raúl Castro outlined his economic reform plans, which included removing "the excess of prohibitions and regulations," and he explicitly emphasized "the country's priority…to meet the basic needs of the population." Do you think Raúl has started to make good on the expectations he has raised?

6. The one exception to the prohibiting of U.S. trade with Cuba has been the billion-dollar agribusiness that burgeoned after Hurricane Michelle devastated the island in 2001. Under the Nethercutt Amendment, Cuba can buy agricultural products for "cash only," resulting in some billion dollars in trade deals for American companies. In your opinion, is this likely to lead to pressure by other American industries to be allowed to deal with Cuba, i.e. the oil industry?

NOTES: ....
....
....
....
....
....
....
....

READINGS

Burki, Shahid Javed, and Erikson, Daniel P., eds, **Transforming Socialist Economies: Lessons for Cuba and Beyond.** New York, Palgrave Macmillan, 2005. 288 pp. $94.95 (hardcover). Experts examine what Cuba can learn from the experiences of economic transition in Russia, Central Asia, Eastern Europe, China and Vietnam.

Domínguez, Jorge I., Pérez Villanueva, Omar Everleny, and Barberia, Lorena, eds., **The Cuban Economy at the Start of the Twenty-First Century.** Cambridge, MA, Harvard University Press, 2004. 456 pp. $24.99 (paper). American and Cuban economists share their perspectives on the major challenges confronting the Cuban economy.

Erikson, Daniel P., **The Cuba Wars: Fidel Castro, the United States, and the Next Revolution.** New York, Bloomsbury Press, 2008. 320 pp. $28.00 (hardcover). The book unravels the multiple arguments that swirl about Cuba in Miami, Washington and Havana, and examines what lies ahead for U.S.-Cuban relations under the Obama Administration.

Falcoff, Mark, **Cuba the Morning After: Confronting Castro's Legacy.** Washington, DC, American Enterprise Institute, AEI Press, 2003. 285 pp. $25.00 (hardcover). A major study of U.S.-Cuba relations warns that America is ill-prepared for the serious dilemmas and even threats posed by a post-Castro Cuba.

Latell, Brian, **After Fidel: Raul Castro and the Future of Cuba's Revolution**, updated edition. New York, Palgrave Macmillan, 2007. 304 pp. $14.95 (paper). A compelling dual biography of Fidel and Raúl Castro that sheds new light on their complex relationship.

Pérez-Stable, Marifeli, ed., **Looking Forward: Comparative Perspectives on Cuba's Transition.** University of Notre Dame Press, 2007. 336 pp. $27.00 (paper). This volume considers the possible consequences of change in Cuba across a range of political, economic and social dimensions, and draws lessons for the future.

Ziegler, Melanie M., **U.S.–Cuban Cooperation Past, Present, and Future.** University Press of Florida, 2007. 192 pp. $59.95 (hardcover). A concise survey of how and why the U.S. and Cuba cooperate despite ongoing antagonisms.

TO LEARN MORE ABOUT THIS TOPIC AND TO ACCESS WEB LINKS TO RESOURCES GO TO www.greatdecisions.org/topic7

Human rights in a new era: wars for peace?
by David C. Morrison

Morally straight-forward in principle, an internation-ally mandated "responsibil-ity to protect" victims of state oppres-sion through armed human-itarian inter-vention has no shortage of complexities in practice.

Houses destroyed by Cyclone Nargis are seen in a village in the hardest-hit Irrawaddy Delta, Myanmar, on May 7, 2008. Some 138,000 people are known dead and tens of thousands more are listed as missing, and the UN estimates more than 2 million people are homeless. AP PHOTO/BURMA NEWS AGENCY VIA XINHUA NEWS AGENCY

In May 2008, the most deadly named cyclone ever to hit the north Indian Ocean slammed into Burma—now officially called Myanmar. The immediate toll is still uncertain—the country's insular ruling generals deliberately stopped counting—but has been pegged at 138,000 deaths. The tragedy of this unavoidable natural disaster paled, however, beside the avoidable humanitarian disaster that loomed ahead when the Burmese junta refused landing rights to the foreign ships and planes that flocked to succor an estimated 2.4 million destitute and displaced Burmese.

That the off-coast humanitarian flotilla numbered U.S. Navy relief forces only compounded the paranoia infecting Myanmar's rulers, given to bizarre irrationality at the best of times. "What the generals truly fear is that if they allow U.S. warships and foreign forces to come to the aid of cyclone survivors, people will soon rise up and the regime would be overthrown," a Burmese dissident paper, *The Irrawaddy*, suggested at the time. Meanwhile, Burmese officers began

expropriating for themselves what supplies did make it through, even as experts darkly forecast a million or more deaths from disease, starvation and exposure.

As it dawned on the world that a suffering populace was the least of this odd government's concerns, frustrated would-be samaritans began speaking openly of forcing the door, delivering assistance at the tip of a bayonet, if necessary. Most outspoken on this score was French Foreign Minister Bernard Kouchner—a founder of the international care group, Doctors Without Borders—who repeatedly urged recourse to a novel doctrine the United Nations had endorsed more or less in passing three years before. Called Responsibility to Protect, or R2P for short, the new concept built on a controversial type of foreign action called "humanitarian intervention," or using military force against countries whose noncompliant administrators refuse to stop tormenting their own people.

In response to the atrocities committed during World War II, the UN General Assembly in 1948

DAVID C. MORRISON *has spent a quarter century researching and reporting on security issues, including a decade in Washington as national security correspondent for* National Journal. *He currently writes the daily "Behind the Lines" media roundup column for* The Congressional Quarterly Homeland Security *online magazine.*

adopted the Universal Declaration of Human Rights, specifying basic rights and fundamental freedoms to which people everywhere are entitled. However, the pressing issue today is what to do when countries do not respect the rights of their people. What recourse do nations and the people horrified by such atrocities have to enforce such rules?

A classic mission of humanitarian intervention was Washington's dispatch to crumbling, starving, war-torn Somalia in late 1992 of 25,000 U.S. troops as the kernel of a multinational force charged with safeguarding relief efforts and, if possible, restoring some order. Such was the chaos that the mis-

sion grew less humanitarian and more interventionary. After 18 Army Rangers were killed in an ambush, President Bill Clinton (1993–2001) terminated "Operation Restore Hope," which had been initiated by his lame-duck predecessor. Somalia remains today a cockpit of anarchy and Islamist militancy, in whose doings Washington dabbles from a discreet distance.

Another case study from the 1990s—very much the golden age of American humanitarian intervention—is the U.S.-North Atlantic Treaty Organization (NATO) air campaign mounted in 1999 to forestall feared ethnic cleansing in Serbia's largely Albanian Kosovo province. "This is probably the

first war that has not been waged in the name of 'national interests,' but rather in the name of principles and values," Czech writer-politician Vaclav Havel applauded. Although the Chinese Embassy in Belgrade was accidentally bombed, alongside other "collateral" death and damage, "Operation Allied Force" succeeded, to the extent that an Albanian Kosovar government—which has its own human rights irregularities, and is sustained by thousands of foreign troops, declared independence in February 2008, although Serbia continues to reject Kosovo statehood.

Responsibility to Protect is a bid to entrench in global practice a normative understanding that countries bear

R2P: Responsibility to protect

"THE CLINTON ADMINISTRATION BURST with moral purpose when it arrived in the White House," David Milne, professor of American politics, wrote in the *Los Angeles Times*. "It took a well-intentioned but disastrous intervention in Somalia to denude Clinton's foreign policy of its altruistic core, leading to indecision and drift further down the line."

The starkest symptom of this do-gooder drift was that Administration's determined turning of half a blind eye to the genocidal slaughter taking place in Rwanda in mid-1994. Some 800,000 minority Tutsis had been murdered by majority Hutu nationalists by the time the butchery ended—and then only because a Tutsi-led insurgency drove the genocidalists, and millions of Hutu refugees, out of Rwanda. The United Nations was just as impotent in confronting 100 days of horror playing out on the front pages of the world. With no major power pushing for action, a pitifully weak pre-positioned peacekeeping force was powerless to stem the long-cresting wave of horror.

Visiting Rwanda four years later, a contrite U.S. President offered what is called "the Clinton apology," a ritualistic acknowledgment of failure, blaming his and the world's inaction on an inability to "fully appreciate" the fury of these particular killing fields.

For his part, haunted by the ghosts of Rwanda and earlier UN ineffectiveness in blocking Bosnia massacres—such as the 1995 Serbian extermination of 8,000 Bosniak men and youths at Srebrenica—then UN Secretary General Kofi Annan posed a tough question in his 2000 "Millennium Report" to the UN General Assembly: "If humanitarian intervention is, indeed, an unacceptable assault on sovereignty," he wondered, "how should we respond to a Rwanda, to a Srebrenica—to gross and systematic violations of human

rights that offend every precept of our common humanity?"

Seeking answers, Canada sponsored an International Commission on Intervention and State Sovereignty (ICISS), tasked to "foster a global political consensus" on humanitarian intervention. At the fore of this effort was the International Crisis Group, a conflict-prevention organization with international headquarters in Brussels, Belgium. More than any other, Gareth Evans, the former Australian foreign minister, remains the standard-bearer for what the ICISS termed in its 2001 final report "Responsibility to Protect"—or, in shorthand, R2P.

In a bit of legerdemain not unknown on the leading edges of international law, panelists had strived to identify a nascent norm: "Growing state and regional organization practice as well as Security Council precedent do suggest an emerging norm, or guiding principle," they wrote, "which can be usefully described in the commission's language, as 'the responsibility to protect.'" Their profoundest innovation, though, was shifting the terms of discussion from a nation's debatable "rights"—to intervene, to be sovereign—to every government's "responsibility" to protect people from abuse. Only if oppressive regimes cannot otherwise be persuaded to bear this burden would "responsibility" for redress shift to conscientious bystanders.

"Once activists have agreed on the proper framework and content for a 'new' norm, they often set about to legitimize the norm throughout the international community," a skeptical Heritage Foundation account observes. Indeed, observers on all sides have been frankly astonished at how rapidly the hitherto unrecognized norm embraced as "R2P" has been absorbed by the lumbering UN policy mechanism.

Central provisions of the ICISS report were folded into the 2005 UN World Summit's "outcome document," while a Security Council resolution a year later detailed the protection due civilian populations during armed conflict. In 2007, Annan's successor, Ban Ki-moon, named a special adviser on

absolute responsibility to protect their people; if they fail in that, their sovereignty is effectively ceded to outside actors who will. Six criteria determine R2P applicability: Parties to any intervention must act only as a "last resort" and with the "right intentions," using "proportionate means" that have a "reasonable prospect" of success. The mission must also be blessed with the "right authority," meaning some sort of international sanction, preferably by the UN Security Council. Most importantly, coercion can be countenanced only for a "just cause," defined as addressing "large-scale" losses of life, genocidal or not, or ethnic cleansing, "whether carried out by killing, forced expulsion, acts of terror or rape."

On paper, this is a morally laudable, imminently civilized approach to coping with the outbreaks of barbarity so regularly visited upon populations the world over. The ethnic slaughter of Bosnian Muslims and the wholly unimpeded extermination of 800,000 Tutsis in Rwanda both occurred half a century after Nazi death camps prompted the world to firmly declare "never again." The Rwandan horror show, exemplified by thousands of hacked bodies carried downriver into neighboring lands, in particular inspired the formulation of R2P.

It is really not that complicated, genocide-chronicler Samantha Powers urges: "If we are ever to prevent genocide and not merely ritually lament it after the fact, we have to improve our capacity to imagine the costs of inaction, and to act upon evidence of direct and immediate mortal threats."

Mission creep

Few would admit being in favor of mass murder, but not everyone favors R2P. One school of policy analysts—and not merely noninterventionist "realist" conservatives—believes it marks a dangerous ceding of state sovereignty while serving as a cover for major-power domination. When weighing the right to impose a moral order on an unruly neighbor, answers tend to depend

the Responsibility to Protect. Each new iteration advanced and altered the original concept; environmental disasters, for instance, were dropped in 2005 as an accepted reason to intervene.

National and international foreign policy and humanitarian groups, meantime, have turned their considerable energies to decrying, discussing and/or propagating R2P. The Council on Foreign Relations, for one, hailed UN acceptance of R2P as "marking the end of a 350-year period in which the inviolability of borders and the monopoly of force within one's own borders were sovereignty's formal hallmarks." Increasingly, Lee Feinstein, then senior fellow at the Council on Foreign Relations, added, the individual weighs more heavily in the rights balance than does the nation-state.

Washington's signing off on these UN resolutions hardly makes a coercive protection enthusiast out of the U.S.—which as "the indispensable nation" is fated to lead most rescue missions. "We do not accept that either the UN as a whole, or the Security Council, or individual states, have an obligation to intervene under international law," then ambassador to the UN John Bolton (2005–2006) asserted at the time. (China and Russia signed off on the World Summit report, too, significantly, but are equally iffy about acting on R2P.) In any event, burdened by its post-9/11 interventions, the Bush Administration owned little remaining capacity to address purely humanitarian crises.

Elsewhere in the General Assembly, Canada, Australia, Sweden, Switzerland and Britain are termed R2P's most active Western proponents. The goals being, at least nominally, so laudable, few actors, including a skeptical Bush Administration, have shown much appetite for damning R2P. Critics on the left—convinced that the new "norm" is merely novel sheep's clothing for imperialist wolves and a cloak for powerful interveners wielding hypocritical standards to dominate weaker nations—are more outspoken. The "logical lesson"

of the 1938 "appeasement" of the Nazis at Munich "is not that we should plunge madly into war on all sides to defend minorities, which is precisely what Hitler claimed he was doing," Belgian critic Jean Bricmont goes so far as to argue in his *Humanitarian Imperialism: Using Human Rights to Sell War*.

A photograph of a young Rwandan child is displayed in a gallery of genocide victims, Kigali Memorial Centre in Kigali, Rwanda, Feb. 19, 2008. JASON REED/REUTERS /LANDOV

In any event, the U.S. invasion and occupation of Iraq—justified in retrospect, absent the promised weapons of mass destruction, as the democracy-promoting overthrow of a ruthless dictator—now points to the pitfalls awaiting overambitious interventionary urges, whatever their motivation.

A Russian soldier stands guard at a checkpoint as EU observers are present to watch Russian troops pull back in the Georgian village of Karaleti, some 90 km (56 miles) west of Tbilisi, Georgia's capital, Oct. 8, 2008. AP PHOTO/SHAKH AIVAZOV

on whose doors are being kicked in.

A case in point: in August 2008, Russia earned international condemnation by bringing crushing force to bear in the long-running standoff between Georgia and two breakaway ethnic enclaves (which it continues to garrison to this day, having largely withdrawn from Georgia proper). Moscow responded to a torrent of criticism with a wounded innocence that was not perhaps as farcical as it first appeared.

"When Russian forces crossed into South Ossetia," which abuts Russia but is inside Georgia, Moscow claimed that its purpose was "to protect an endangered minority, many of whom hold Russian passports," Mary Dejevsky, chief editorial writer, notes in *The Independent* (London). "It is quite hard to argue that there is one law for assisting Albanians in Kosovo and quite another for Russians and Ossetians in Georgia."

Similarly, China has been repeatedly blamed for not pressing the Sudanese government over Darfurian atrocities. "Would those advocating a more interventionist China," Dejevsky further wonders, "be so enthusiastic if Beijing applied it, say, to Taiwan, or overseas Chinese in parts of Southeast Asia?"

Back to typhoon-traumatized Myan-

mar, such powers as China, Vietnam, South Africa and Russia are said to have argued in closed councils against granting Kouchner's call to involve the UN Security Council in the aid standoff. According to Reuters, "China's envoy compared the crisis to a deadly heat wave in France in 2003, questioning why the Security Council should step in now when it did not do so in the French case." Obviously, R2P was not brought

to bear on the Irrawaddy Delta. Rather, a controlled system of supply was finally instituted and aid mostly reached the needy. Widespread death was averted, while the junta's unhappy hammerlock on its people remained unaffected.

More calls to invoke R2P were excited by another of 2008's many political crises. After decades of Robert Mugabe's misrule (1980 to present), Zimbabwe was already spiraling into a humanitarian crisis when the founder-president refused to countenance opposition party gains in a sickeningly violent June 2008 election. Again, the prospect of humanitarian intervention to jump-start a democratic transition in Zimbabwe was raised in the UN Security Council. However, aside from a condemnatory statement, even the prospect of sanctions against Zimbabwe was vetoed by both Russia and China in the Security Council. As it happened, the political temperature eased in Zimbabwe, regional organizations got involved, for better or for worse, and the parties are now butting heads over the formation of a national unity government.

It is said that to one equipped with only a hammer, every problem looks like a nail. The current popularity of the notion of humanitarian intervention may flow from the same impulse: in-

Zimbabwe's President Robert Mugabe is interviewed during the 63rd session of the United Nations General Assembly, Sept. 24, 2008, at UN headquarters in New York City. AP PHOTO/SETH WENIG

vading countries is something the U.S. is good at; reforming and rebuilding them—well, not so good. As Martin Jacques, *The Times* (London) columnist charged in *The Guardian*: "Even when the very thought is ridiculous and utterly impractical, the call for military intervention, on the part of political leaders and media commentators alike, is seemingly the invariable reflex action."

The near-simultaneous rejections of R2P missions in both Myanmar and Zimbabwe signal a subtle shift in power from the West to the rest, and as Jacques also believes, a sign that the sun is setting on a post-cold-war era of sole-superpower intervention— humanitarian or otherwise. However, such a conclusion may be premature.

More likely, as *World Politics Review* judges, these two cases simply "demonstrate that the doctrine is not yet ready for prime time." The U.S. was comfortable helping storm-battered Burmese and decrying Mugabe's thuggery, but evinced no interest in parachuting troops into either disaster area, or into the ongoing one-sided ethnic-tribal war in Darfur, supported by the Sudanese government. Nations on all sides decry the some 300,000 dead since 2003 as well as the 2 million internally displaced in Darfur, the result of acts that the U.S. has formally proclaimed to be genocide. There is a broad rhetorical consensus for some sort of military intervention—an end point that seems fated never to arrive.

The key question remains: who is going to make it happen? At the end of even the most high-flown debate, world politics still comes down to national power—mighty countries get to make most of the decisions. Conversely, post-9/11, the mightiest of them all suffers severely from interventionary overstretch and, with the abuse of detainees at Abu Ghraib and Guantánamo Bay, has diminished world trust in its charitable good intentions.

"To put the matter starkly," journalist and policy analyst David Reiff writes in *The New Republic*, "the [U.S.] no longer enjoys enough moral credibility in the world as a whole to in-

Iraqi train passengers leave al-Alawi railway station, central Baghdad, Iraq, on Oct. 30, 2008. The Iraqi Railways have launched for the first time since the U.S.-led invasion an urban service inside the capital Baghdad—which officials say indicates security has improved. AP PHOTO/HADI MIZBAN

tervene in Darfur in a way that would avoid deepening the civilizational crisis in which we find ourselves."

Above all, do no harm

The unwieldy roadblock in this case is the almost six-year-old U.S. intervention in Iraq. Although not promi-

At least 5 million Iraqis have fled their neighborhoods in fear since the 2003 U.S.-led invasion, and some are still leaving. This little boy has lived his whole life in an abandoned building on this street in Karrada, Baghdad. MERCED SUN-STAR/MCT / LANDOV

nent in the President George W. Bush (2001–2009) Administration's prewar pitch to sell the pending invasion, the very real suffering of the Iraqi people under Baath party oppression emerged as a justification once it became clear undisclosed weapons of mass destruction were a phantasm. Whatever the other arguable merits of the occupation of Iraq, the human rights community is conspicuously not buying this *ex post facto* justification. As Gary J. Bass, professor of politics, notes in *Freedom's Battle*, intervention in 1988, when the Iraqi government was exterminating its Kurdish citizens, might have qualified, but Washington in those days was Saddam Hussein's ally.

Checking the usual criteria, Human Rights Watch judged in 2004 that "despite the horrors of Saddam Hussein's rule, the invasion of Iraq cannot be justified as a humanitarian intervention." It does not help that many more Iraqi people have died from conditions generated by the occupation than likely would have had Hussein been left in power. Humanitarian-intervention enthusiasts, a commentator counsels, might do well to heed the first principle of the medical profession: Above all, do no harm.

But the harm was done, exacerbated, some contend, by then British Prime

'Wars for peace': a roll call of battles fought

"**HUMANITARIAN INTERVENTIONS** are not just a new-fangled experiment from the 1990s. Humanitarian interventions have a deep history, which is worth understanding both for its own sake and for the light it casts on current debates," writes Gary J. Bass. His *Freedom's Battle: The Origins of Humanitarian Intervention*, goes all the way back to the early 1800s to trace these beginnings, focusing on Western interventions to halt much-decried "atrocities" committed in the decaying Ottoman Empire: on behalf of Greek independence in 1825, Lebanon's Maronite Christians in 1860, Bulgarian nationalists in 1876 and—most ineffectually—Armenians in the 1915 genocide.

In each of these cases, not particularly surprisingly, the humanitarian cause célèbre supported a Christian minority writhing under the thumb of a Muslim imperium. And, in the first three instances, at least, the intervening powers' attempted good deeds arguably also arose from nonphilanthropic national interest in the fate of the Ottoman state, "the sick man of Europe." Pure philanthropy is a lot to ask of any nation; humanitarian incursions today, too, are often dogged by fierce debate over interveners' real reasons for jumping in. In international as in private affairs, motives are more often mixed than not.

Moving forward, David Chandler, professor of international relations, argues in *From Kosovo to Kabul and Beyond: Human Rights and International Intervention* that modern human rights-based "solidarity" movements and the notion of a "right to intervene" were born of the late 1960s Biafran famine, itself a product of Nigeria's crushing of the independence bid of the Igbo people. With African states sworn to uphold postcolonial borders and no cold-war stakes at issue, Igbo secessionists found themselves without foreign allies. They had, in fact, effectively lost their war when, in 1968, the first iconic photographs of potbellied starving Biafran babies hit the Western press, sparking an unprecedented international relief drive.

The Biafran war did much to shape the international humanitarian landscape of today. The campaign to assist southeastern Nigeria was the International Red Cross's first large-scale undertaking, Oxfam's second field operation and inspired the birth in France of Doctors Without Borders in 1971. Coming full circle, that last group's guiding light, Bernard Kouchner, now France's foreign minister, was appointed UN administrator for Kosovo after the 1999 NATO intervention.

The Biafran relief effort, unfortunately, stumbled upon the ironies that entangle all such endeavors. By reviving the rebels' spirits and fortunes, the global spotlight on starving Igbos and the aid delivered to them allowed the war stutter on until the inevitable Biafran surrender in early 1970. The subsequent general slaughter of Igbos—widely predicted by the relief community—failed to materialize, but the war's death toll totaled some 3 million, mostly from disease and famine.

Biafra could be considered a trial run for future "wars for peace," albeit a test model with no outside government involvement. Even the UN stayed out. By contrast, the later endeavors briefly cataloged below were mounted by foreign governments of varying ideology and incentive, with or without international sanction. These interventions also share the mixed motives and unintended consequences that have afflicted these ambiguous missions since the days of the Turks.

INDIA IN BANGLADESH (1971): West Pakistan's brutal suppression of a secessionist movement in the noncontiguous province then called East Pakistan sparked the exodus of some 10 million refugees into India, which lay between Pakistan's two halves. Amidst considerable alleged rape and pillage, the Pakistani Army had methodically murdered as many as 35,000 Bengals in Dhaka alone, systematically targeting urban intellectuals, including teachers, students and doctors—an atrocity much publicized by the Indian government (and ignored by Washington, which supported West Pakistan). New Delhi's armed interjection into its neighbor's civil war, also known as the third Indo-Pakistan war, was driven less by humanitarian concerns than the calculation that it was worth going to war to foster an independent East Pakistani state to receive back the extensive flood of refugees. Pakistan's defeat in late 1971 and the creation of Bangladesh, the world's third-largest Muslim state, saw that goal achieved.

TANZANIA IN UGANDA (1978–79): Ugandan dictator Idi Amin's (1971–79) abuses need no rehearsal here; his misrule is even today a byword for capricious cruelty. After the slowly collapsing Amin regime struck across the border at exiles who had found sanctuary in Tanzania, its President Julius Nyerere mobilized a "people's defense force," 100,000 strong, which crossed in the other direction alongside Ugandan rebel units in October 1978. By the following April, Amin's army and its Libyan allies were routed. Amin fled to Saudi Arabia and Uganda descended into decades of continuing civil war and disorder. Nyerere withdrew his forces in mid-1981, basically as soon as he could, ignoring the pleas of Uganda's embattled strong-arm civilian president. However, he was roundly denounced by the then Organization of African Unity for having breached state sovereignty.

VIETNAM IN CAMBODIA (1979–89): The barbarity of Khmer Rouge rule in Cambodia—far exceeding Amin's crimes—is no less notorious. Again, this domestic genocide was not, at least directly, what elicited intercession. In bloody border conflicts from 1975 on, a freshly reunified Vietnam fended off incursions by the newly installed Khmer regime. In December 1978, Vietnam's seasoned army finally blitzed into Cambodia, promptly installing a government

Kurdish women use snow-covered areas to wash clothing in the refugee camp near Sirnak, Turkey, April 8, 1991. ©PATRICK ROBERT/SYGMA/CORBIS

tantly, establishing a "no-fly zone" over northern Iraq—enforced by U.S., British and French interceptors, which downed several of Hussein's fighters. In October 1991, Iraqi forces withdrew from Kurdistan, and, thanks to continuing U.S. protection, Iraqi Kurdistan assumed the de facto autonomy it enjoys to this very day, some six years after the subsequent U.S. occupation of the rest of Iraq.

U.S. IN SOMALIA (1992–93): In the last month of his term, as a weak UN mission struggled to sort out the famine-ridden Somalian "failed state," President George H.W.Bush (1989–93) authorized U.S. forces to spearhead a multinational force, to which the U.S. contributed 25,000 out of 37,000 troops. The operation was an undisputed success, at least in facilitating aid delivery. However, thanks to conflicting UN directives and seemingly inevitable "mission creep," the focus shifted to quelling the chaotic multifaction civil war raging in Mogadishu. Anti-American criticism increased as gunship attacks caused mounting civilian casualties, while domestic critics questioned continuing a seemingly thankless mission. When 18 Army Rangers died grisly deaths in a botched October 1993 sortie to capture a warlord, the new Clinton Administration quickly announced plans to pull out, a maneuver completed six months later.

NATO IN KOSOVO (1999): NATO had mounted a small-scale bombing operation during the Serbian-led ethnic cleansing of Muslims in Bosnia earlier in the 1990s, but such feeble stabs at stemming the bloodshed were nothing compared to "Operation Allied Force," launched when the same drama seemed about to play out in the largely Armenian province of Kosovo. Led by the U.S., this campaign, which some dubbed "humanitarian bombing," was directed first at knocking out Serbia's military and civilian infrastructure, followed by deterring Serbian troops on the ground in Kosovo. The high altitudes at which the 38,000 raids were flown averted NATO losses, but multiplied unintended civilian deaths. After two-plus months, Serbia agreed to a peacekeeping force while most Serbs fled Kosovo. U.S. troops account for one tenth of the 16,000 peacekeepers still in Kosovo, which declared independence in February 2008.

U.S. IN HAITI (1994, 2004): These two interventions—by no means Washington's first in this Caribbean island—wound up entailing no armed combat, but were classic "humanitarian" invasions, attendant ambiguities and all. Determined in part to stem Florida-bound refugee "boat people" amidst spiraling human rights abuses, the Clinton Administration secured UN approval to forcefully restore Haiti's deposed popularly elected president, Jean-Bertrand Aristide (1991, 1994–96, 2001–2004). A last-minute accord allowed more than 15,000 U.S. troops to land unopposed in September 1994, Aristide was reinstalled in October 1994 and the U.S. turned peacekeeping operations over to the UN the following March. A far-murkier brief 2004 UN-approved "intervasion" by 2,000 U.S. and 1,700 other troops sought to restore order after Aristide's eventual flight from office—a capitulation much sought by U.S. President George W. Bush.

led by a former Khmer official while remaining there for a decade of running skirmishes with dispersed Khmer units. During this time, for their own reasons, the UN, U.S. and China continued to recognize the Khmer Rouge as Cambodia's legitimate government. Finally, in the early 1990s, UN peacekeepers were authorized to defuse the fighting and repatriate the many refugees. A tribunal in Phnom Penh is now weighing judgment on surviving Khmer Rouge leaders.

U.S. IN KURDISTAN (1991–present): Iraqi dictator Saddam Hussein's (1979–2003) savage response to a Kurdish uprising in northern Iraq, following his crushing defeat in the U.S.-led Persian Gulf war, sent millions of Kurds streaming into Turkey for fear of yet another Baghdad-directed extermination drive. Washington responded with "Operation Provide Comfort," airdropping much needed survival supplies and, more impor-

Didn4 I hear a NOISE?

WAR ON TERROR

HUMAN RIGHTS

Minister Tony Blair's (1997–2007) insistence on flatly categorizing the Iraq occupation as a humanitarian coup. "The notion of national sovereignty as sacred is gaining ground, helped in no small part by the disastrous results of the American invasion of Iraq," Clinton-era Secretary of State Madeleine Albright (1997–2001) mourned in *The New York Times*. "Indeed, many of the world's necessary interventions in the decade before the invasion—in places like Haiti and the Balkans—would seem impossible in today's climate."

Two other factors clouding these waters are "mission creep," always an institutional danger, and the fact that "homeland security," not human rights, per se, is very much the flavor of the decade. *The Harvard Journal of Human Rights* spotlights attempts to expand the R2P criteria to circumstances beyond its originally intended scope, a "duty to prevent" potential security disasters, particularly nuclear ones, for instance, or to unleash preemptive strikes on suspected terrorist targets.

President Bush's post-9/11 pronouncement of a doctrine of preemptive attack to quell potential future threats has not paved the way for humanitarian interveners today. Some fear, as Andrew Clapham, professor of international law, notes in *Human Rights: A Very Short Introduction*, that human rights "are becoming instrumentalized,

deployed as excuses for intervention by powerful countries in [the] political, economic and cultural life of weaker countries from the South." It seems that Burma's misanthropic self-serving leaders are not the only ones reacting to this apprehension.

Innately suspicious of major powers' real motives—and given that only very strong states can afford humanitarian intervention—critics on the left are not hesitant to disparage what they view as naked imperialism wearing a halo of compassion. "I'm not going to say that there aren't circumstances under which the use of military force to prevent genocide might be called for, but the issue always is who decides that it's legitimate to do so," foreign policy critic Chalmers Johnson argues. Only international law and global councils can confer that legitimacy. He adds: "If you yourself say, 'I'm invading Panama but this is humanitarian intervention'; well, no, that's imperialism."

Many on the right, by contrast, could not care less how U.S. military expeditions launched in service of American national interests are viewed elsewhere. They seek, above all, a free hand to make such decisions unilaterally. "The U.S. should continue to assert that it needs no authorization from the UN to use its military as it sees fit to protect the American people," a Heritage Foundation analy-

sis asserts in connection with R2P.

On both flanks, the basic sticking point is sovereignty, which is jealously guarded by most states and serves as an obvious impediment to general acceptance of the new norm. "Properly understood, R2P is an ally of sovereignty, not an adversary. Strong states protect their people, while weak ones are either unwilling or unable to do so," UN Secretary General Ban Ki-moon reassures. However, this misses the point since it is precisely seeming disregard for sovereign rights of the "weak" that raises the hackles of critics.

After Vietnam pushed the genocidal Khmer Rouge regime out of Cambodia in 1978, and Tanzania invaded Uganda to overthrow the cruelly dictatorial Idi Amin in 1979, significantly, both governments claimed self-defense, denying any philanthropic inspiration. "The reason for these denials is obvious," a contributor to *International Intervention in the Post-Cold War World* explains. "To recognize the legitimacy of humanitarian intervention would have created a precedent that at some other point in time could be turned against the intervening state."

War, whatever you call it

Less-doctrinaire types occupying the liberal middle ground worry about doing away with humanitarian intervention altogether. It takes a cold heart to stand by while potentially preventable savagery plays out 24/7 on cable news channels. "The problem here is that while no one wants imperialism to win, no one in his right mind can want liberty to fail either," reasons historian Michael Ignatieff, an advocate of humanitarian intervention.

These are hardly fresh concerns. David Reiff notes that "19th century European colonialism, particularly the so-called second imperialism of the last part of that century, was also explicitly undertaken in the name of humanitarian imperative"—namely squelching the slave trade and improving public health—which explains the exaggerated sighing at the time about "the white man's burden."

Interestingly, while Reiff has no

problem with coercive do-good operations per se, he does insist they be "called by their right name, not sanitized by the term humanitarian intervention." Others similarly object to euphemizing armed humanitarian intervention for altogether practical reasons. "Let's have no illusions; let's make no pretenses: That is not a peacekeeping operation; that is ... an offensive military action. It is an act of war, and will be interpreted by the adversary in those terms," an ex-UN undersecretary firmly advises.

Failure to be at least relatively up front about realities on the ground can lure intervening nations into quagmires they would rather never visit, leaving their citizens feeling they have been sold a false bill of goods. "Domestic support for military action can be sustained only if presidents speak frankly from the outset about the costs and risk, and explain the mission carefully, and prepare the American people for sacrifice," Stewart M. Patrick, senior fellow at the Council on Foreign Relations, suggests, adding: "From Somalia to Iraq, such candor has been conspicuously absent in Washington."

This is but one of many practical factors demanding consideration in pondering these missions. The philosophical, moral and geopolitical conundrums teased out in the debate over

U.S. Marines draw their weapons on a Somali gunman, forcing him to lay down his weapon near the city's Green Line, Dec. 11, 1992. Marines were patrolling further into disputed territory of Somalia's capital, Mogadishu. AP PHOTO/JOHN GAPS III

R2P are simple compared to the hard dilemmas posed by actually entering another country and forcing its leaders to do what seems right while comforting and rehabilitating millions of victims. However willing, political scientists are not going to stop genocide in Darfur. If anyone ever does, it will be thousands of expensively trained, equipped and transported soldiers, engineers and "nation builders," backed by determined national will.

A major deterrent for would-be interveners is the continued absence of a supranational armed force willing and able to conduct life-risking combat to make — not simply to keep — a peace in situations where no single powerful nation has reason really to act. The dream of an autonomous UN army has always been around but has never solidified into reality, a lack regretted by a pair of former ambassadors writing in *Foreign Affairs,* who note that "Whatever the U.S. skepticism about the UN, developing the organization's capacity to deal with international crises would help free Washington from its self-appointed task of unilaterally invading and rebuilding countries."

Outside of the UN, several supranational armies are in formation. A NATO Response Force, 25,000 strong, can deploy on five days' notice, sustaining operations for 30 days or longer if resupplied. The European Union, receiving voluntary contributions from its member states, has at least 13 operational 1,500-troop strong Battle Groups in place for rapid response deployment, while more are being formed. Boasting as many as 20,000 soldiers, an African Standby Force is slated to stand up in 2010, while the 16-member Economic Community of West African States is planning a

Human Rights !

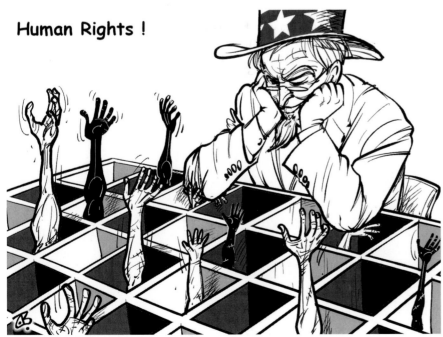

CAGLECARTOONS.COM/EMAD HAJJAJ

A nurse with Médecins Sans Frontières/Doctors Without Borders (MSF) attends to a patient under a mosquito net at the MSF hospital in Muhajariya, South Darfur, Sudan, April 3, 2008. REUTERS /LANDOV

similar institution of 6,500 fighters.

No nation has ever owned the logistical reach and strategic might that is wielded by the U.S. Pentagon today. As witnessed by the nation-building duties forced upon it by the occupations of Iraq and Afghanistan, not to mention earlier tours in Kosovo, Haiti and elsewhere, this war machine increasingly is no stranger to noncombat, humanitarian operations.

Whatever the ultimate fortunes of the R2P model, as *The Boston Globe* reported in July 2008, "U.S. military strategists are rewriting decades-old military doctrine to place humanitarian missions on a par with combat, part of a new effort to win over distrustful foreign populations and enlist new global allies." Meanwhile, the Joint Chiefs of Staff are now undertaking to draft formal military doctrine for "stability operations," and craft new curricula for the service colleges.

Militarizing aid

Assuming the will exists to re-leash the dogs of war in some distant hell hole, and that a qualified, adequate and deployable army exists to carry out the task, there remain a scary plethora of ways to inadvertently make any bad situation worse. One cautionary tenet advanced by strategic thinkers is

to jump in as early as possible. Swift action hopefully will save more threatened civilians lives; and it is usually cheaper to roll back the evildoers before they become firmly entrenched.

Moreover, as Chaim Kaufmann, professor of international relations, cautions in *The Use of Force: Military Power and International Politics*, "in many cases impartiality is morally and politically untenable." If the interveners cannot find the good guy, if both sides are equally repugnant, Robin Hood

should probably stay home because to go in neutral is a prescription for a military morass overseas and rapidly evaporating public support at home.

International aid agencies strive never to take sides, at least openly. However frustrating or counterintuitive in practice, a professed indifference to politics is their passport to establishing life-saving feeding stations and medical clinics in geopolitical disaster zones that would otherwise be strictly off limits. Incidentally, humanitarian intervention has few fans among professional relief workers.

"There is a real risk of militarizing and politicizing aid and, thus, of extending the violence," the Doctors Without Borders' legal director warned in 2008 when intervention was being mulled over in Myanmar. "Convoys cannot be protected without entering into conflict at some point with those who are controlling the territory, as was the case in Somalia in 1992." Humanitarian intervention, she added, "is a soft word whose efficiency is more to cover for military activities than humanitarian relief."

Those who would do good at gun point, need also take care that they do not inadvertently make things easier for those committing serious human rights abuses. Although little publicized, one country did intervene in Rwanda dur-

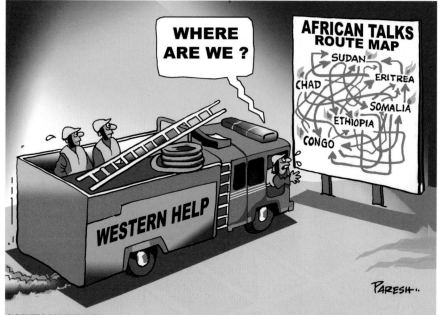

Children play at the prison in Naivasha, Rift Valley Province, Kenya, in Feb. 2008. This area was an epicenter of ethnic violence triggered by disputed presidential-election results when incumbent President Mwai Kibaki, of the Kikuyu tribe, defeated Raila Odinga, of the Luo, in December 2007. AP PHOTO/MARCUS BLEASDALE/VII

ing the 1994 butchery. Having withdrawn UN forces, the Security Council authorized a French mission organized to establish a "safe zone" in the country's southwest. However, one seriously overlooked problem with "Operation Turquoise" was that Tutsi genocide survivors could only reach this zone by passing through Hutu checkpoints where they were subject to identification and murder.

Another disturbing wrinkle is that the Hutu regime was on the brink of breaking before a Tutsi-led offensive when France's involvement — much as international relief activities did for Biafran secessionists a quarter century before — inspired the Hutus to continue fighting. France denies responsibility for additional preventable deaths. At the very best, the Africanist Mahmood Mandani judges, Turquoise may have saved Tutsi lives "but it also rescued the political and military leadership of the genocide, who slipped through French lines into the eastern Congo."

Undoubtedly, such situations pose genuinely excruciating quandaries. Some observers helpfully advise that

the ideal time to stop genocide is as it is brewing, not after it is actually being conducted. Like so much good advice, this is wisdom read in a rearview mirror. The world is a vast and messy panorama of potential crises and carnage. Unfortunately, atrocity prevention is fated to be a hope, not a promise.

R2P proponents proffer as an ultimate goal building a climate of deterrence in which malefactor regimes will know that the world will step in if inhuman savagery runs out of hand. Although unprovable, some analysts believe Bernard Kouchner's loud campaign for intervention in Burma is what turned the junta toward grudging compromise on the provision of relief.

For others, the wave of postelection violence that swept Kenya in early 2008 reinforces this paradigm. Over 1,000 people died, and hundreds of thousands were displaced, setting Kenya on a course to collapse when former UN Secretary General Kofi Annan and other world leaders intervened. In this instance, it was not military intercession, but skillful mediation that yielded a power-sharing agreement between

the clashing ethnically aligned political parties. While basic divisions in Kenyan society continue to fester, the apocalyptic bloodbath feared in January 2008 has been averted, at least for now. In a world where responsibility and protection alike are in short supply, such small triumphs may have to suffice.

"The instinct to embrace a 'responsibility to protect' is fundamentally a moral one," a Stimson Center assessment of "the impossible mandate" reasonably concludes. "Nations are right to call for countries to stand up to their sovereign responsibilities and to shield citizens from mass violence and killings. No nation should shy away from that position." However, the Washington think tank adds, "realists and [those who are] schooled in pragmatic thinking rightly question how such a norm will work, and if it is embraced, how it will be carried out." ●

OPINION BALLOTS AFTER PAGE 64

QUESTIONS

1. Is there a moral contradiction in going to war to enforce peace? Do you think "just war" theory covers such contingencies?

2. Precisely what criteria do you think should be applied to qualify for humanitarian interventions? Number of deaths? Amount of publicity given particular atrocities? Degree to which other "hard" national interests come into play?

3. Can it really be justifiably claimed that, at this date, an "international norm" exists that imposes a general "responsibility" to mount humanitarian interventions?

4. You broke it, you own it, the saying goes. Are interveners duty-bound to stay on for "nation building" after the immediate violence is squelched? How would you apply your views on this question to the specific case of Iraq?

5. Has the code of state sovereignty generally accepted since the mid-17th century outlived its relevance? What government actions or inactions do you believe could justify depriving a nation of this assumption of territorial inviolability?

6. Do you have any reservations about applying the principles enunciated in this discussion to the U.S.? Imagine European nations deciding to intervene in the civil rights conflict in the early 1960s or to free detainees from Guantánamo Bay.

7. Should the U.S. reevaluate its traditional devotion to the principle of absolute national sovereignty and embrace the concept of "responsibility to protect" as an actionable global norm?

8. Do you think the U.S. should spearhead faltering efforts to establish a United Nations-commanded "rapid deployment force" not constrained by national governments' domestic considerations and hesitations about mobilizing for crises? What are the pros and cons of such a force?

NOTES: ....
....
....
....
....
....
....
....
....
....
....
....
....

READINGS

Bass, Gary J., **Freedom's Battle: The Origins of Humanitarian Intervention.** New York, Knopf, 2008. 528 pp. $35.00 (hardcover). A highly readable account of European and American intercessions in the Ottoman Empire's governance of Greece, Syria, Bulgaria and Armenia, this book reviews this "forgotten history" to root the "human rights movement" not in the post–World War II era, but in the 19th century.

Bricmont, Jean, **Humanitarian Imperialism: Using Human Rights to Sell War.** New York, Monthly Review Press, 2006. 192 pp. $17.95 (paper). Arguing very much from a Third Worldist perspective, Bricmont cannot imagine a humanitarian intervention that does not boil down to self-serving domination of vulnerable states. However tendentious, the Belgian's approach to the material is also admirably concise and strongly argued.

Chandler, David, **From Kosovo to Kabul and Beyond: Human Rights and International Intervention.** London, Pluto Press, 2006. 340 pp. $28.95 (paper). Covering the cases of Iraq, Afghanistan, Bosnia, Somalia, Kosovo and East Timor, Chandler focuses on how the rights of individuals have come to be awarded higher priority than those of the sovereign state, and why this shift has seemingly come so quickly.

Donnelly, Jack, **International Human Rights,** 3rd ed. Boulder, CO, Westview Press, 2006. 272 pp. $28.00 (paper). Provides informative overview of human rights issues since World War II, as well as the challenges posed by globalization and global terrorism, and explores the emergence of nonstate actors such as the UN.

Orbinksi, James, **An Imperfect Offering: Humanitarian Action for the Twenty-First Century.** New York, Walker, 2008. 448 pp. $27.00 (hardcover). Written by the former head of Médecins Sans Frontières, the book relates "how to be in relation to the suffering of others" through personal experiences on humanitarian missions to Afghanistan, Russia, Rwanda and Somalia, among other nations.

Weiss, Thomas G., **Humanitarian Intervention: Ideas in Action.** Cambridge, Britain, Polity, 2007. 176 pp. $19.95 (paper). Research director for the commission that gave rise to the "Responsibility to Protect" doctrine, Weiss here locates the normative evolution of the concept in the context of the war on terror and, one reviewer remarks, "appears to be struggling to sustain optimism for the future."

TO LEARN MORE ABOUT THIS TOPIC AND TO ACCESS WEB LINKS TO RESOURCES GO TO www.greatdecisions.org/topic8

INDEX TO GREAT DECISIONS TOPICS
1998 ● 2008

TOPIC 1/IRAQ

ISSUE A: In the debate about whether the U.S. should withdraw its forces from Iraq, and if so, how quickly, what are the most important factors for the U.S. to consider? (Rank in order of importance, with 1 being most important and 6 being least important)

	#1	#2	#3	#4	#5	#6
1. Political stability in Iraq	57%	20%	10%	8%	4%	3%
2. Impact of U.S. policy on the actions of Iraq's neighbors	14%	28%	36%	14%	6%	2%
3. Perceptions of the U.S. status as a major power	3%	4%	8%	14%	30%	41%
4. Public opinion in the U.S.	12%	8%	12%	22%	24%	23%
5. Economic stability in Iraq, especially regarding the safety of its oil supply	14%	35%	23%	13%	9%	6%
6. How other nations view the U.S.'s responsibility in Iraq	6%	9%	14%	29%	24%	19%

ISSUE B: There is substantial discussion about the size of the American military force in Iraq. Should the U.S.:

1. Continue with the surge and send more troops into Iraq	12%
2. Make deep cuts in troop level and keep the remaining forces in secure bases outside the sectarian and ethnic fault lines	71%
3. Withdraw all military troops immediately	17%

ISSUE C: Should the U.S. remain insistent that the Iraqi government moves steadily forward with efforts toward accommodation and an end to sectarian and ethnic differences and violence?

Yes_____88%   No_____12%

TOPIC 2/EUROPEAN INTEGRATION

ISSUE A: How do you feel about the continued expansion of the European Union (EU)? (Choose one)

1. The EU is already too big.	7%
2. The EU should continue to expand.	73%
3. The EU is just the right size.	20%

ISSUE B: The EU has a common currency. Should it have a common foreign and defense policy?

Yes _____69%   No _____ 31%

ISSUE C: Do you agree or disagree with the following statements?

	AGREE STRONGLY	AGREE	DISAGREE	DISAGREE STRONGLY
1. Turkey should be a member of the EU	20%	61%	16%	3%
2. Muslim populations in Europe are diverse	14%	52%	31%	3%
3. The EU is a crucial ally of the U.S.	57%	39%	3%	0%
4. The new generation of leaders will change policy in the EU	10%	69%	21%	1%
5. The strong euro hurts the dollar	13%	43%	40%	3%
6. As the EU expands and becomes more diverse, it becomes stronger	23%	59%	17%	1%

TOPIC 3/BLACKLISTING THE ENEMY

ISSUE A: Reflecting on actual incidents of politico-religious mass violence with which you are familiar, the crucial criteria for defining such incidents as "terrorism" are: (Rank in order of *preference, with 1 being the most significant and 4 being the least*)

	#1	#2	#3	#4
1. The victims number "innocent" nonuniformed civilians going about their daily business	29%	21%	26%	24%
2. The act is committed with the stated basis of advancing or proclaiming a particular ideological or theological cause	26%	25%	31%	18%
3. The scenario is clearly directed at influencing public attitudes via fear and social disruption	32%	39%	21%	9%
4. The attackers are nonstate actors not serving as soldiers of a recognized government	16%	15%	21%	48%

ISSUE B: Whatever their specific merits, charges of "state terrorism" levied against, say, the U.S. or Israel are invalid because terrorism is technically not a national-level crime. The Geneva Conventions exist precisely to sanction military abuses and "crimes against humanity" committed by governments.

Yes _____ 53%   No _____47%

ISSUE C: Applying the definitional criteria that make the most sense to you, would you personally label these countries as "terrorist" based on actions you know them to have committed:

	YES	NO	MAYBE		YES	NO	MAYBE		YES	NO	MAYBE
Cuba	6%	81%	13%					Israel	30%	44%	27%
Iran	54%	16%	30%	Libya	32%	42%	26%	Pakistan	33%	30%	37%
Syria	50%	18%	32%	Russia	20%	51%	29%	Myanmar/			
Sudan	64%	16%	20%	U.S.	19%	56%	25%	Burma	43%	26%	31%
North Korea	40%	31%	29%	China	22%	53%	26%	Venezuela	15%	46%	39%

TOPIC 4/RUSSIA AND 'PUTINISM'

ISSUE A: As a matter of policy, do you believe the U.S. should:

	YES	NO
1. Actively seek a closer and more stable relationship with Russia?	97%	3%
2. Attempt to have friendly relations with the former Russian republics but avoid meddling in Moscow's "sphere of influence?"	87%	13%
3. Make strong efforts to establish close ties to those former Russian republics that could be of most use to the U.S. for security reasons or to promote stable access to fossil fuels for the U.S. and its European allies?	70%	30%

ISSUE B: Do you agree or disagree with the following statements?

	YES	NO

1. Vladimir Putin has shored up the Russian state so effectively that the economy will prosper and the government

will be able to assert itself within the Commonwealth of Independent States (CIS) and the international community after he steps down at the end of his second term.	75%	25%
2. Russia must make sure that it plays the dominant role in the CIS in order to maintain its rightful place in the world and keep its economy shored up and its energy flowing.	63%	37%
3. Russia should be allowed to act as it sees fit in its own interests in situations such as the Chechyna conflict and what it saw as the electoral conflict in Ukraine.	42%	58%

TOPIC 5/U.S. DEFENSE POLICY

ISSUE A: How should the U.S. pay for expanding the size of its ground forces? (Check all that apply)

1. Cut programs from the Navy and Air Force	27%
2. Increase the size of the defense budget	25%
3. Revisit the decision to expand the size of the Army and the Marines	48%

ISSUE B: What sort of defense strategy should the U.S. adopt? *(Check only one)*

1. A preventive war strategy	3%
2. A strategy of containment and deterrence	8%
3. A cooperative world order approach	39%
4. Some combination of the three	50%

ISSUE C: Should the U.S. maintain global military superiority, no matter what the cost?

Yes _____ 26%   No _____ 46%   Maybe _____ 28%

TOPIC 6/LATIN AMERICA

ISSUE A: How much does Latin America matter to the U.S.?

Great deal _____ 71%   Somewhat _____ 27%   Not much _____ 3%

ISSUE B: Do you think that Latin America should be a priority for the next U.S. Administration?

Yes _____ 92%   No _____ 8%

ISSUE C: What are the most important issues for the U.S. to address vis-à-vis Latin America? *(Rank in order of importance, with 1 being most important and 6 being least important)*

	#1	#2	#3	#4	#5	#6
Illegal immigration	22%	14%	16%	15%	17%	17%
Trade relations	24%	27%	24%	17%	6%	3%
Drug trafficking	10%	19%	17%	24%	20%	9%
Protecting the U.S. border against terrorists	11%	8%	13%	15%	23%	31%
Supporting democracy in the region	8%	15%	18%	16%	19%	25%
Alleviating poverty and income inequality	31%	18%	13%	11%	13%	14%

TOPIC 7/U.S.-CHINA ECONOMIC RELATIONS

ISSUE A: How important to the U.S. is the trade deficit with China?

Very important ___ 61%   Important _____ 36%   Not important _____ 4%

ISSUE B: Does the fact that a product is made in China affect your decision on whether or not to buy it? (*Check only one*)

1. I buy products made in China.	50%
2. I don't buy products made in China.	16%
3. I don't care where the products I buy are made.	34%

ISSUE C: Globally, do you see China's surging economy as (*check only one*):

1. A threat, competing for scarce global resources	15%
2. A boon, lifting the global economy	13%
3. Both	71%

ISSUE D: In terms of the U.S., do you see China's surging economy as (*check only one*):

1. A threat, taking jobs from the U.S.	16%
2. A boon, providing cheap goods to the U.S.	11%
3. Both	74%

TOPIC 8/FOREIGN AID

ISSUE A: If foreign aid is measured as a percentage of a donor country's GDP, the U.S. is lagging behind other countries that give aid. However, looking at aid in dollar terms, the U.S. is by far the country donating the most money. Do you think (check only one):

1. The U.S. gives more than enough foreign aid.	28%
2. The U.S. gives just enough foreign aid.	25%
3. The U.S. should give more foreign aid.	48%

ISSUE B: Which is more effective? *(Check only one)*

1. Foreign aid from government or UN sources	20%
2. Foreign aid from private sources	81%

ISSUE C: Do you agree or disagree with the following statements

	AGREE STRONGLY	AGREE	DISAGREE	DISAGREE STRONGLY
Third World debt should be erased.	8%	38%	49%	6%
The U.S. should support free trade.	30%	62%	8%	1%
Outright foreign aid is counterproductive	7%	35%	48%	10%

ISSUE D: Should a donor country use foreign aid to promote a political agenda?

Yes _____ 7%   No _____ 44%   Maybe _____ 48%

How to get more out of Great Decisions

A brief look at some of our supplementary materials for GREAT DECISIONS, NATIONAL OPINION BALLOT REPORT and our most recent HEADLINE SERIES. Order today or visit our online bookstore at **www.fpa.org.**

GREAT DECISIONS **TEACHER'S GUIDE**

Many educators use **Great Decisions** as supplementary material in the classroom or lecture hall to stimulate debate and to promote global awareness. This book provides ideas and lesson plans on how to promote learning about the world.

$27.50 plus S&H
ISBN# 978-0-87124-227-3
ID# 31597

GREAT DECISIONS **TELEVISION SERIES** ON DVD

Foreign policy experts and global thinkers discuss the **Great Decisions** topics, raising policy issues. Broadcast on PBS, the popular series is available as a two-disc DVD set.

$40 plus S&H
ID# 31598

NATIONAL OPINION BALLOT REPORT 2008

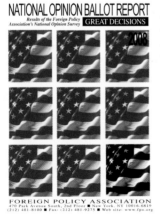

A **National Opinion Ballot Report** is produced each year based on the tabulation of opinion ballots submitted by participants in the **Great Decisions** program. Since 1955, opinion ballots for each topic have been included with **Great Decisions** to enable those interested to make their views known. Each year FPA sends the National Opinion Ballot Report to the White House, the departments of State and Defense, members of Congress, the media and concerned citizens. **Free upon request.**

Headline Series

Since the first issue in 1935, FPA has published 330 insightful and concise *Headline Series*. The list of authors represents a who's who of foreign policy experts and leading journalists. Each issue of the pocket-size *Headline Series* is devoted to a single geographic area or topic of global concern.

Available as single copies, on standing order (four consecutive issues) or in bulk at a discount, these inexpensive, succinct and well-researched books demystify the complexities of international affairs. Many provide background for **Great Decisions** topics.

HEADLINE SERIES 331
MEXICO'S STRUGGLE WITH 'DRUGS AND THUGS'
by George Grayson

This *Headline Series* deals with the hot-button issue of the armed conflict taking place between Mexico's rival drug cartels and the Mexican government forces who are trying to put an end to the wildly profitable supply route for cocaine and other illegal drugs making their way into the United States. It examines Mexican efforts to get a real handle on both the demand and supply sides of the problem and considers possible approaches to halting the escalating killings of innocent victims and other heinous acts taking place daily in the "war zone."

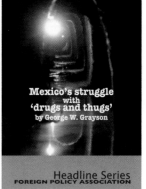

GEORGE W. GRAYSON is the Class of 1938 Professor at the College of William & Mary. He is also a Senior Fellow at the Center for Strategic & International Studies (Washington, D.C.) and an Associate Scholar at the Foreign Policy Research Institute (Philadelphia). The Penn State University Press recently published his book *Mexican Messiah,* a biography of Andrés Manuel López Obrador, the populist candidate who, even though he lost the mid-2006 contest for chief executive, declared himself to be Mexico's "legitimate president" and continued to barnstorm the country.

$8.99 plus S&H; (Winter 2009)
ISBN# 978-0-87124-224-2; ID# 31593

HEADLINE SERIES 332
AFRICAN SOLUTIONS TO AFRICAN PROBLEMS
by Robert Nolan

As African governments seek to curb conflict, integrate their growing economies and usher in a new era of democratic leadership, most agree the African Union has a critical role to play for the continent. From peacekeeping missions in Sudan and Somalia to regional trade deals with Europe and the U.S., Africa's leaders increasingly call for "African solutions to African problems." What role can the African Union play as an incubator for such solutions and on the world stage, and is a United States of Africa on the horizon?

This *Headline Series,* as well as its accompanying blog featuring interviews, photos, video and more, is critical reading for those interested in the future of Africa.

ROBERT NOLAN is editorial producer of the Great Decisions Television Series and online editor at the Foreign Policy Association. A former Peace Corps volunteer in Zimbabwe, Nolan's work on African issues has appeared in the *Village Voice,* the *Christian Science Monitor* and AllAfrica.com, as well as the anthology *Africa Par Adventure*.

$8.99 plus S&H; (available Spring 2009)
ISBN# 978-0-87124-225-9; ID# 31594

BECOME A MEMBER

Associate Member — $250
- Complimentary Great Decisions briefing book and issues of the occasional Headline Series
- Advance mailing of the annual National Opinion Ballot Report and Great Decisions Updates
- Free admission to all Associate events for member and family
- Savings of 40% on guest registration for Associate events

National Associate Member — $75 (Open to residents outside the New York, New Jersey, Connecticut tristate area.)
- Complimentary issue of the Headline Series
- Advance mailing of the annual National Opinion Ballot Report and Great Decisions Updates

Support FPA's efforts to improve global affairs education.
Make a fully tax-deductible contribution to the Foreign Policy Association's Annual Fund 2009. To contribute to the Annual Fund 2009, contact an individual-giving specialist at 800-628-5454 x 225.
Gifts over $500 are listed in the Annual Report.

All financial contributions are tax-deductible to the fullest extent of the law under section 501 (c)(3) of the IRS code.

COMPLETE THIS FORM AND RETURN TO: Foreign Policy Association, 470 Park Avenue South, New York, N.Y. 10016 **OR FAX TO: (212) 481-9275**

□ MR.   □ MRS.   □ MS.   □ DR.   □ PROF.

NAME _____

ADDRESS _____

_____**APT/FLOOR** _____

CITY _____ **STATE** _____ **ZIP** _____

TEL _____

E-MAIL _____

□ AMEX   □ VISA   □ MC   □ CHECK   (PAYABLE TO FOREIGN POLICY ASSOCIATION)

CARD NO.

[   ][   ][   ][   ][   ][   ][   ][   ][   ][   ][   ][   ][   ][   ][   ][   ]

SIGNATURE OF CARDHOLDER   **EXP. DATE**

TO **ORDER DIRECTLY** CALL: **(800) 477-5836**
OR **ORDER ONLINE:** WWW.GREATDECISIONS.OR
FOR **MEMBERSHIP** CALL **(800) 628-5754 X228**

PRODUCT	QTY	PRICE	COST
GREAT DECISIONS 2009 TEACHER'S GUIDE		$27.50	
GREAT DECISIONS 2009 DVD		$40	
MEXICO'S STRUGGLE WITH DRUGS AND THUGS HS 331		$8.99	
ASSOCIATE MEMBERSHIP		$250	
NATIONAL ASSOCIATE MEMBERSHIP		$75	
ANNUAL FUND 2009			

SUBTOTAL $

S & H $

TOTAL $

SHIPPING AND HANDLING

If order totals	Delivery charge
up to $20.00	$7.00
$20.01–50.00	$8.50
$50.01–80.00	$10.00

$80.01–120.00	$12.50
$120.01–150.00	$14.50
$150.01 and over	add 10% of subtotal

Have your say in
the Great Decisions blogosphere
at GREATDECISIONS.ORG!

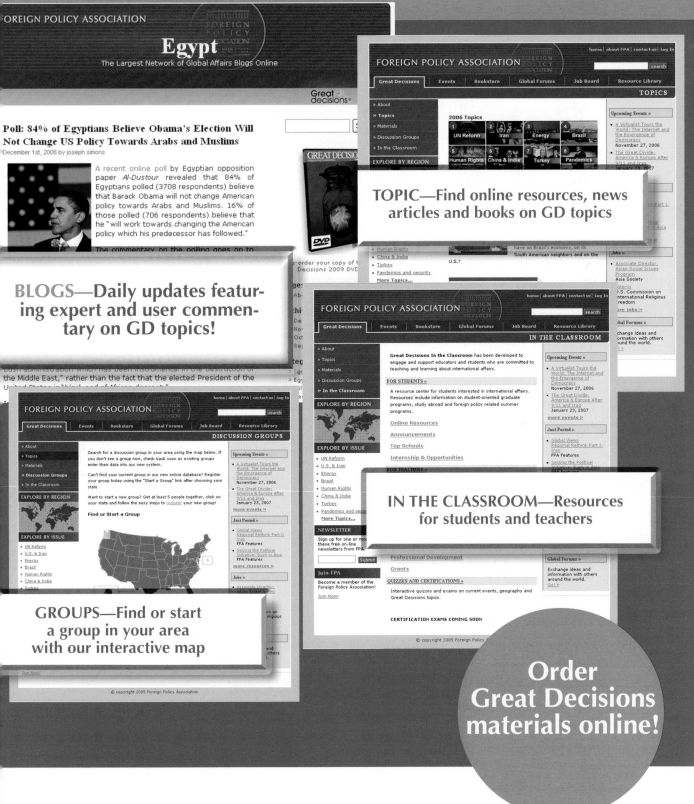

BLOGS—Daily updates featuring expert and user commentary on GD topics!

TOPIC—Find online resources, news articles and books on GD topics

GROUPS—Find or start a group in your area with our interactive map

IN THE CLASSROOM—Resources for students and teachers

Order Great Decisions materials online!

Go beyond the binding to enhance your Great Decisions experience online at GreatDecisions.org!

The Global Order Is Changing.

The 21st century is marked by many competing sources of global power acros
politics, economics, culture, military strength, and more.

Did You Know You Have a Seat at the Table?

The Stanley Foundation wants citizen leaders to discuss the challenges to the globa
order, major issues that cut across national boundaries, and how all of this w
impact American lives. You can help raise awareness, motivate thinking, an
ultimately improve US foreign policy regarding this global transformation.

Join Us in Creating an International System That Works.

The Stanley Foundation provides FREE resources and tools for citizen leaders to hea
and be heard.

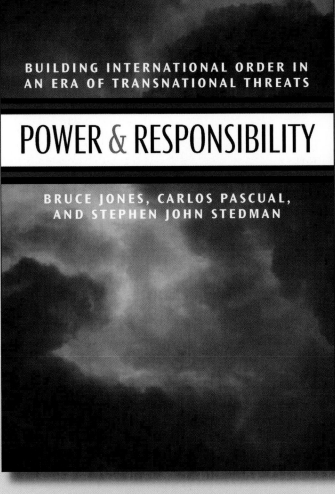

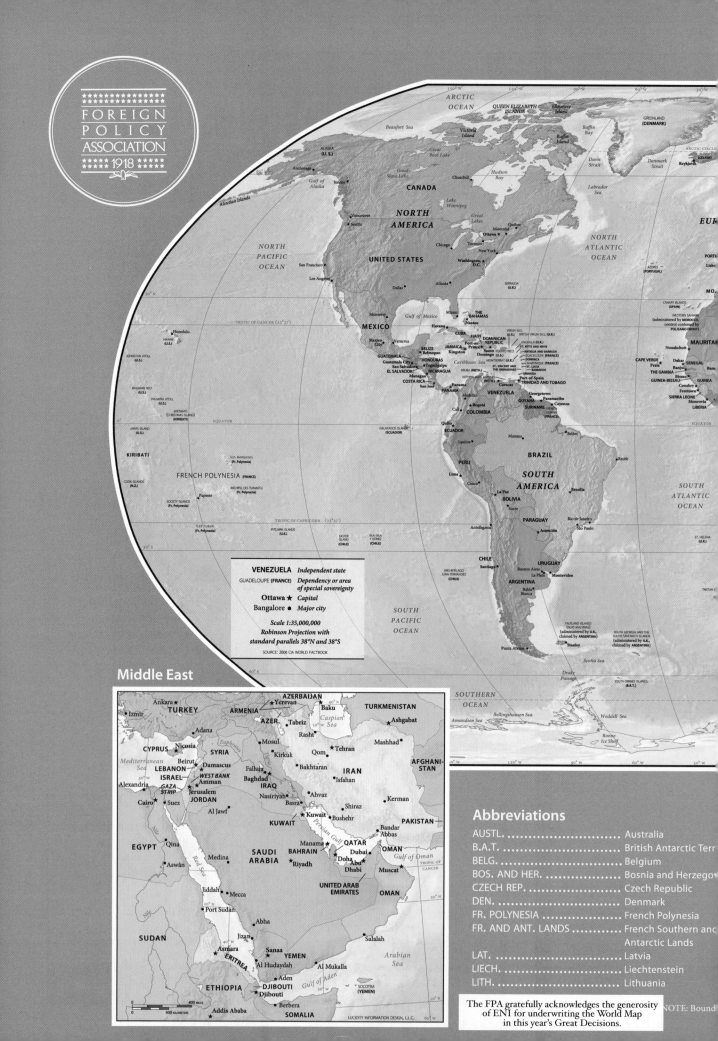

Middle East

VENEZUELA *Independent state*
GUADELOUPE **(FRANCE)** *Dependency or area of special sovereignty*
Ottawa ★ *Capital*
Bangalore ● *Major city*

Scale 1:35,000,000
Robinson Projection with standard parallels 38°N and 38°S

SOURCE: 2006 CIA WORLD FACTBOOK

Abbreviations

AUSTL.	Australia
B.A.T.	British Antarctic Terr
BELG.	Belgium
BOS. AND HER.	Bosnia and Herzegov
CZECH REP.	Czech Republic
DEN.	Denmark
FR. POLYNESIA	French Polynesia
FR. AND ANT. LANDS	French Southern and
	Antarctic Lands
LAT.	Latvia
LIECH.	Liechtenstein
LITH.	Lithuania

The FPA gratefully acknowledges the generosity of ENI for underwriting the World Map in this year's Great Decisions.

NOTE: Bound

LUCIDITY INFORMATION DESIGN, LLC.

You know where
THEIR TURN TO DRIVE meets
YOUR TURN TO COACH?

I'M THERE™

With two teens, Cal Ripken, Jr. knows what

it takes to turn new drivers into safe drivers:

Coaching. So who better to team up with State Farm®

in our efforts to help parents prepare their teens?

We're offering the Parent's Handbook, sample driving lessons and more.

Find it all at **statefarm.com/teendriving**.

Like a good neighbor, State Farm is there.®

State Farm